# Third Grade Math with Confidence

## Student Workbook

## Part A

# Third Grade Math with Confidence

## Student Workbook

## Part A

KATE SNOW

WELL-TRAINED MIND PRESS

Names: Snow, Kate (Teacher), author.

Title: Third grade math with confidence. Student workbook part A / Kate Snow.

Other titles: Student workbook part A

Description: [Charles City, Virginia] : Well-Trained Mind Press, [2023] | Series: Math with confidence | Interest age level: 007-009.

Identifiers: ISBN: 978-1-944481-30-8 (paperback)

Subjects: LCSH: Mathematics--Study and teaching (Elementary) | LCGFT: Problems and exercises. | BISAC: JUVENILE NONFICTION / MATHEMATICS / Arithmetic.

Classification: LCC: QA107.2 .S663 2023 | DDC: 372.7--dc23

Reprinted March 2026 by Versa Press, Inc.

# Table of Contents

# Author's Note

You'll need three books to teach *Third Grade Math with Confidence*. All three books are essential for the program.

- The Instructor Guide contains the scripted lesson plans for the entire year (Units 1-16).
- Student Workbook Part A contains the workbook pages for the first half of the year (Units 1-8).
- Student Workbook Part B contains the workbook pages for the second half of the year (Units 9-16).

**The Student Workbooks are not meant to be used as stand-alone workbooks.** The hands-on teaching activities in the Instructor Guide are an essential part of the program. You'll need the directions in the Instructor Guide to guide your child through the Lesson Activities pages. The icon with two heads means that your child should complete these pages with you, and that she is not expected to complete these pages on her own.

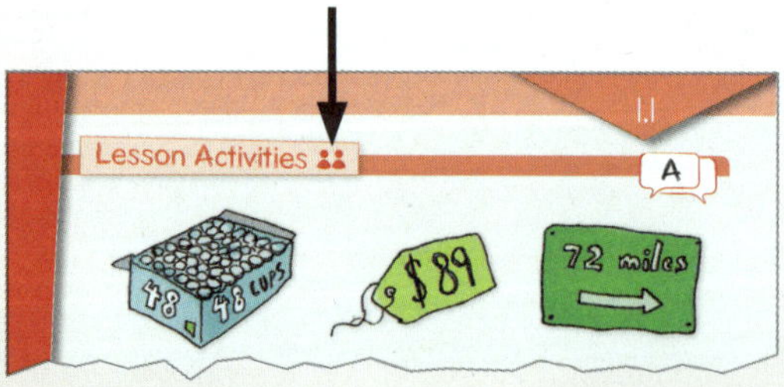


The Practice and Review pages give your child practice with new concepts and review previously-learned skills. The icon with one head means that your child may complete these pages on his own. Most third-graders will be able to complete these workbook pages independently, but some may need help reading and interpreting the directions.

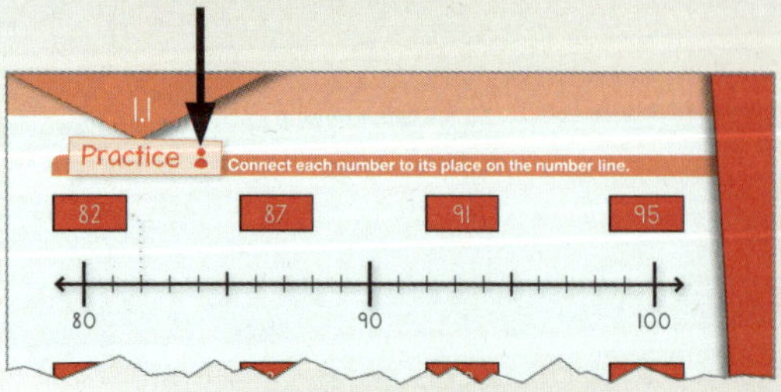


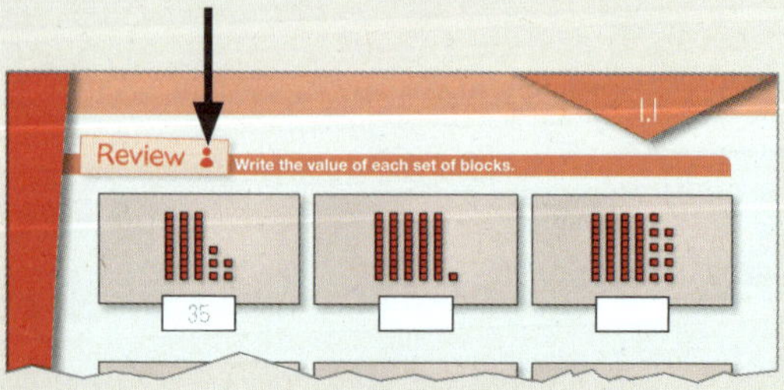

## Lesson Activities

### A

### B

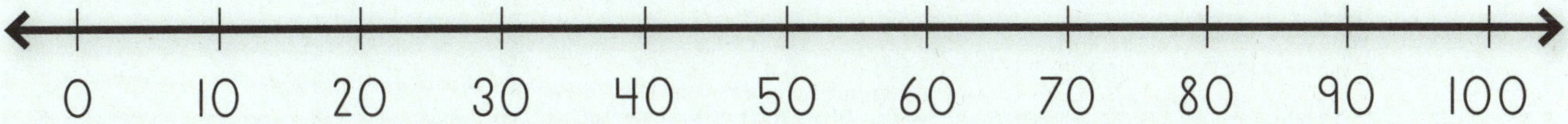


| 62 | 69 | 87 | 23 | 18 | 51 | 45 | 96 |
|---|---|---|---|---|---|---|---|
| | | | | | | | |

### C

## Round to the Nearest Ten Crash

| | | | | |
|---|---|---|---|---|
| 10 | 20 | 30 | 40 | 50 |
| 60 | 70 | 80 | 90 | 100 |

## Practice

**Connect each number to its place on the number line.**

82 | 87 | 91 | 95

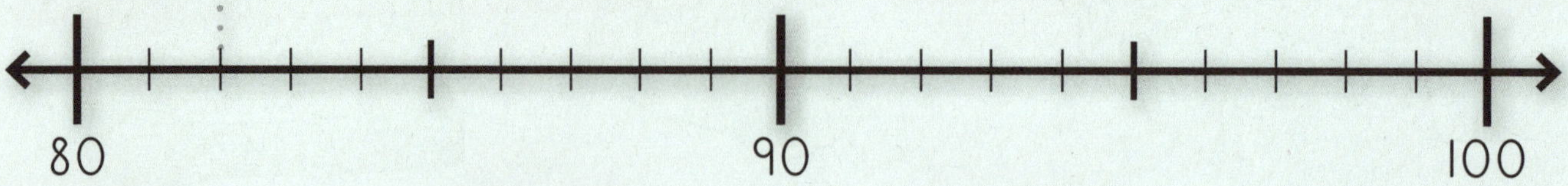


84 | 88 | 93 | 96

**Round each number to the nearest ten. Use the number line to help.**

| 82 | 91 | 88 | 95 | 93 | 84 | 96 | 87 |
|---|---|---|---|---|---|---|---|
| | | | | | | | |

**Round each number to the nearest ten.**

About ☐ golf balls

About ☐ pencils

About ☐ crayons

About ☐ blocks

About ☐ stickers

About ☐ rubber bands

## Review

Write the value of each set of blocks.

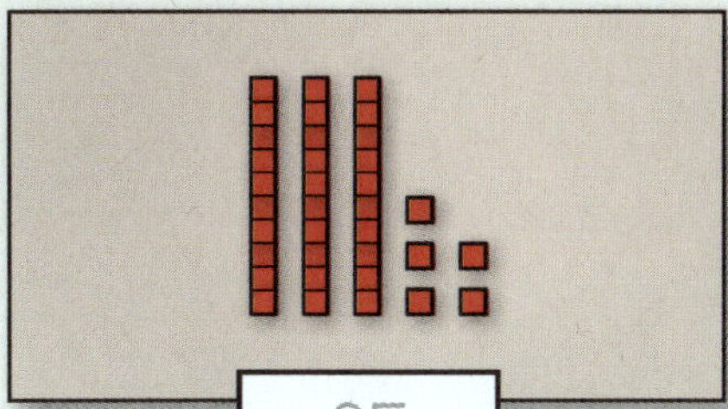

35

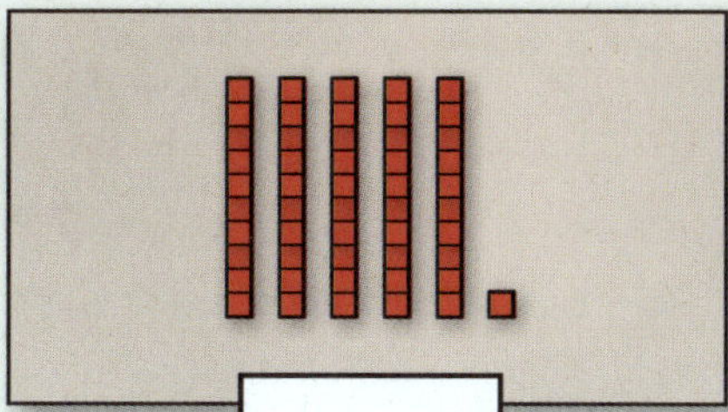

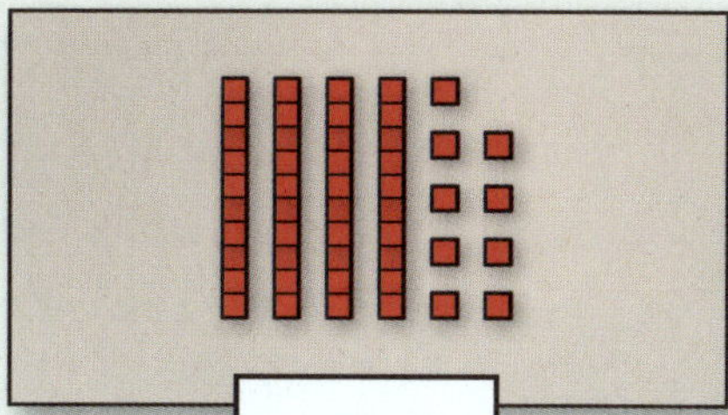

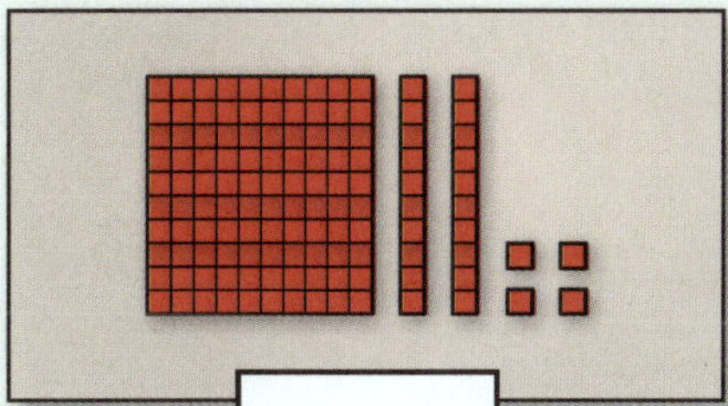

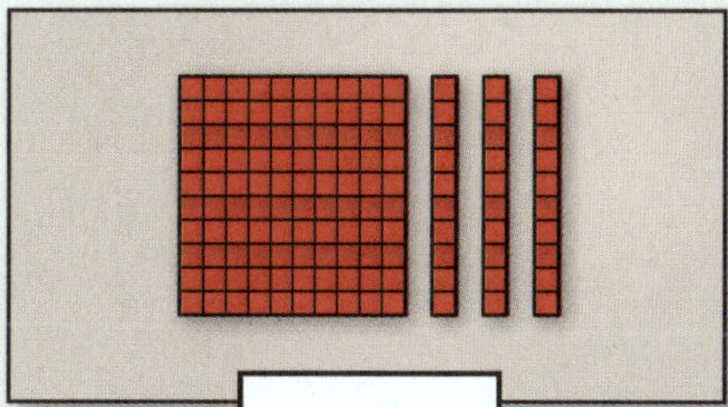

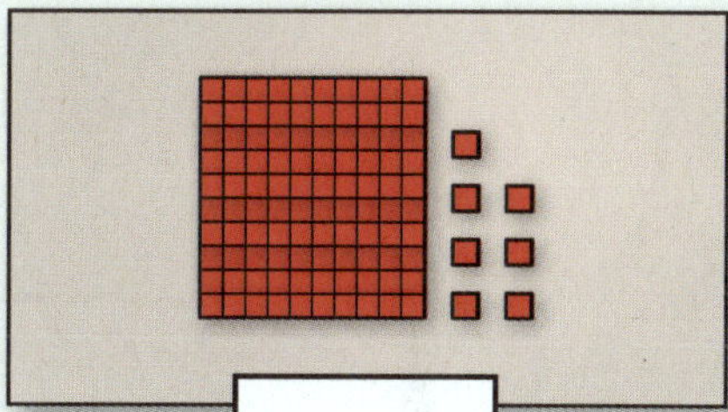

Connect each number to its place on the number line.

91 97 103 108

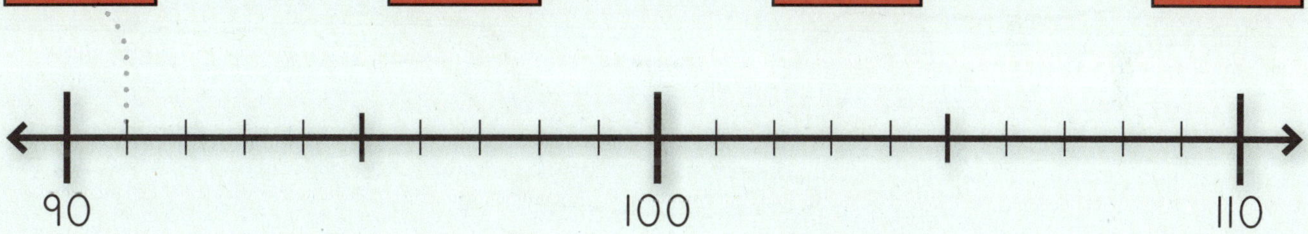


94 99 101 105

Complete.

| | −9 |
|---|---|
| 11 | 2 |
| 15 | |
| 17 | |
| 12 | |

| | −8 |
|---|---|
| 16 | |
| 10 | |
| 14 | |
| 17 | |

| | −7 |
|---|---|
| 14 | |
| 12 | |
| 16 | |
| 13 | |

## Lesson Activities

### A

| | | |
|---|---|---|
| 87 > 42 <br> ↑ <br> greater-than sign | 42 < 87 <br> ↑ <br> less-than sign | 42 = 42 <br> ↑ <br> equals sign |

60 ◯ 100　　　38 ◯ 38　　　49 ◯ 47

### B

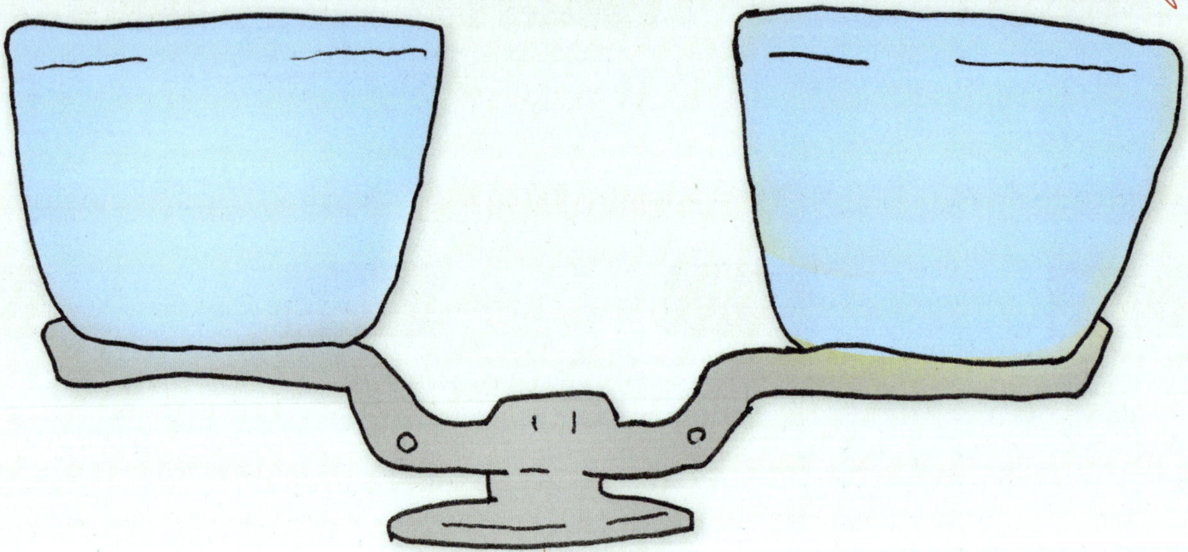

| | |
|---|---|
| 5 ◯ 4 | 3 + 3 ◯ 7 |
| 5 ◯ 8 - 3 | 6 - 4 ◯ 3 |
| 10 ◯ 5 + 4 | 9 - 1 ◯ 2 + 6 |

## Practice

**Complete the circles with <, >, or =.**

| | | |
|---|---|---|
| 30 ○ 40 | 126 ○ 26 | 199 ○ 201 |
| 10 ○ 9 + 6 | 15 - 5 ○ 10 | 10 ○ 6 + 4 |
| 20 + 20 ○ 40 | 10 + 30 ○ 50 | 60 ○ 50 + 9 |
| 100 ○ 30 + 30 | 50 + 50 ○ 100 | 100 ○ 80 + 40 |

**Write a number in the blank that makes the statement true.**

| | | |
|---|---|---|
| 7 + 6 < ☐ | ☐ > 7 + 9 | ★ 7 + 7 = 9 + ☐ |
| 8 + 8 > ☐ | ☐ < 12 - 6 | ★ 12 - 6 > 11 - ☐ |
| 9 + 5 = ☐ | ☐ > 6 + 5 | ★ 5 + 8 < 20 - ☐ |

## Review

**Complete.**

| | +5 |
|---|---|
| 4 | 9 |
| 7 | |
| 8 | |
| 6 | |

| | +7 |
|---|---|
| 7 | |
| 9 | |
| 6 | |
| 8 | |

| | +6 |
|---|---|
| 5 | |
| 8 | |
| 9 | |
| 6 | |

**Connect each number to its place on the number line.**

455 458 461 465 466

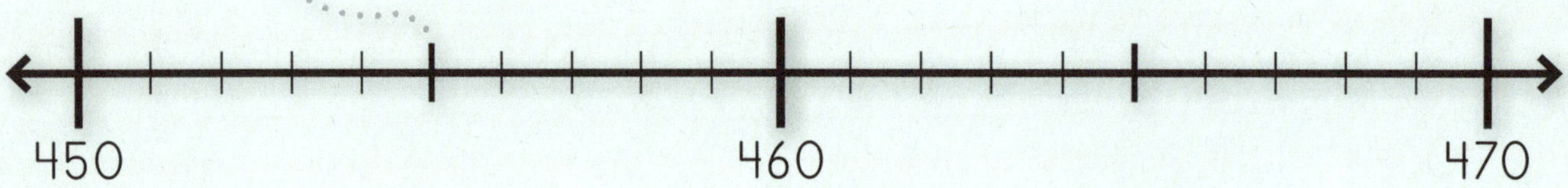


453 457 459 464 468

**Match pairs that equal 100.**

| | |
|---|---|
| 90 | 80 |
| 20 | 25 |
| 70 | 10 |
| 75 | 30 |
| 40 | 99 |
| 1 | 60 |

**Copy the shapes.**

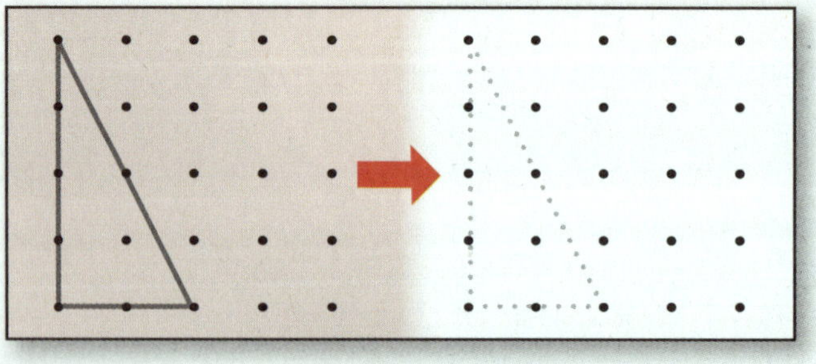

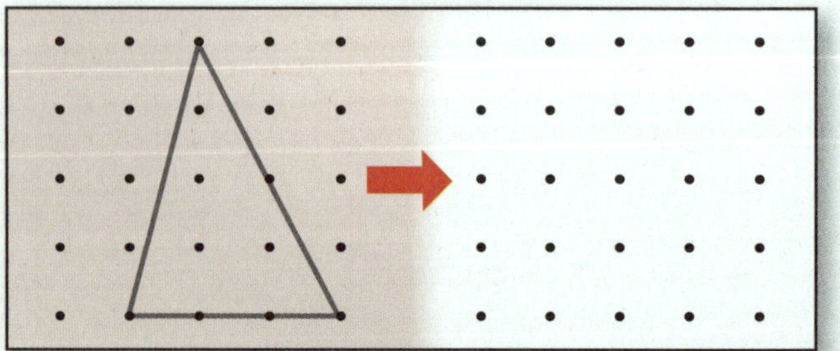

## Lesson Activities

A

12

8 4

☐ + ☐ = ☐

☐ + ☐ = ☐

☐ - ☐ = ☐

☐ - ☐ = ☐

10

8 ☐

☐

9 4

13

☐ 5

B

☐ + 6 = 13

12 - ☐ = 9

☐ - 8 = 7

☐ + ☐ = ☐

☐ - ☐ = ☐

☐ - ☐ = ☐

## Practice

**Use the numbers to complete the blanks. You will use each number once.**

| 0 | 1 | 2 | 3 | 4 | 5 | 6 | 7 | 8 |
|---|---|---|---|---|---|---|---|---|

| | | |
|---|---|---|
| $8 + \square = 9$ | $14 - 8 = \square$ | $\square - 2 = 1$ |
| $10 - \square = 5$ | $3 + 1 = \square$ | $\square - 5 = 3$ |
| $12 + \square = 14$ | $16 - 9 = \square$ | $\square + 6 = 6$ |

**Complete.**

| Whole | Part | Part |
|---|---|---|
| 12 | 6 | $\square$ |
| 15 | 9 | $\square$ |
| 14 | $\square$ | 7 |
| 13 | 9 | $\square$ |
| 15 | 8 | $\square$ |
| 13 | $\square$ | 6 |
| 16 | $\square$ | 8 |
| 12 | $\square$ | 3 |
| 12 | 8 | $\square$ |
| 14 | $\square$ | 8 |
| 13 | 5 | $\square$ |
| 16 | $\square$ | 7 |

## Review

**Round each number to the nearest ten.**

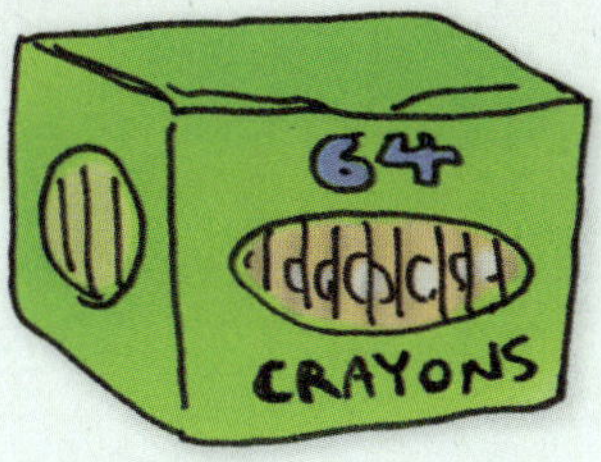


About [ ] crayons

About [ ] stickers

About [ ] packs of crackers

**Complete the sequences.**

Count by [10] s: 10, 20, [ ], 40, [ ], [ ], [ ], 80

Count by [ ] s: 15, 20, 25, [ ], 35, 40, [ ], 50

★ Count by [ ] s: 42, 45, 48, 51, [ ], 57, 60, [ ]

**Complete.**

$ [ ]

$ [ ]

**Complete.**

50 + 40 = [ ]

70 - 20 = [ ]

35 + 10 = [ ]

25 + 25 = [ ]

80 - 40 = [ ]

50 - 20 = [ ]

## Lesson Activities

A

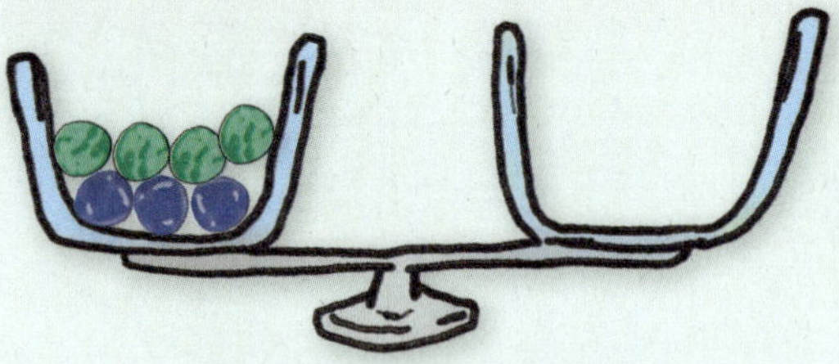

$3 + 4 = \square$

$\square = 3 + 4$

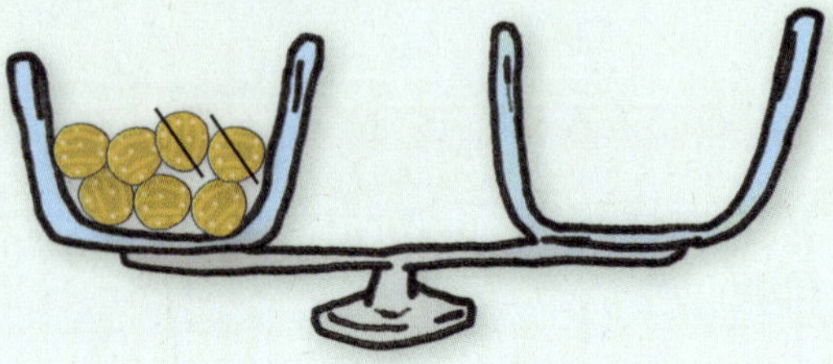

$7 - 2 = \square$

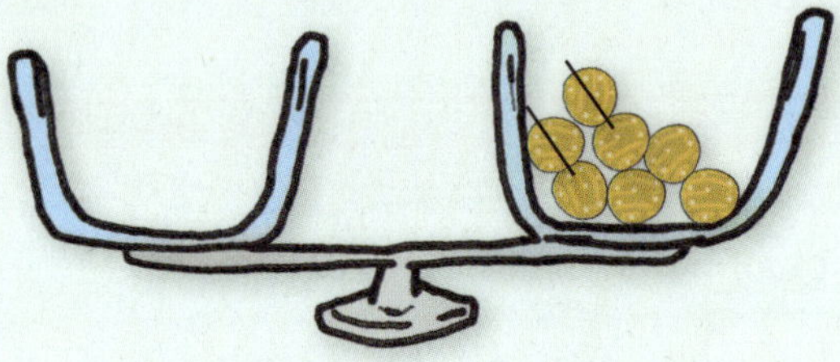

$\square = 7 - 2$

B

$\square = 4 + 4$

$\square = 9 - 5$

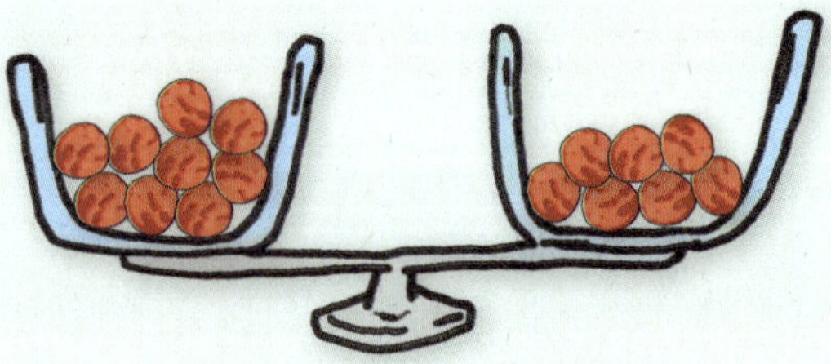

$9 = 7 + \square$

$5 = 8 - \square$

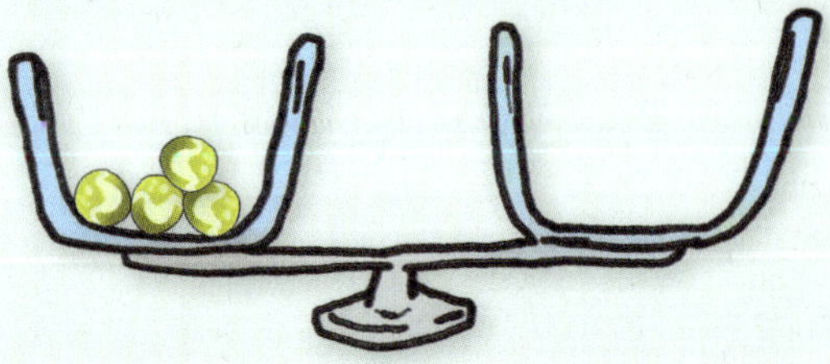

$4 = \square - 2$

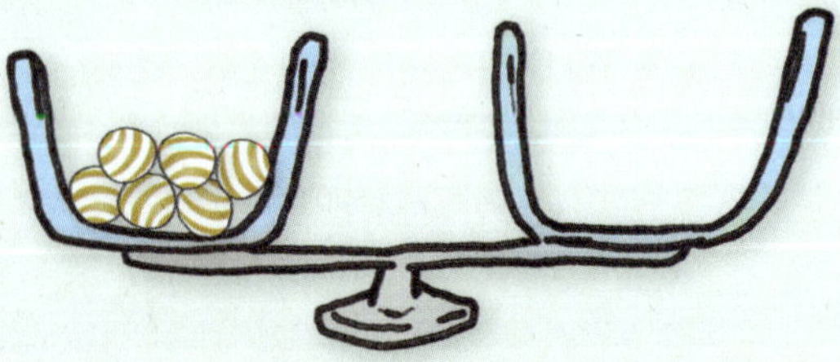

$6 = \square - 4$

## Practice

**Complete.**

| | | |
|---|---|---|
| ☐ = 8 + 4 | ☐ = 7 + 6 | ☐ = 4 + 9 |
| ☐ = 7 + 8 | ☐ = 9 + 9 | ☐ = 8 + 5 |
| ☐ = 16 - 8 | ☐ = 11 - 4 | ☐ = 11 - 9 |
| ☐ = 14 - 9 | ☐ = 13 - 7 | ☐ = 15 - 6 |

**Complete. Draw or cross out marbles on the scale to match each completed equation.**

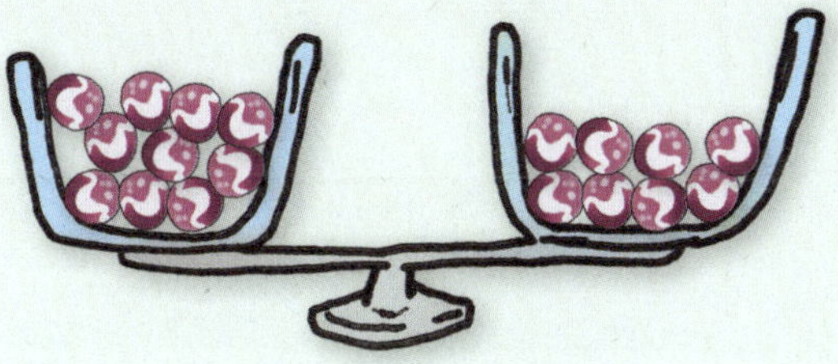

10 = 8 + ☐

7 = 9 - ☐

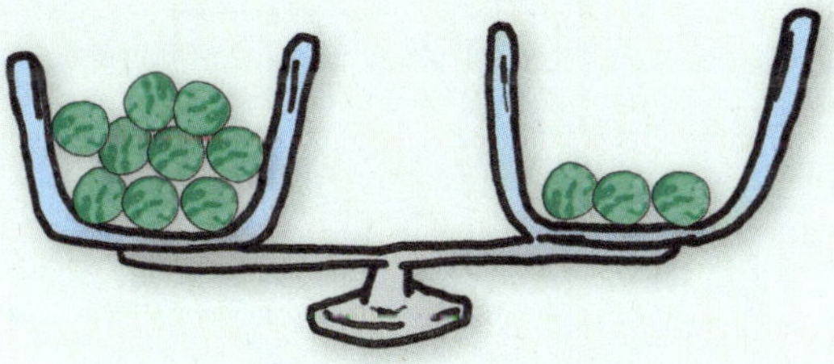

9 = ☐ + 3

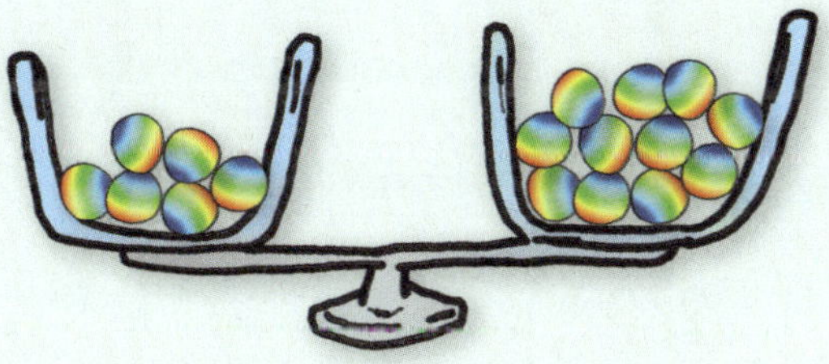

6 = 11 - ☐

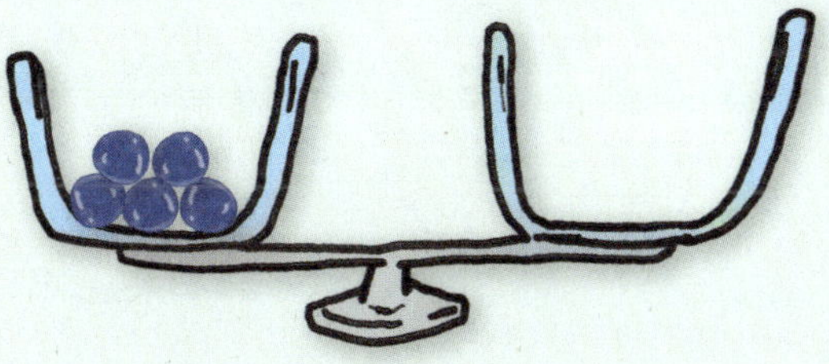

5 = ☐ - 3

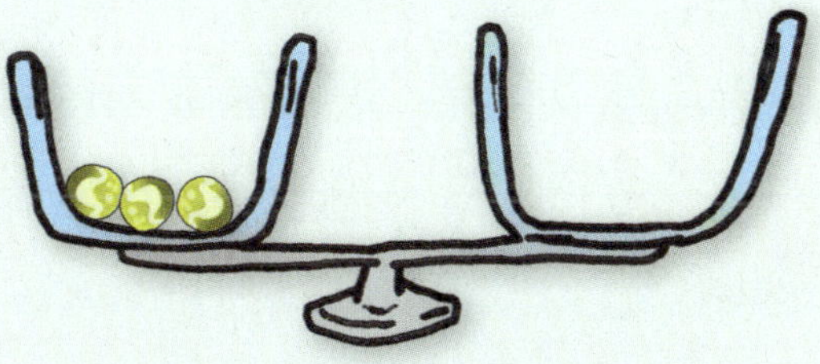

3 = ☐ - 7

## Review

**Use the graph to complete the chart.**

| Subject | Number of People |
|---|---|
| Reading | |
| Math | |
| Science | |

**Color the even numbers green. Color the odd numbers blue.**

**Complete.**

99 + ☐ = 100

98 + ☐ = 100

97 + ☐ = 100

96 + ☐ = 100

95 + ☐ = 100

**Match.**

Eighths | Halves | Fourths | Sixths | Thirds

## Lesson Activities

A

### How to Read Word Problems

1. Read the problem.
2. Identify the goal.
3. Read the problem again.
    - Read slowly and carefully.
    - Imagine what's happening.
    - Stop after each sentence to make sure you understand it.
4. Solve.

B

You have $15.
Then, you earn $10 more.
How much money do you have?

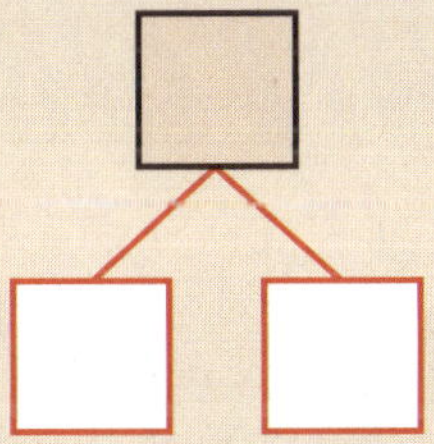

You pay $15 for a book and a box of markers. The book costs $10. How much do the markers cost?

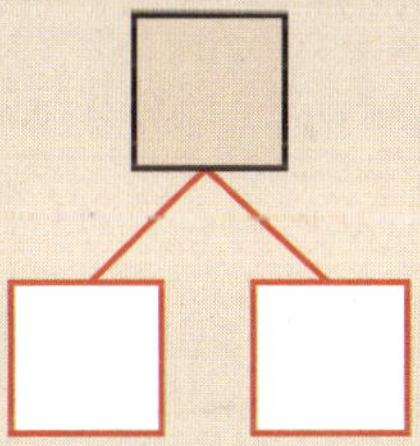

C

You have 10 inches of red ribbon.
You have 6 inches of blue ribbon.
How many more inches of red ribbon do you have than blue?

greater number – lesser number = difference

☐ – ☐ = ☐

## Practice

**Solve. Write the equations you use.**

How much does it cost to buy the squirrel and the teddy bear?

How much more does the whale cost than the snake?

You have $16. Then, you buy the squirrel. How much money do you have left?

How much does it cost to buy 2 monkeys?

How much less does the snake cost than the monkey?

★ How much does it cost to buy all 5 stuffed animals?

## Review

**Match.**

| | |
|---|---|
| 600 + 20 + 4 | 604 |
| 600 + 4 | 640 |
| 600 + 40 | 624 |
| 600 + 40 + 2 | 642 |

| | |
|---|---|
| 900 + 80 | 908 |
| 900 + 8 | 890 |
| 800 + 9 | 980 |
| 800 + 90 | 809 |

**Complete with <, >, or =.**

25 + 25 ◯ 50

50 ◯ 30 + 30

30 + 30 ◯ 59

40 ◯ 100 - 50

101 - 1 ◯ 60 + 40

**Complete.**

$ ☐

$ ☐

**Complete.**

☐ tiles

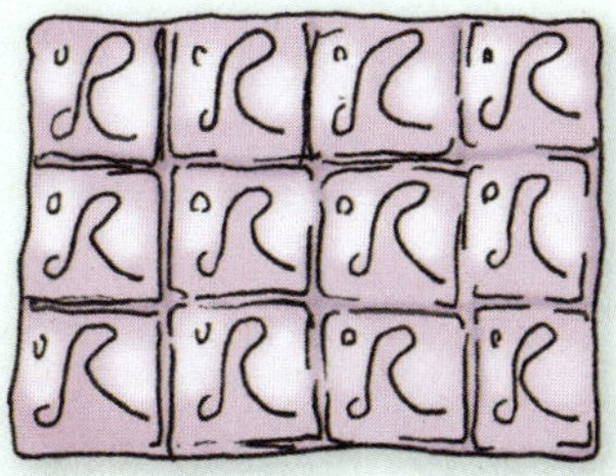

☐ tiles

**Complete.**

1 week = ☐ days

1 day = ☐ hours

1 hour = ☐ minutes

1 minute = ☐ seconds

## Lesson Activities

A

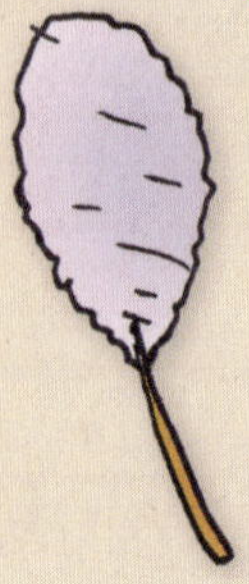

Oscar has $11 to spend at the carnival.
He spends $4 on a snack.
Then, he spends $3 at the arcade.
How much money does he have now?

Arthur has 9 library books.
He takes 6 books back to the library.
Then, he checks out 10 more.
How many library books does he have now?

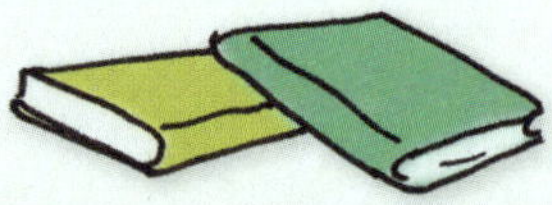

B

The ice cream shop sold 12 ice cream cones.
4 were chocolate.
5 were vanilla.
The rest were strawberry.
How many were strawberry?

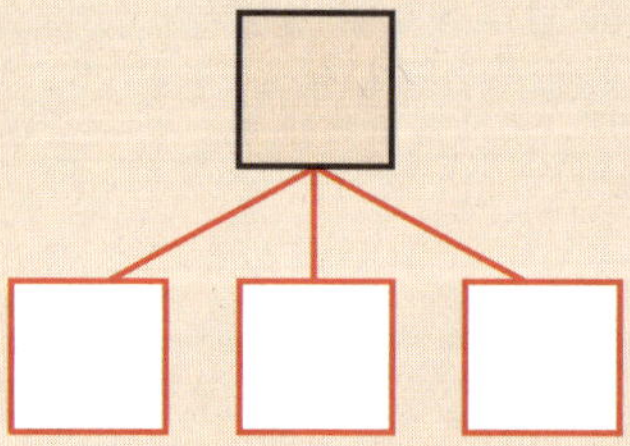

Aman spent 30 minutes on all his chores.
He spent 10 minutes washing dishes.
He spent 5 minutes sweeping.
He spent the rest of the time cleaning his room.
How long did he spend cleaning his room?

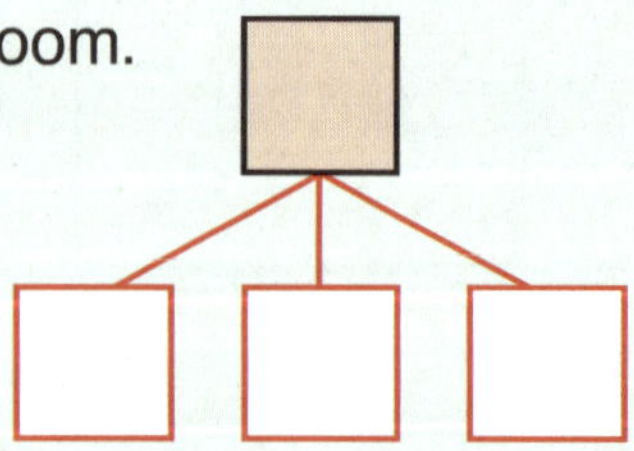

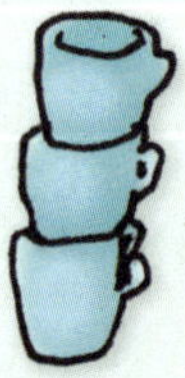

## Practice

**Solve. Complete the Part-Total diagram to match.**

Gabby spends $10 in all at the yard sale.
She spends $4 on a shirt.
She spends $3 on books.
She spends the rest on a board game.
How much does the board game cost?

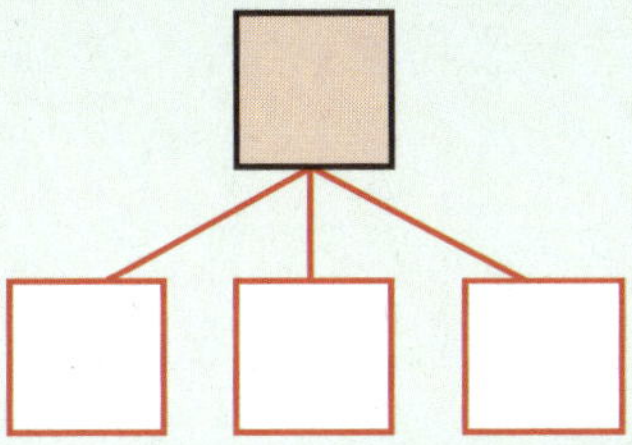

Gavin has 16 googly eyes.
He puts 2 eyes on an octopus.
He puts 8 eyes on a monster.
How many googly eyes does he have left?

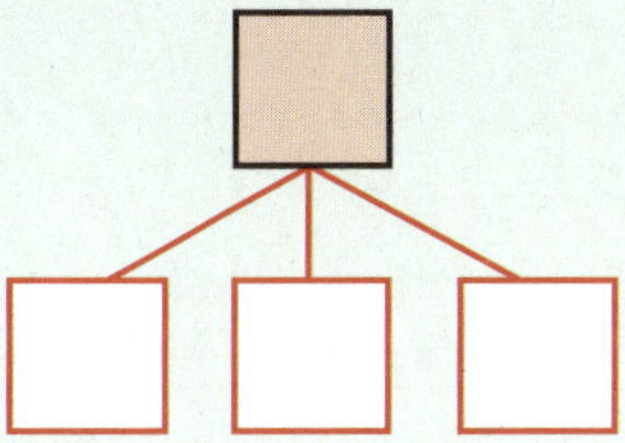

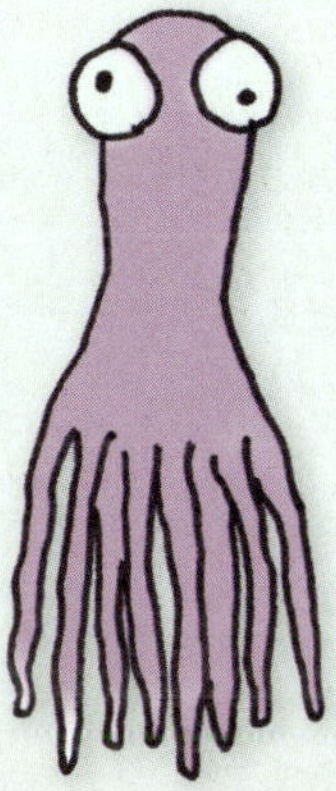

**Solve. Write the equations you use.**

Connor brought 12 cookies for the bake sale.
Josie brought 6 cookies for the bake sale.
They sold 8 cookies.
How many cookies did they have left?

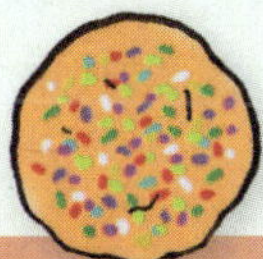

Serena has 10 trading cards.
She gives 4 to her brother.
Then, she buys 9 more.
How many trading cards does she have now?

1.6

## Review

**Draw a shape to match each description.**

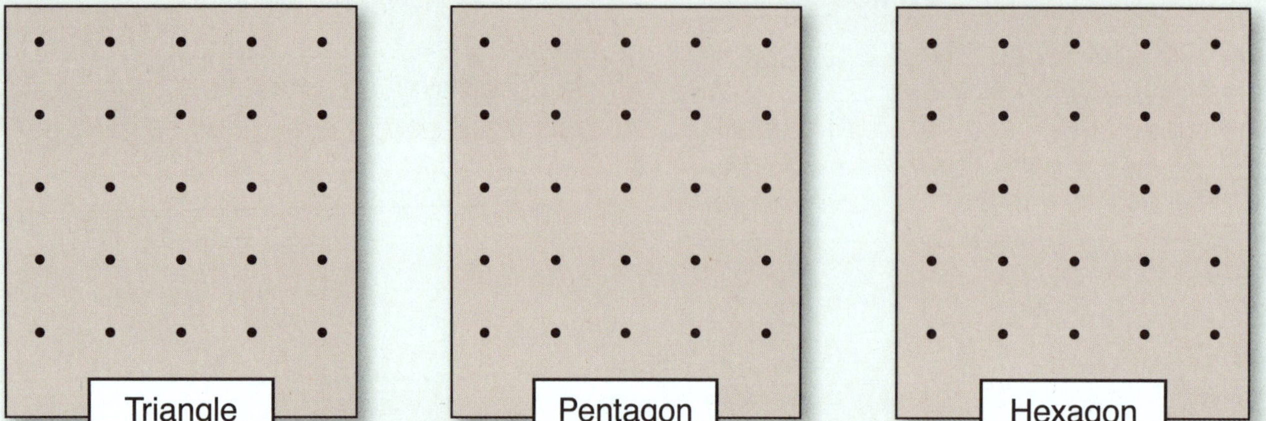

Triangle | Pentagon | Hexagon

**Complete the sequences.**

Count by ☐s: ☐, ☐, 72, 74, 76, ☐, ☐, ☐

Count by ☐s: ☐, ☐, ☐, ☐, 185, 190, 195, ☐

★ Count by ☐s: ☐, ☐, 42, 49, 56, ☐, ☐, ☐

**Draw lines to divide each cake into equal parts.**

Halves | Fourths | Eighths | Thirds | Sixths

## Lesson Activities

**A**

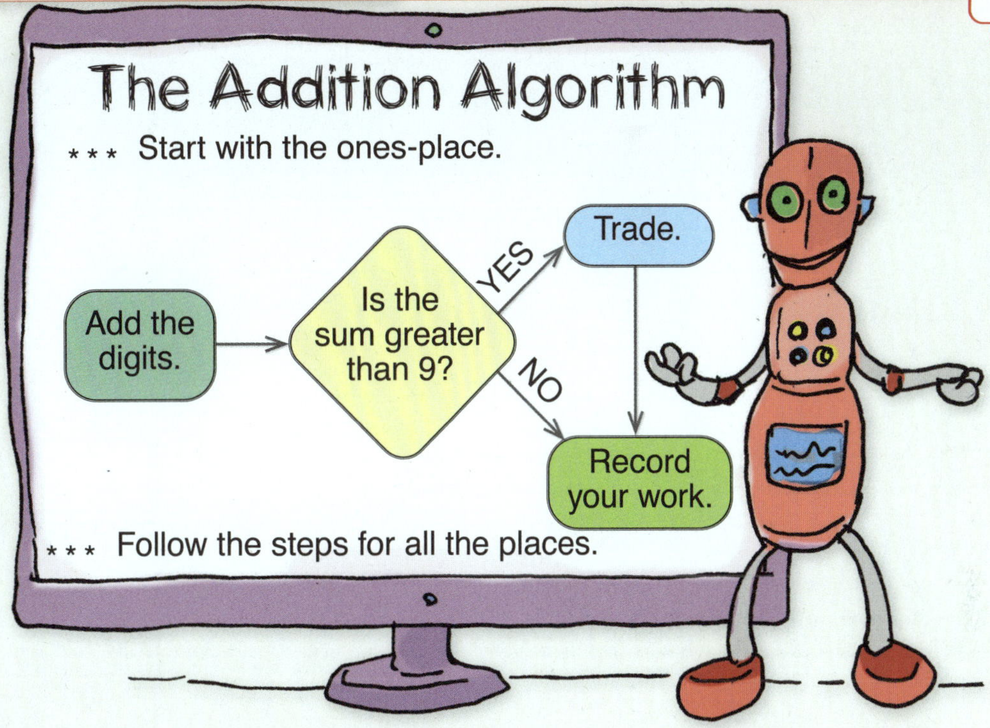


| | 3 | 9 |
|---|---|---|
| + | 5 | 7 |
| | | |

| | 2 | 6 |
|---|---|---|
| + | 6 | 8 |
| | | |

| | 5 | 7 |
|---|---|---|
| + | 5 | 2 |
| | | |

| | 7 | 6 |
|---|---|---|
| + | 8 | 4 |
| | | |

**B**

## Leaf Fight

| | | |
|---|---|---|
| + | | |
| | | |

| | | |
|---|---|---|
| + | | |
| | | |

| | | |
|---|---|---|
| + | | |
| | | |

| | | |
|---|---|---|
| + | | |
| | | |

| | | |
|---|---|---|
| + | | |
| | | |

| | | |
|---|---|---|
| + | | |
| | | |

| | | |
|---|---|---|
| + | | |
| | | |

| | | |
|---|---|---|
| + | | |
| | | |

## Practice

Complete.

| | 8 | 0 |
|---|---|---|
| + | 3 | 6 |
| | | |

| | 6 | 3 |
|---|---|---|
| + | 2 | 4 |
| | | |

| | 4 | 5 |
|---|---|---|
| + | 2 | 6 |
| | | |

| | 7 | 8 |
|---|---|---|
| + | 2 | 9 |
| | | |

## Review

Use a ruler to measure in inches.

☐ inches

☐ inches

☐ inches

Complete.

1 foot = ☐ inches

1 yard = ☐ inches

1 yard = ☐ feet

1 meter = ☐ centimeters

Write a.m. or p.m. for each time.

Storytime 10:15 ☐

Soccer Practice 4:30 ☐

Complete.

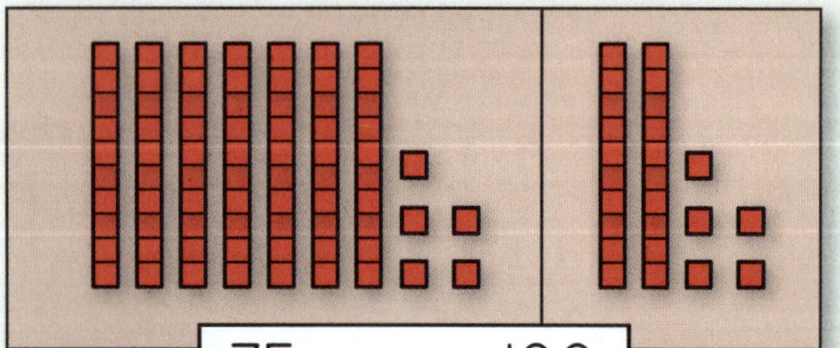

75 + ☐ = 100

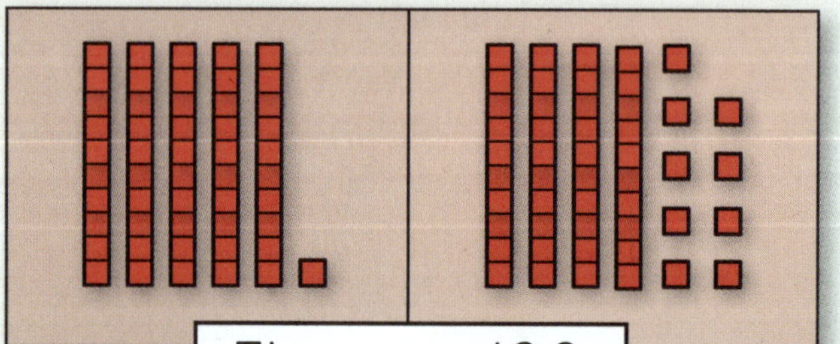

51 + ☐ = 100

## Lesson Activities

A

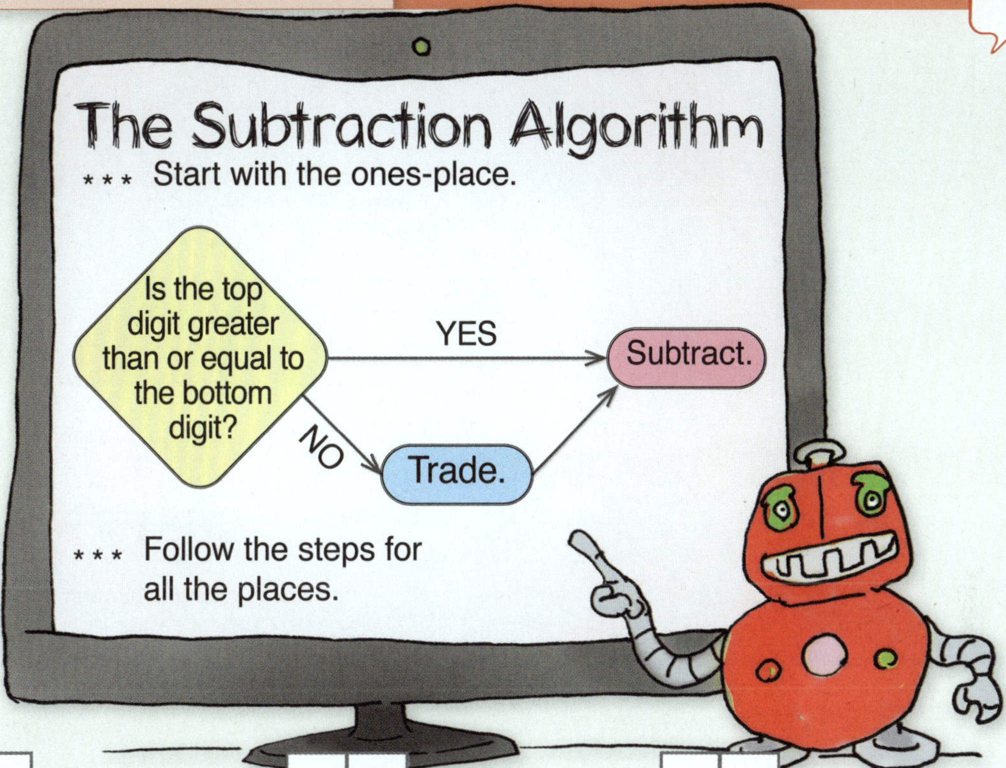


$$\begin{array}{r} 72 \\ -\ 29 \\ \hline \end{array} \qquad \begin{array}{r} 96 \\ -\ 58 \\ \hline \end{array} \qquad \begin{array}{r} 80 \\ -\ 47 \\ \hline \end{array} \qquad \begin{array}{r} 65 \\ -\ 23 \\ \hline \end{array}$$

B

## Leaf Fight

# 1.8

## Practice

Complete.

|   | 4 | 2 |
|---|---|---|
| - | 1 | 6 |
|   |   |   |

|   | 8 | 0 |
|---|---|---|
| - | 2 | 7 |
|   |   |   |

|   | 8 | 4 |
|---|---|---|
| - | 3 | 5 |
|   |   |   |

|   | 9 | 0 |
|---|---|---|
| - | 8 | 3 |
|   |   |   |

## Review

Use a ruler to measure in centimeters.

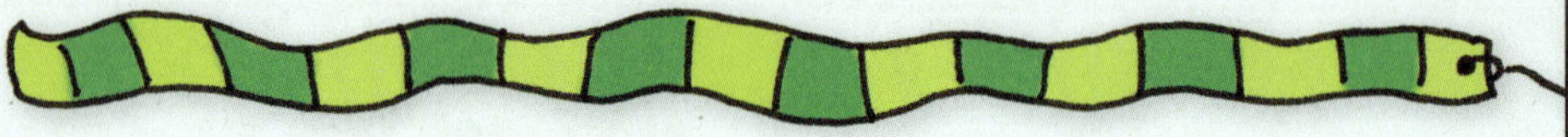

☐ centimeters

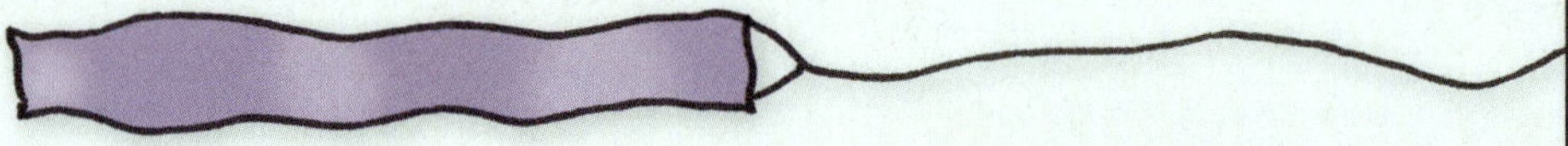

☐ centimeters

☐ centimeters

Write the time.

☐ : ☐

☐ : ☐

☐ : ☐

☐ : ☐

Complete.

☐ ¢

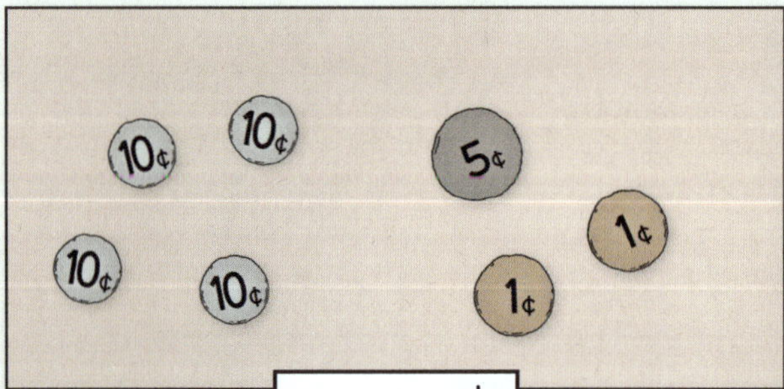


☐ ¢

## Lesson Activities

A

### Points Scored in Last Night's Game

| Player | Points |
|---|---|
| Arjun | 6 |
| Brynn | 10 |
| Claire | 3 |
| Dan | 7 |
| Eve | 4 |

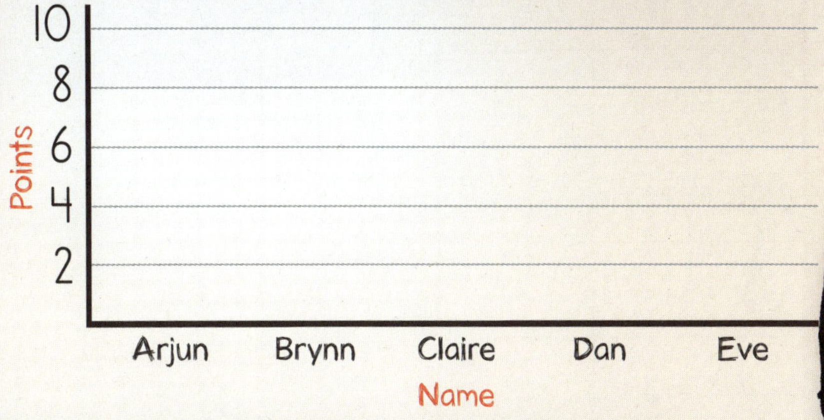


B

### Points Scored This Season

| Player | Points |
|---|---|
| Arjun | 20 |
| Brynn | 35 |
| Claire | 22 |
| Dan | 19 |
| Eve | 6 |

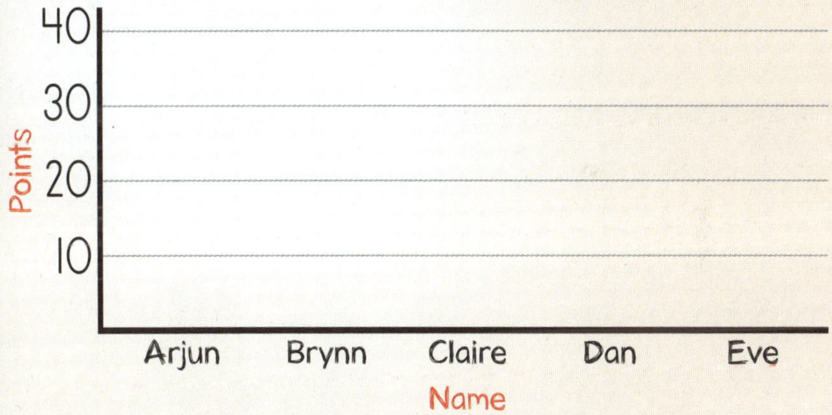


C

How many more points has Brynn scored than Dan this season?

How many points has the team scored in all this season?

## Practice

**Use the chart to make a bar graph.**

| Type of Tree | Number of Trees |
|---|---|
| Maple | 49 |
| Oak | 25 |
| Pine | 32 |
| Gingko | 17 |

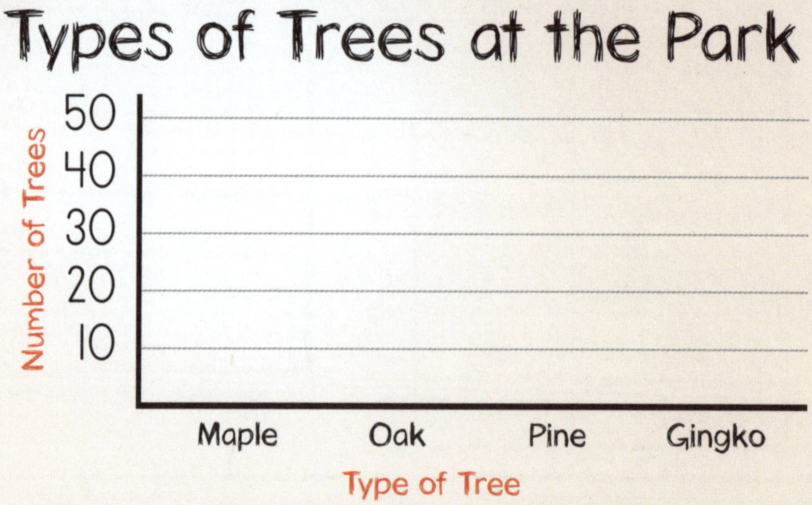


**Use the chart to solve. Write the equations you use.**

How many trees are maples or oaks?

How many more pine trees than gingko trees are there?

If the park plants 9 more oak trees, how many oak trees will there be?

How many trees are listed in all in the chart?

## Review

**Use a ruler to draw a line that matches each length.**

5 inches

9 centimeters

**Complete.**

| | 3 | 7 |
|---|---|---|
| + | 5 | 6 |
| | | |

| | 8 | 4 |
|---|---|---|
| + | 1 | 7 |
| | | |

| | 9 | 2 |
|---|---|---|
| - | 3 | 5 |
| | | |

| | 8 | 0 |
|---|---|---|
| - | 4 | 7 |
| | | |

**Round to the nearest ten.**

| | |
|---|---|
| 16 | |
| 27 | |
| 43 | |
| 85 | |
| 96 | |

**Write each amount of money two ways.**

$ ______ ______ ¢

$ ______ ______ ¢

**Write the time.**

___ : ___

___ : ___

# Unit Wrap-Up

## Complete the fact family to match the Part-Total diagram.

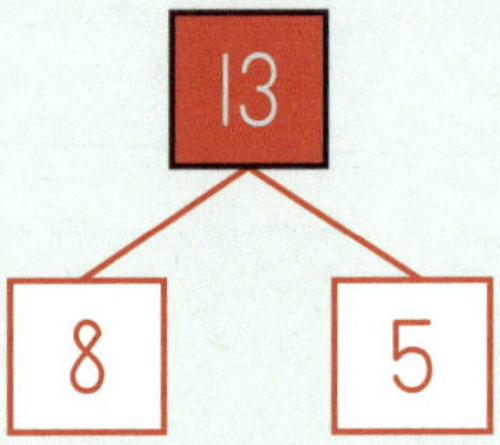


☐ + ☐ = ☐

☐ + ☐ = ☐

☐ - ☐ = ☐

☐ - ☐ = ☐

## Match.

| | |
|---|---|
| The sum of 7 and 4 | 3 |
| The difference between 7 and 4 | 11 |
| The sum of 7, 4, and 2 | 13 |

## Round to the nearest ten.

| | |
|---|---|
| 47 | |
| 19 | |
| 65 | |
| 97 | |

## Complete with <, >, or =.

10 - 7 ◯ 5

10 + 15 ◯ 20

9 ◯ 20 - 10

35 ◯ 20 + 10

## Complete.

7 + ☐ = 12 ☐ = 8 + 8 12 = 7 + ☐

10 - ☐ = 7 ☐ = 15 - 6 10 = 14 - ☐

## Unit Wrap-Up

**Complete.**

|   | 4 | 2 |
|---|---|---|
| + | 3 | 9 |
|   |   |   |

|   | 8 | 7 |
|---|---|---|
| - | 3 | 5 |
|   |   |   |

|   | 8 | 5 |
|---|---|---|
| + | 4 | 8 |
|   |   |   |

|   | 8 | 0 |
|---|---|---|
| - | 4 | 7 |
|   |   |   |

**Carlos made a chart to show how high the kids in his family can jump. Use the chart to complete the graph.**

| Name | Centimeters |
|---|---|
| Carlos | 25 |
| Ana | 34 |
| Rafael | 19 |

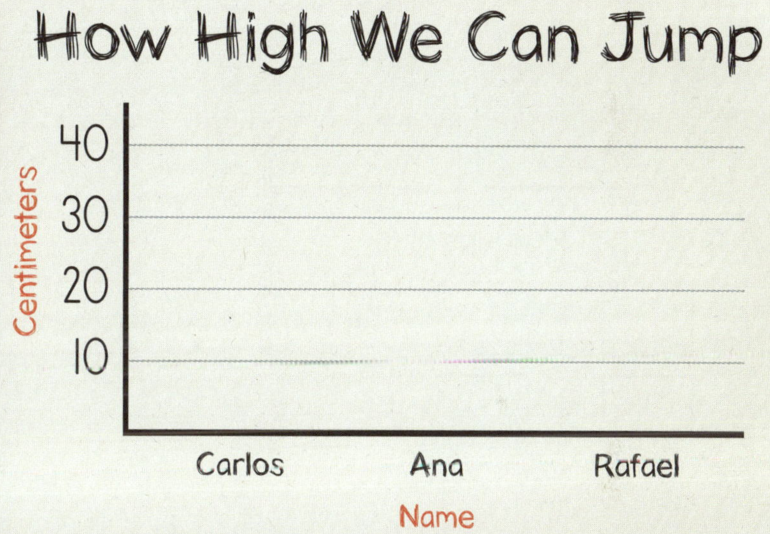


**Solve. Write the equations you use.**

Ana can jump 34 centimeters high. Rafael can jump 19 centimeters high. How much higher can Ana jump than Rafael?

15 birds are sitting in a tree. 6 are red, 5 are brown, and the rest are yellow. How many birds are yellow?

# Lesson Activities

## A

**Repeated Addition**

3 groups of 4

$4 + 4 + 4 = \square$

**Multiplication**

3 groups of 4

$3 \times 4 = \square$

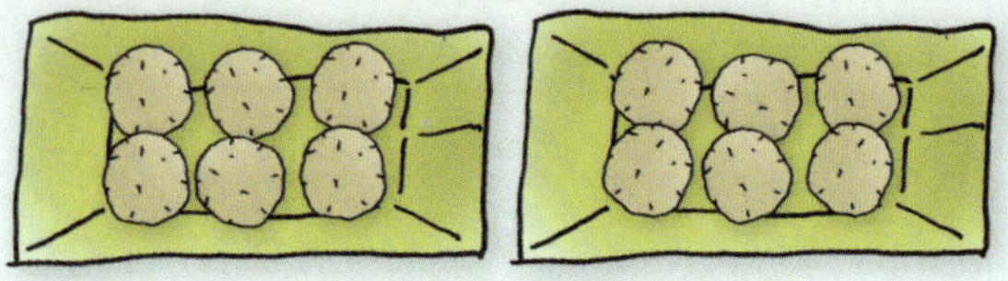

2 groups of 6

$\square + \square = \square$

$\square \times \square = \square$

5 groups of 3

$\square + \square + \square + \square + \square = \square$

$\square \times \square = \square$

## B

| Cookie Order | Multiplication Equation |
|---|---|
| 3 boxes of 6 | |
| 4 boxes of 4 | |
| 1 box of 8 | |
| 2 boxes of 7 | |
| 5 boxes of 2 | |

## Practice

**Complete.**

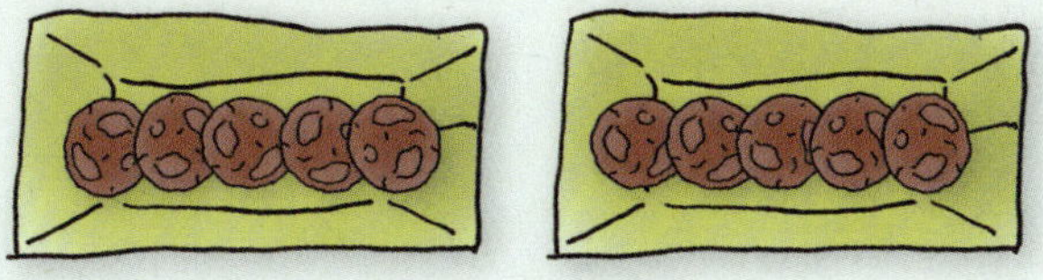

2 groups of 5

$2 \times 5 = \square$

3 groups of 3

$3 \times 3 = \square$

4 groups of 2

$4 \times 2 = \square$

4 groups of 4

$\square \times \square = \square$

5 groups of 4

$\square \times \square = \square$

4 groups of 5

$\square \times \square = \square$

5 groups of 1

$\square \times \square = \square$

5 groups of 0

$\square \times \square = \square$

1 group of 9

$\square \times \square = \square$

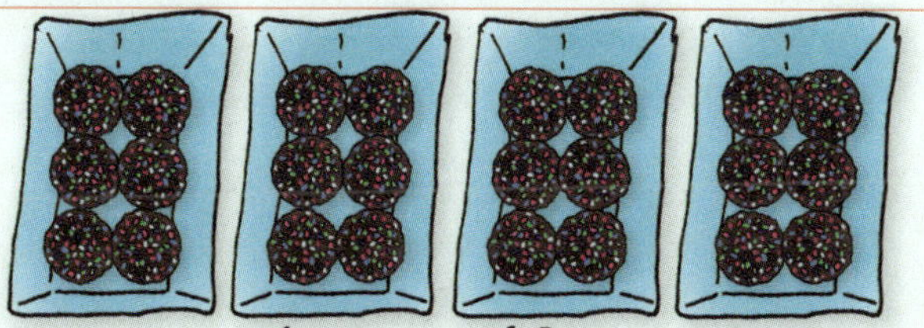

4 groups of 6

$\square \times \square = \square$

## Review

Complete.

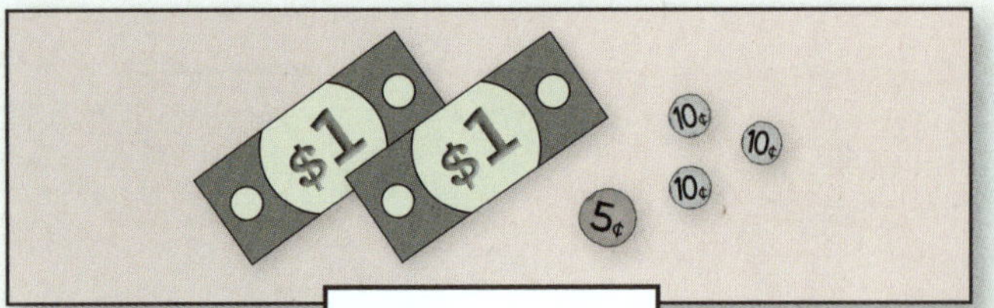

$

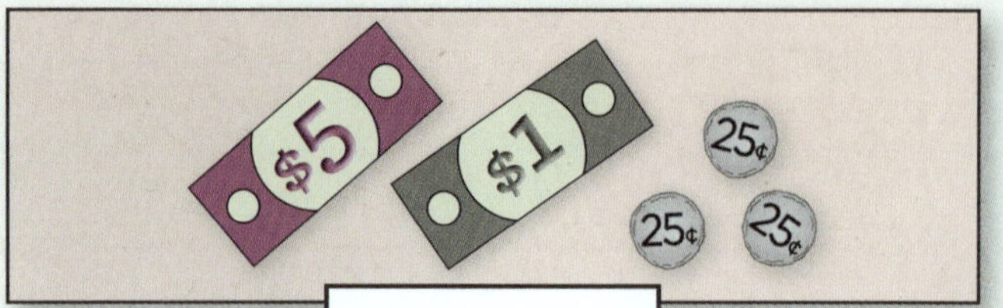

$

Complete.

| | Double |
|---|---|
| 10 | 20 |
| 11 | |
| 40 | |
| 42 | |
| 45 | |
| 50 | |

Write the value of the base-ten blocks.

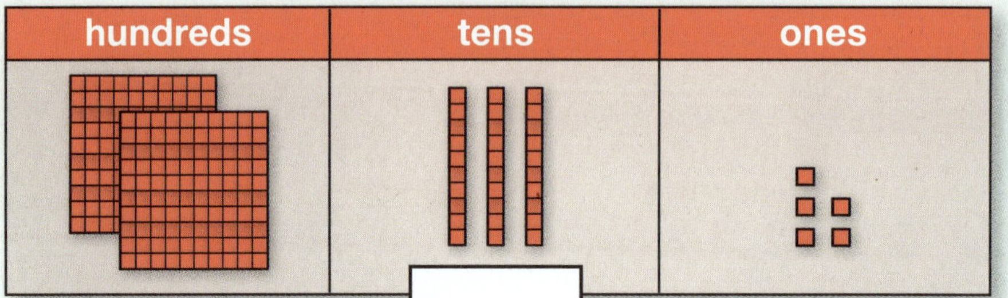

Complete.

| | 3 | 7 |
|---|---|---|
| + | 2 | 3 |
| | | |

| | 8 | 0 |
|---|---|---|
| - | 4 | 7 |
| | | |

| | 5 | 2 |
|---|---|---|
| - | 1 | 8 |
| | | |

| | 6 | 8 |
|---|---|---|
| + | 9 | 4 |
| | | |

Match.

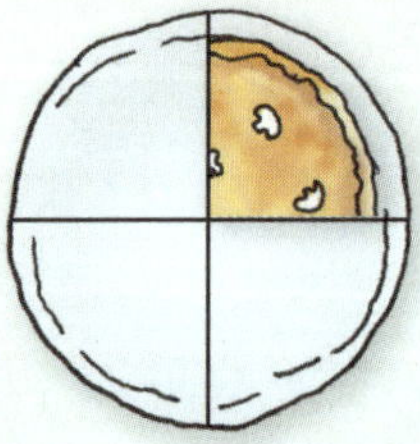

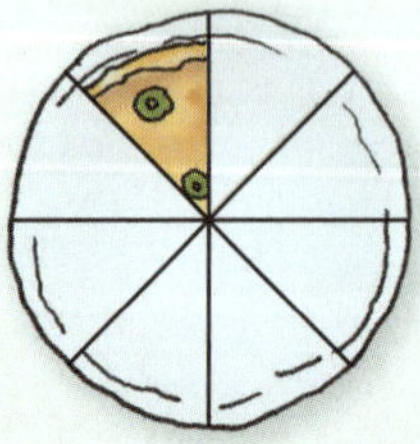

$\frac{1}{8}$

$\frac{1}{3}$

$\frac{1}{4}$

## Lesson Activities

**A**

3 groups of 5

☐ × ☐ = ☐

5 groups of 3

☐ × ☐ = ☐

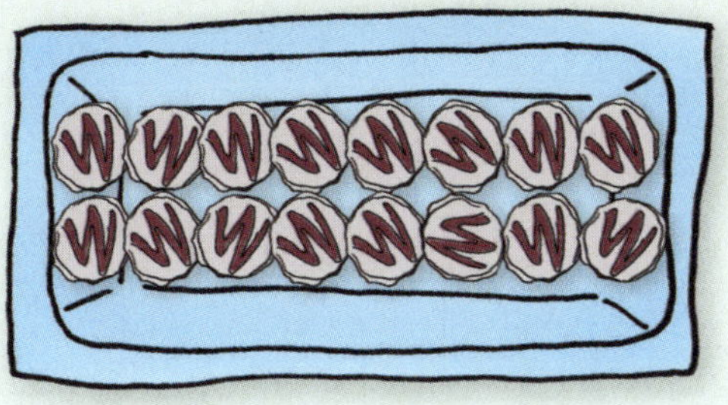

☐ × ☐ = ☐

☐ × ☐ = ☐

**B**

| Order (Rows x Columns) | Total Squares |
|---|---|
| 3 × 3 | |
| 7 × 2 | |
| 1 × 6 | |
| 5 × 5 | |
| 3 × 8 | |

## Practice

**Write an equation to match each array.**

☐ × ☐ = ☐

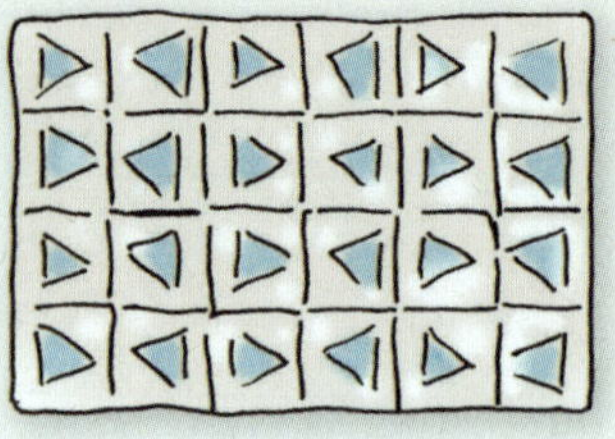

☐ × ☐ = ☐

☐ × ☐ = ☐

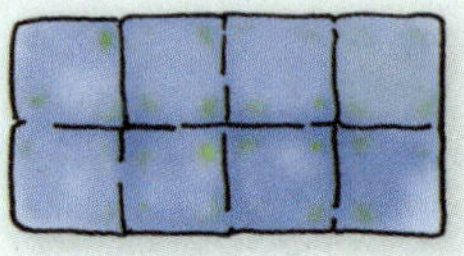

☐ × ☐ = ☐

**Draw an array to match each equation. Then, complete the equation.**

$2 \times 6 =$ ☐

$4 \times 5 =$ ☐

$5 \times 6 =$ ☐

$3 \times 7 =$ ☐

## Review

### Complete.

□ ¢

□ ¢

### Write the time.

□ :

□ :

### Write a.m. or p.m. for each time.

Breakfast 7:30 □

Lunch 12:30 □

Dinner 6:00 □

### Solve.

Greyson helped his mom plant 50 flower bulbs.
32 were tulips.
The rest were daffodils.
How many were daffodils?

### Match.

$\frac{3}{4}$

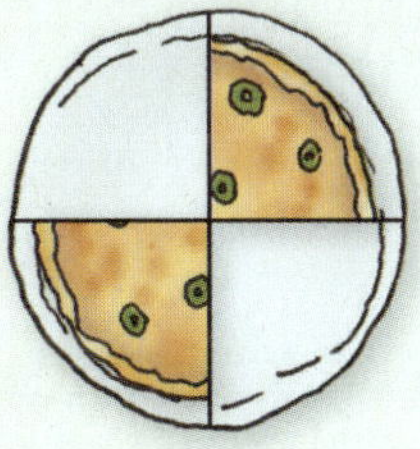

$\frac{4}{4}$

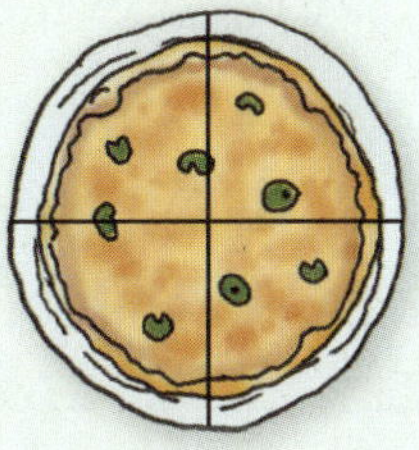

$\frac{2}{4}$

## Lesson Activities

### A

$1 \times 2 = \square$

$2 \times 2 = \square$

$3 \times 2 = \square$

$4 \times 2 = \square$

$5 \times 2 = \square$

$6 \times 2 = \square$

$7 \times 2 = \square$

$8 \times 2 = \square$

$9 \times 2 = \square$

$10 \times 2 = \square$

### B

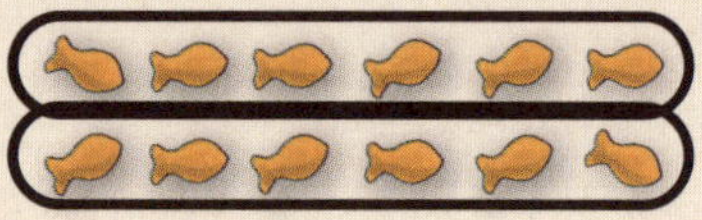

2 groups of 6

$2 \times 6 = \square$

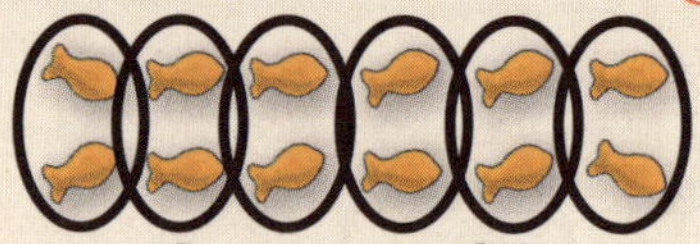

6 groups of 2

$6 \times 2 = \square$

$10 \times 2 = \square$

$2 \times 10 = \square$

$8 \times 2 = \square$

$2 \times 8 = \square$

$9 \times 2 = \square$

$2 \times 9 = \square$

### C

## Multiplication Crash (×2)

| | | | | |
|---|---|---|---|---|
| 2 | 4 | 6 | 8 | 10 |
| 12 | 14 | 16 | 18 | 20 |

## Practice

**Complete.**

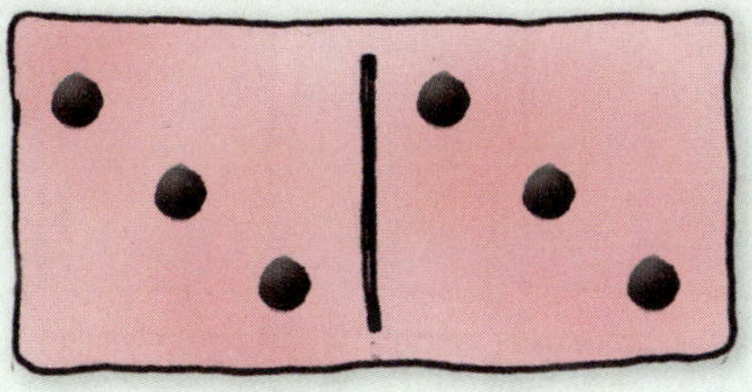

$2 \times 3 =$ ☐

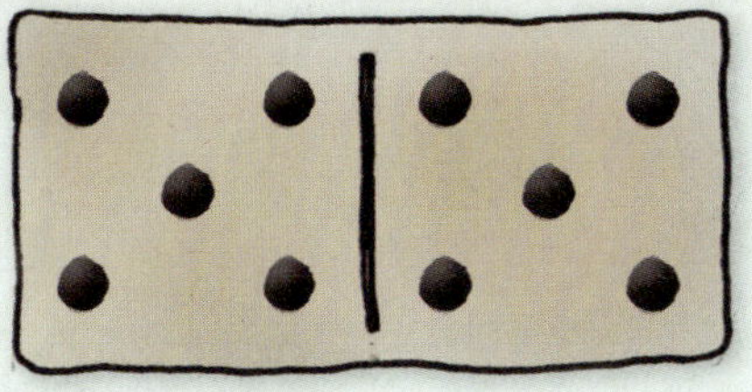

$2 \times 5 =$ ☐

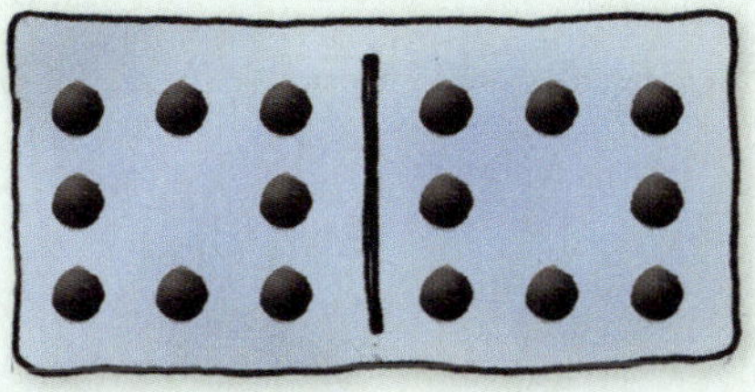

$2 \times 8 =$ ☐

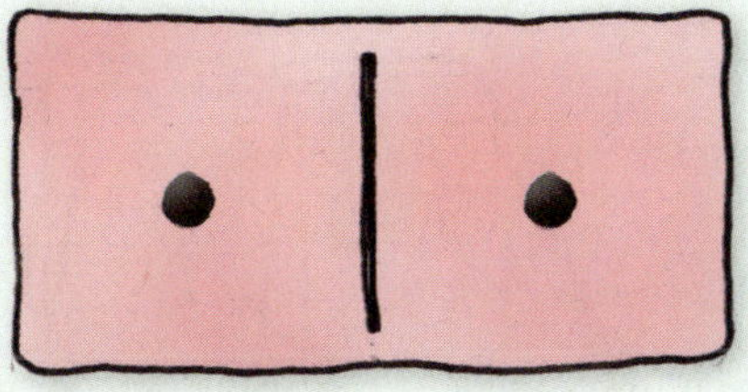

$2 \times 1 =$ ☐

$2 \times 7 =$ ☐

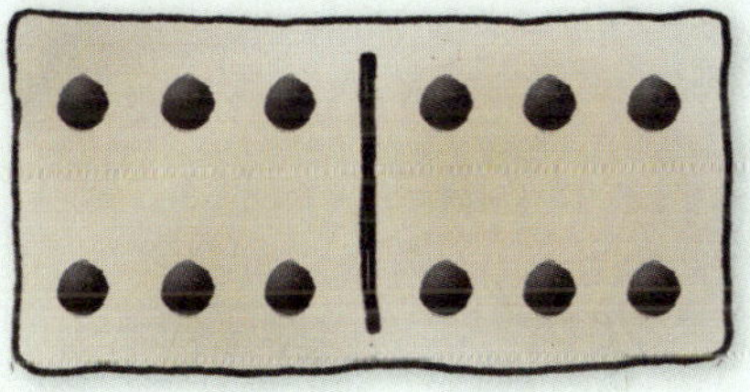

$2 \times 6 =$ ☐

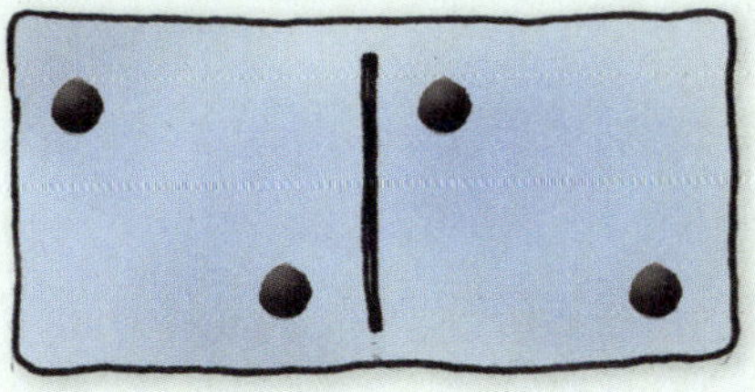

$2 \times 2 =$ ☐

$2 \times 9 =$ ☐

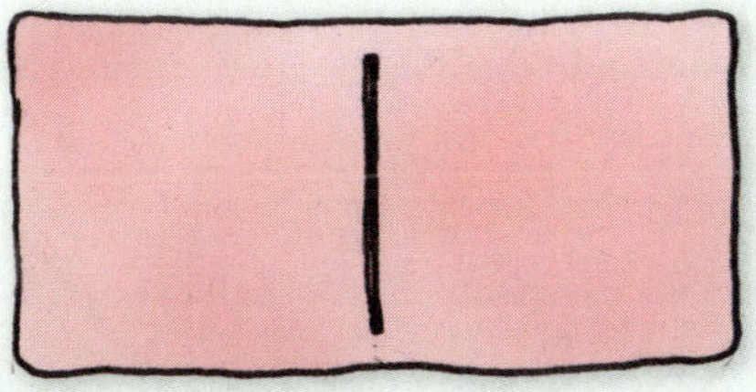

$2 \times 0 =$ ☐

$2 \times 4 =$ ☐

## Review

**Complete the sequences.**

| Count by 1s | 317 | 318 | | | | | | 324 |
|---|---|---|---|---|---|---|---|---|
| **Count by 2s** | 540 | 542 | | | | | | 554 |
| **Count by 5s** | 900 | 905 | | | | | 930 | |

**Complete.**

3 + 4 = ☐

30 + 40 = ☐

300 + 400 = ☐

8 - 2 = ☐

80 - 20 = ☐

800 - 200 = ☐

6 + ☐ = 10

60 + ☐ = 100

600 + ☐ = 1,000

**Complete.**

$ ☐

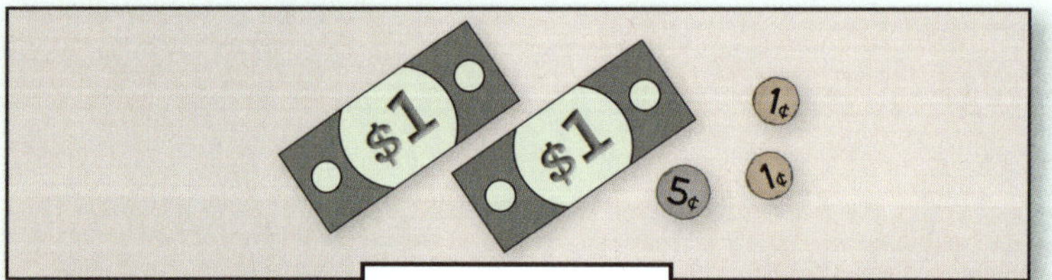


$ ☐

**Solve.**

Tia practiced violin for 15 minutes on Monday, 30 minutes on Tuesday, and 25 minutes on Wednesday. How many minutes did she practice?

## Lesson Activities

A

# Multiplication Bingo (×2)

| B | I | N | G | O |
|---|---|---|---|---|
| 2 | 8 | 20 | 14 | 18 |
| 10 | 20 | 16 | 6 | 4 |
| 16 | 14 | 12 | 10 | 18 |
| 8 | 2 | 18 | 20 | 16 |
| 14 | 6 | 4 | 4 | 12 |

| B | I | N | G | O |
|---|---|---|---|---|
| 12 | 10 | 6 | 20 | 4 |
| 18 | 6 | 2 | 14 | 8 |
| 16 | 8 | 10 | 4 | 12 |
| 20 | 4 | 14 | 8 | 18 |
| 16 | 2 | 10 | 6 | 2 |

B

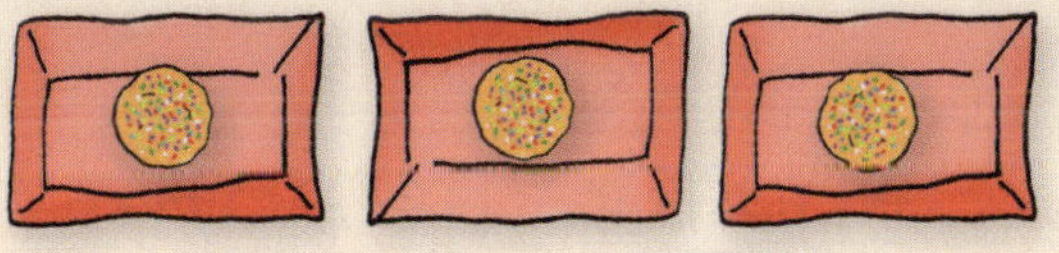

$3 \times 1 = \square$

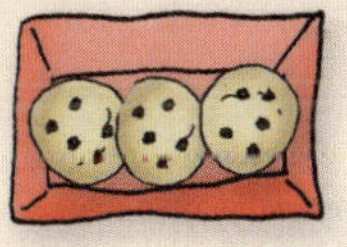

$1 \times 3 = \square$

$6 \times 1 = \square$ $1 \times 7 = \square$ $250 \times 1 = \square$

C

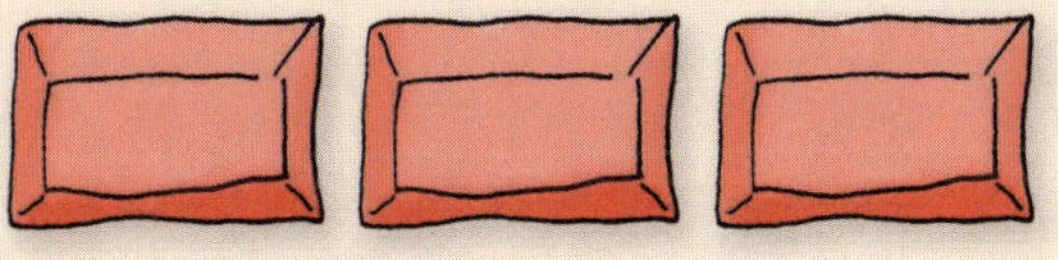

$3 \times 0 = \square$

$0 \times 3 = \square$

$6 \times 0 = \square$ $0 \times 7 = \square$ $250 \times 0 = \square$

## Practice

**Match.**

| | | |
|---|---|---|
| 1 × 2 | | 2 × 2 |
| | 0 | |
| 2 × 3 | 2 | 1 × 8 |
| 6 × 0 | 4 | 10 × 0 |
| 10 × 1 | 6 | 2 × 5 |
| 4 × 2 | 8 | 2 × 1 |
| | 10 | |
| 4 × 1 | | 6 × 1 |

**Complete.**

2 × 10 = ☐ 1 × 5 = ☐ 6 × 2 = ☐

9 × 0 = ☐ 2 × 9 = ☐ 1 × 8 = ☐

8 × 2 = ☐ 2 × 5 = ☐ 7 × 2 = ☐

★ 1 × 396 = ☐ ★ 37 × 0 = ☐ ★ 0 × 200 = ☐

## Review

**Complete the sequences.**

| Count by 100s | 200 |  | 400 |  |  |  |  | 900 |
|---|---|---|---|---|---|---|---|---|
| **Count by 50s** | 250 | 300 | 350 |  | 450 |  |  | 600 |
| **Count by 10s** | 570 |  | 590 |  | 610 |  |  | 640 |

**Copy the shapes.**

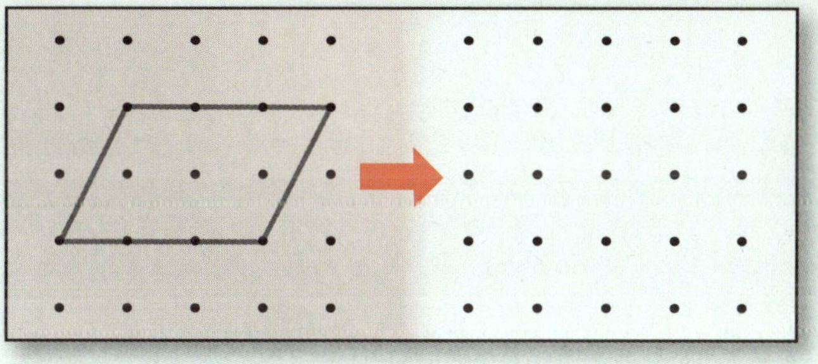

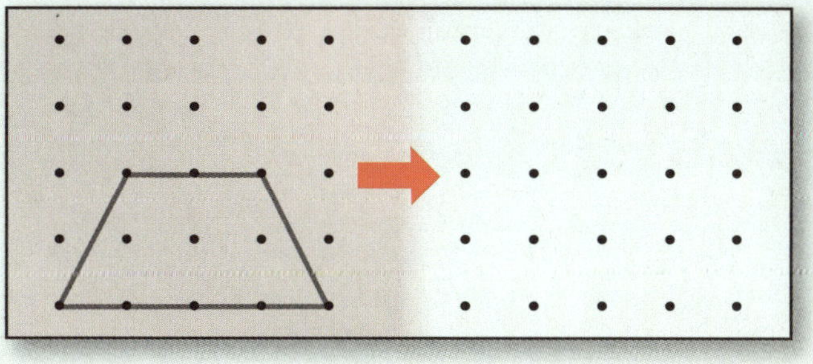

**Complete.**

|   | 7 | 8 |
|---|---|---|
| + | 6 | 2 |
|   |   |   |

|   | 7 | 6 |
|---|---|---|
| - | 2 | 9 |
|   |   |   |

**Solve.**

Luna had $53. Then, she spent $27.
How much did she have left?

**Complete with <, >, or =.**

600 ◯ 500

2 ◯ 200

301 ◯ 300

301 ◯ 301

## Lesson Activities

**A**

$4 \times 10 =$ ☐

4 tens = ☐

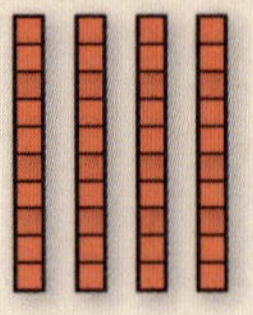

$6 \times 10 =$ ☐ $9 \times 10 =$ ☐ $8 \times 10 =$ ☐

$3 \times 10 =$ ☐ $7 \times 10 =$ ☐ $10 \times 10 =$ ☐

**B**

## Tic-Tac-Toe Crash (×10)

| | | |
|---|---|---|
| 10 | 20 | 30 |
| 40 | 50 | 60 |
| 70 | 80 | 90 |

**C**

| | 1 | 0 |
|---|---|---|
| × | | 2 |
| | | |

| | 1 | 0 |
|---|---|---|
| × | | 5 |
| | | |

| | 1 | 0 |
|---|---|---|
| × | | 1 |
| | | |

| | 1 | 0 |
|---|---|---|
| × | | 7 |
| | | |

| | 1 | 0 |
|---|---|---|
| × | 1 | 0 |
| | | |

## Practice

**Complete.**

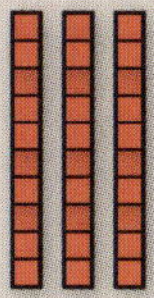

$3 \times 10 =$ ☐

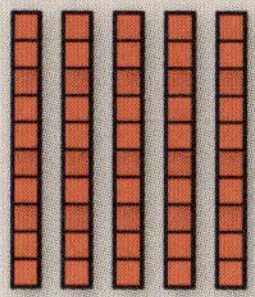

$5 \times 10 =$ ☐

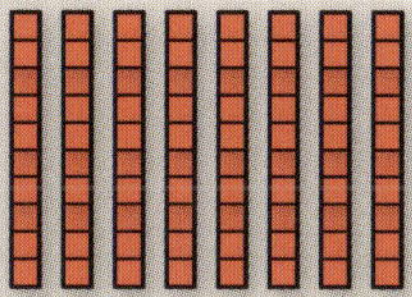

$8 \times 10 =$ ☐

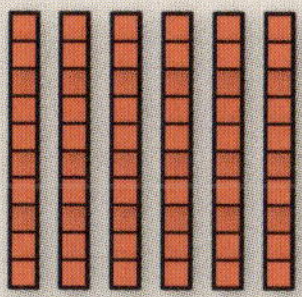

$6 \times 10 =$ ☐

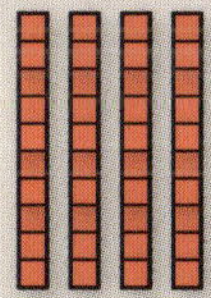

$4 \times 10 =$ ☐

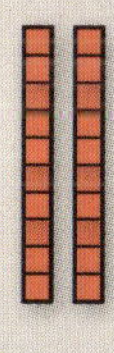

$2 \times 10 =$ ☐

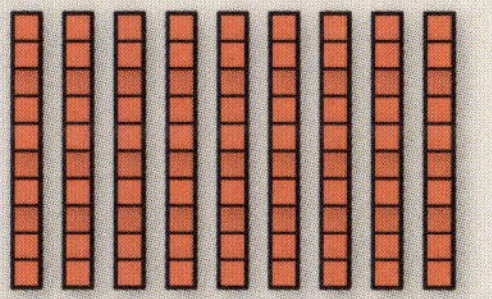

$9 \times 10 =$ ☐

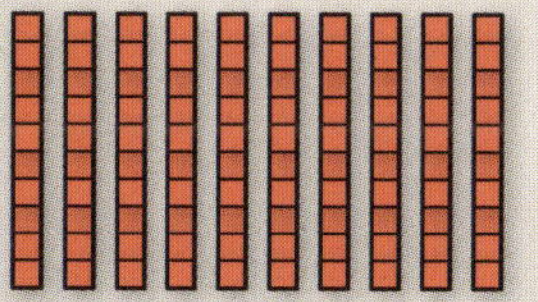

$10 \times 10 =$ ☐

★ $14 \times 10 =$ ☐

★ $30 \times 10 =$ ☐

## Review

**Complete.**

| | | |
|---|---|---|
| ☐ = 7 + 8 | 10 = 14 - ☐ | 5 = ☐ - 4 |
| ☐ = 12 - 3 | 17 = 12 + ☐ | 2 = ☐ - 9 |
| ☐ = 9 + 9 | 3 = 8 - ☐ | 8 = ☐ - 5 |

Complete.

**Round each number to the nearest ten.**

| 9 | 43 | 72 | 58 | 65 | 36 | 99 | 22 |
|---|---|---|---|---|---|---|---|
| | | | | | | | |

**Match.**

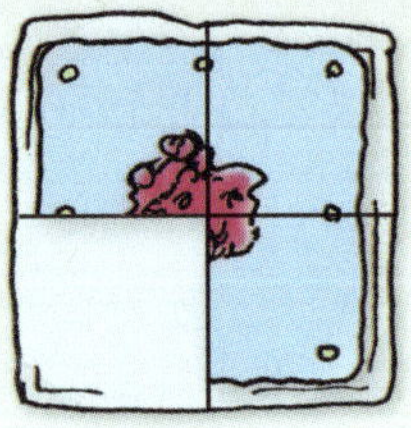

$\frac{3}{6}$

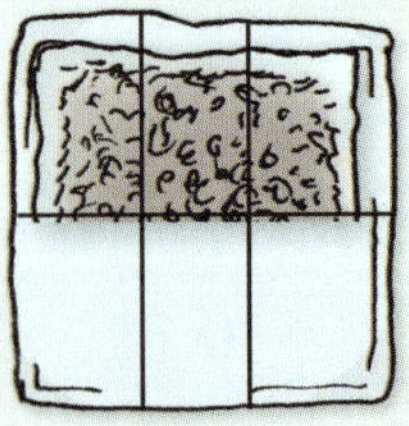

$\frac{3}{3}$

$\frac{3}{4}$

$\frac{3}{8}$

**Complete with <, >, or =.**

40 + 20 ◯ 70

100 ◯ 50 + 50

86 - 6 ◯ 70 + 4

11 ◯ 20 - 7

36 + 42 ◯ 36 + 43

100 - 37 ◯ 100 - 82

## Lesson Activities

**A**

$$9 \times 2 = 18$$

factors ↑↑  product ↑

**B**

### Shopping List

☐ packs of scissors

☐ × ☐ = ☐

☐ packs of pencils

☐ × ☐ = ☐

☐ boxes of markers

☐ × ☐ = ☐

☐ packs of staplers

☐ × ☐ = ☐

**C**

Julius has 2 bags of erasers.
Each bag has 8 erasers.
How many erasers does he have in all?

Lila packed 6 bags of apples.
Each bag had 10 apples.
How many apples did she pack in all?

# 2.6

## Practice

**Complete.**

$$\begin{array}{r} 10 \\ \times\ 3 \\ \hline \end{array} \qquad \begin{array}{r} 10 \\ \times\ 7 \\ \hline \end{array} \qquad \begin{array}{r} 10 \\ \times\ 5 \\ \hline \end{array} \qquad \begin{array}{r} 10 \\ \times\ 2 \\ \hline \end{array} \qquad \begin{array}{r} 10 \\ \times\ 8 \\ \hline \end{array}$$

$$\begin{array}{r} 10 \\ \times\ 4 \\ \hline \end{array} \qquad \begin{array}{r} 10 \\ \times\ 10 \\ \hline \end{array} \qquad \begin{array}{r} 10 \\ \times\ 1 \\ \hline \end{array} \qquad \begin{array}{r} 10 \\ \times\ 9 \\ \hline \end{array} \qquad \begin{array}{r} 10 \\ \times\ 6 \\ \hline \end{array}$$

$$\begin{array}{r} 2 \\ \times\ 7 \\ \hline \end{array} \qquad \begin{array}{r} 6 \\ \times\ 0 \\ \hline \end{array} \qquad \begin{array}{r} 2 \\ \times\ 9 \\ \hline \end{array} \qquad \begin{array}{r} 8 \\ \times\ 2 \\ \hline \end{array} \qquad \begin{array}{r} 1 \\ \times\ 5 \\ \hline \end{array}$$

**Solve. Write a multiplication equation to match.**

Lucas drew 4 robots.
He drew 3 heads on each robot.
How many heads did he draw?

___ × ___ = ___

Kali drew 5 cacti.
She drew 2 arms on each cactus.
How many arms did she draw?

___ × ___ = ___

## Review

**Complete.**

| Count by 100s | | | | 600 | | | | 1,000 |
|---|---|---|---|---|---|---|---|---|

| Count by 50s | | | 700 | 750 | | | | |
|---|---|---|---|---|---|---|---|---|

| Count by 10s | | | | 900 | 910 | | | |
|---|---|---|---|---|---|---|---|---|

**Complete.**

| | 4 | 7 |
|---|---|---|
| + | 9 | 3 |
| | | |

| | 8 | 4 |
|---|---|---|
| - | 4 | 9 |
| | | |

**Write the time.**

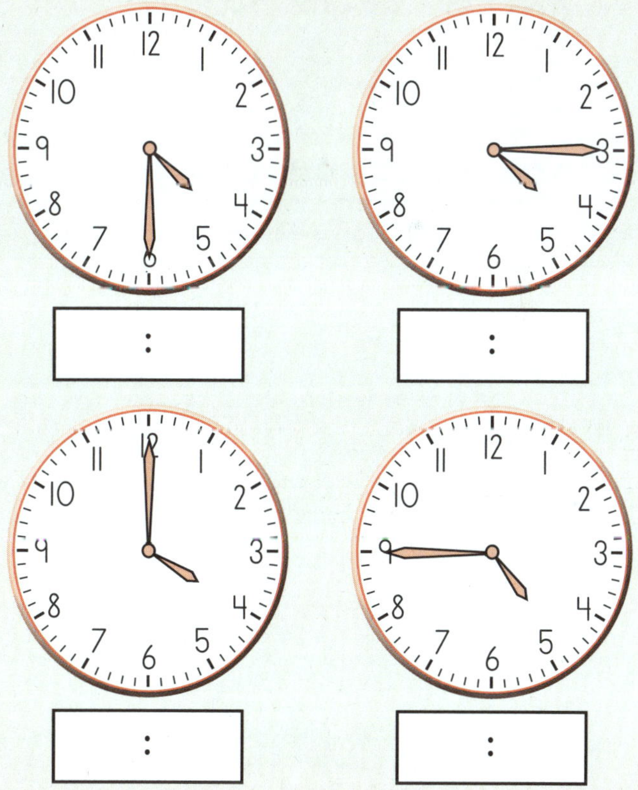

**Use a ruler to measure in centimeters.**

[ ] centimeters

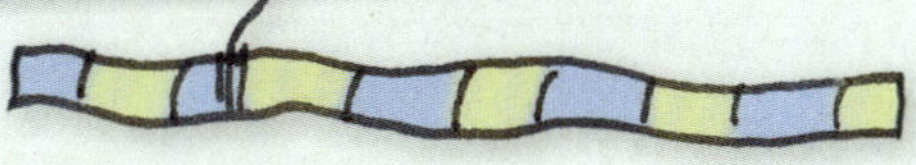

[ ] centimeters

## Lesson Activities

A

| | |
|---|---|
| 1 × 5 = | 6 × 5 = |
| 2 × 5 = | 7 × 5 = |
| 3 × 5 = | 8 × 5 = |
| 4 × 5 = | 9 × 5 = |
| 5 × 5 = | 10 × 5 = |

B

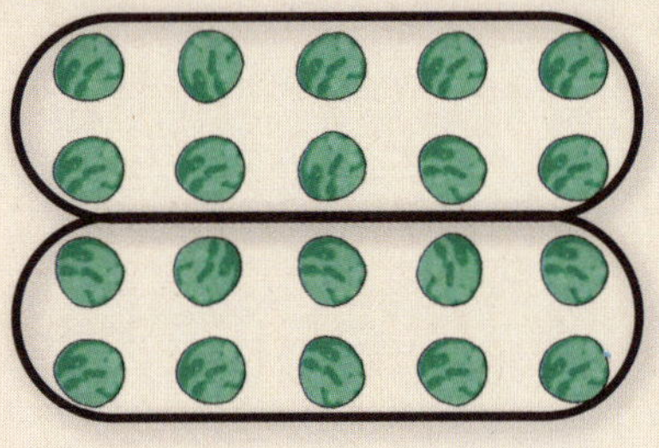

4 × 5 =

5 × 5 =

Start

8 × 5 =

9 × 5 =

6 × 5 =

7 × 5 =

C

### Multiplication Cover Up

| | | | | | | | | | | |
|---|---|---|---|---|---|---|---|---|---|---|
| Player 1 | 5 | 10 | 15 | 20 | 25 | 30 | 35 | 40 | 45 | 50 |
| Player 2 | 5 | 10 | 15 | 20 | 25 | 30 | 35 | 40 | 45 | 50 |

## Practice

**Draw a circle around groups of $10. Then, complete.**

4 × 5 = ☐

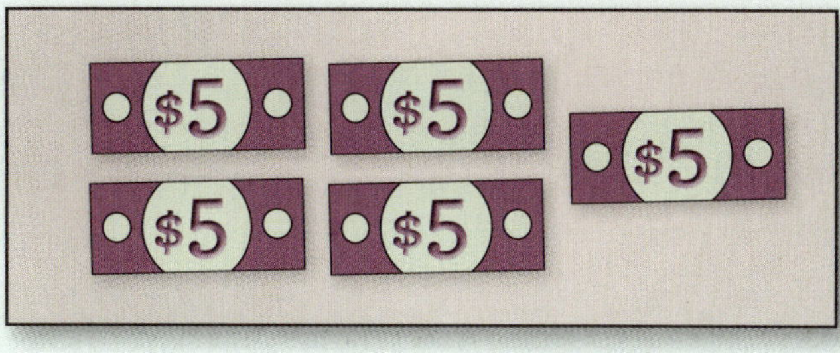


5 × 5 = ☐

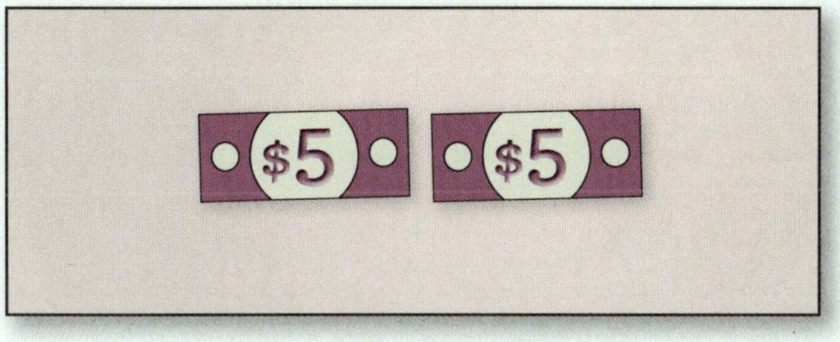


2 × 5 = ☐

3 × 5 = ☐

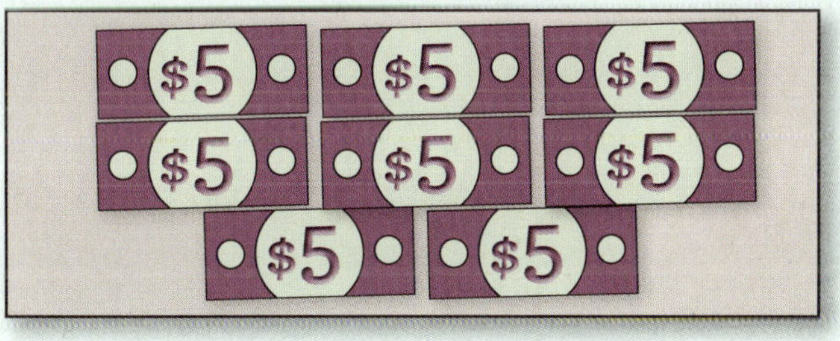


8 × 5 = ☐

9 × 5 = ☐

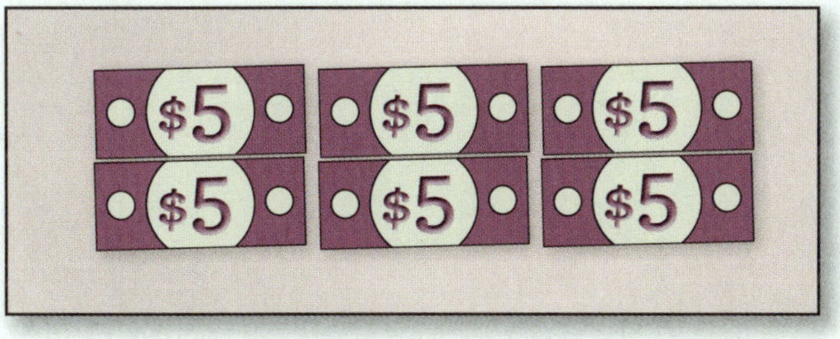


6 × 5 = ☐

7 × 5 = ☐

★ 20 × 5 = ☐

★ 21 × 5 = ☐

2.7

## Review

**Solve. Write the equations you use.**

Naomi has $11.
She earns $3 for helping in the garden.
Then, she spends $6 at the toy store.
How much money does she have left?

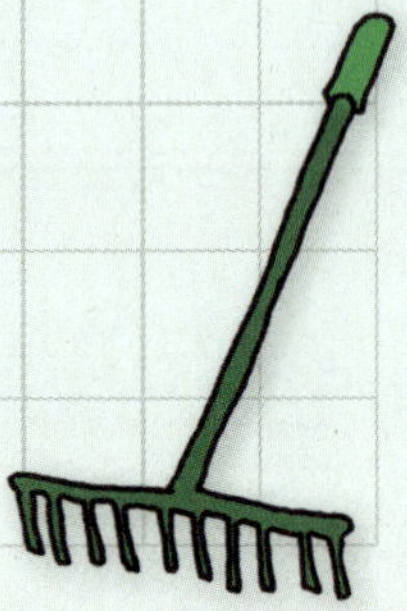

Sam brought 48 cupcakes to the bake sale.
Xander brought 36 cupcakes to the bake sale.
How many more cupcakes did Sam bring than Xander?

**Complete.**

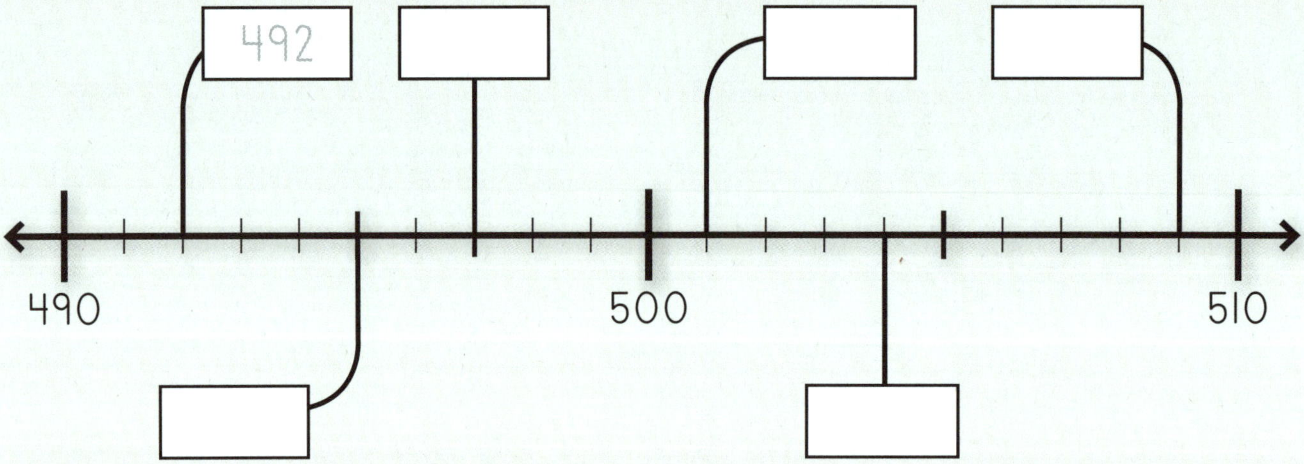


**Complete.**

1 foot = ☐ inches

1 yard = ☐ feet

1 yard = ☐ inches

1 meter = ☐ centimeters

**Complete.**

| | |
|---|---|
| 7 × 2 = ☐ | 6 × 10 = ☐ |
| 10 × 9 = ☐ | 2 × 8 = ☐ |
| 5 × 10 = ☐ | 6 × 2 = ☐ |
| 9 × 2 = ☐ | 10 × 8 = ☐ |

## Lesson Activities

A

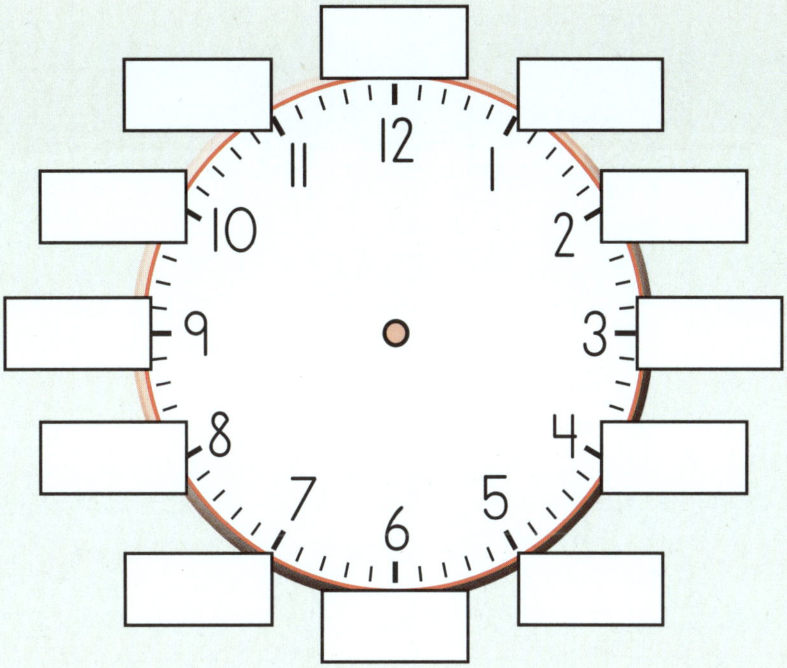


B

## Practice

**Complete.**

| | | | | |
|---|---|---|---|---|
| $3 \times 5 =$ | $5 \times 5 =$ | $6 \times 5 =$ | $2 \times 5 =$ | $8 \times 5 =$ |
| $1 \times 5 =$ | $9 \times 5 =$ | $4 \times 5 =$ | $7 \times 5 =$ | $10 \times 5 =$ |
| $10 \times 9 =$ | $8 \times 2 =$ | $10 \times 6 =$ | $1 \times 7 =$ | $9 \times 2 =$ |

**Write the time.**

___ : ___

___ : ___

___ : ___

___ : ___

**Solve. Write a multiplication problem to match.**

Simon put 5 pieces of candy in each bag. He filled 6 bags. How many pieces of candy did he use?

☐ × ☐ = ☐

Each movie ticket costs $10. How much does it cost to buy 6 movie tickets?

☐ × ☐ = ☐

## Review

**Complete.**

|   | 5 | 3 |
|---|---|---|
| + | 4 | 9 |
|   |   |   |

|   | 5 | 3 |
|---|---|---|
| - | 4 | 9 |
|   |   |   |

**Match.**

| | |
|---|---|
| 700 + 2 | 720 |
| 700 + 20 + 8 | 702 |
| 700 + 20 | 782 |
| 700 + 8 | 728 |
| 700 + 80 | 708 |
| 700 + 80 + 2 | 780 |

**Kai made a chart to show the height of the kids in his family. Use the chart to complete the graph and answer the questions.**

| Name | Height (Inches) |
|---|---|
| Cooper | 28 |
| Audrey | 36 |
| Kai | 47 |

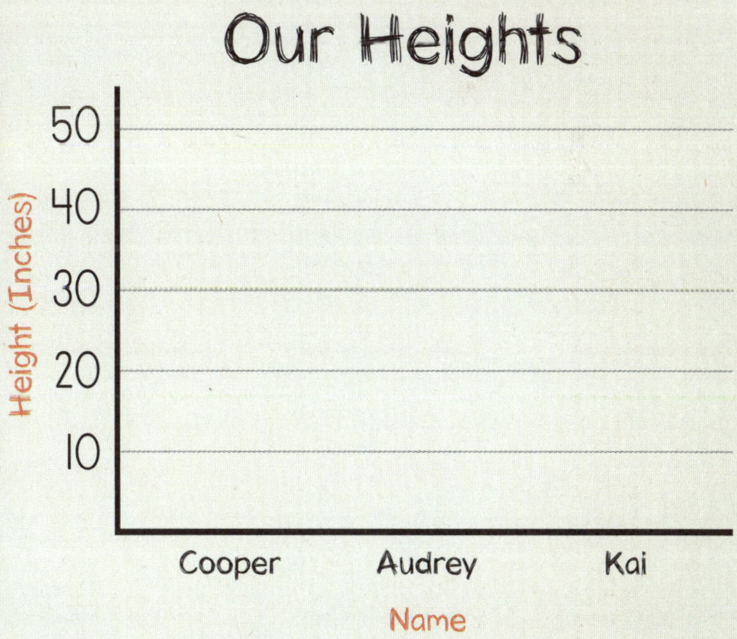


How much taller is Kai than Cooper?

How much shorter is Audrey than Kai?

# Unit Wrap-Up

**Write an equation to match each array.**

☐ × ☐ = ☐

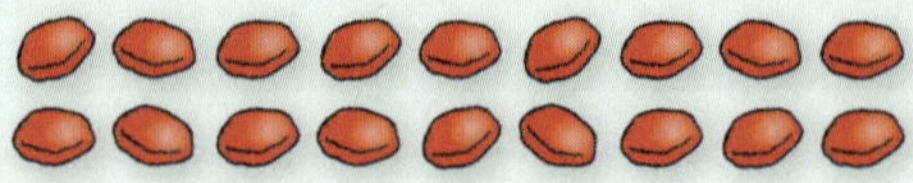

☐ × ☐ = ☐

**Draw an array to match each equation. Then, complete the equation.**

$2 \times 7 =$ ☐

$5 \times 8 =$ ☐

**Complete.**

| 1 × 5 | 2 × 8 | 10 × 7 | 6 × 2 | 7 × 5 |
|---|---|---|---|---|
| 10 × 6 | 10 × 9 | 7 × 2 | 3 × 5 | 4 × 0 |
| 5 × 5 | 9 × 2 | 10 × 8 | 9 × 5 | 10 × 0 |

## Unit Wrap-Up

**Match.**

| | | |
|---|---|---|
| 6 × 5 | 10 | 2 × 10 |
| 4 × 5 | 20 | 4 × 10 |
| 10 × 5 | 30 | 1 × 10 |
| 2 × 5 | 40 | 5 × 10 |
| 8 × 5 | 50 | 3 × 10 |

**Use the chart to answer the questions.**
**Write a multiplication equation for each question.**

**MENU**

Drink .................. $2
Nachos............... $5
Taco Plate .......... $10

How much do 4 drinks cost?

☐ × ☐ = $☐

How much do 8 drinks cost?

☐ × ☐ = $☐

How much do 6 orders of nachos cost?

☐ × ☐ = $☐

How much do 9 orders of nachos cost?

☐ × ☐ = $☐

How much do 3 taco plates cost?

☐ × ☐ = $☐

How much do 7 taco plates cost?

☐ × ☐ = $☐

## Lesson Activities

**A**

13 tens = ☐

10 tens = ☐

3 tens = ☐

12 tens = ☐ 18 tens = ☐ 20 tens = ☐

**B**

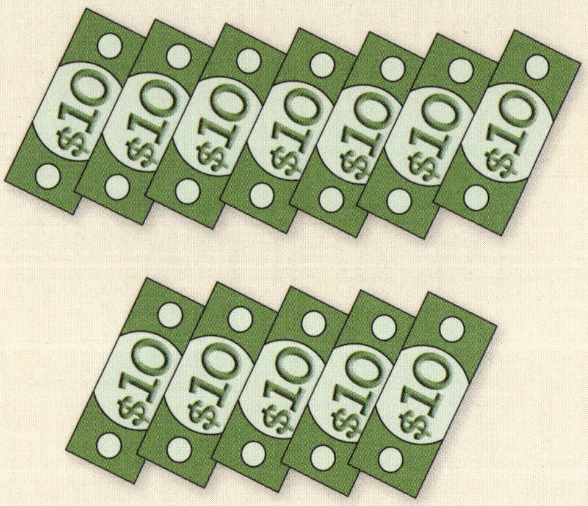

70 + 50 = ☐

7 tens + 5 tens = ☐ tens

Start

| | |
|---|---|
| 70 + 63 = ☐ | 85 + 42 = ☐ |
| 70 + 53 = ☐ | 85 + 40 = ☐ |
| 70 + 50 = ☐ | 80 + 40 = ☐ |

C

# Four in a Row

| | | | | |
|---|---|---|---|---|
| 160 | 60+90 | 70+60 | 120 | 80+60 |
| 120 | 90+70 | 150 | 80+80 | 160 |
| 80+50 | 140 | 70+70 | 90+50 | 80+90 |
| 140 | 90+30 | 130 | 90+90 | 150 |
| 70+80 | 180 | 130 | 70+50 | 170 |

## Practice

**Color the problems that equal the number in the star.**

| 100 | 110 | 120 | 130 |
|---|---|---|---|
| 50 + 50 | 60 + 50 | 90 + 40 | 70 + 60 |
| 10 + 90 | 40 + 70 | 60 + 60 | 30 + 90 |
| 40 + 60 | 20 + 90 | 30 + 80 | 50 + 80 |
| 70 + 40 | 30 + 80 | 50 + 70 | 50 + 60 |
| 80 + 30 | 50 + 70 | 40 + 80 | 90 + 40 |

## Review

**Connect each number to its place on the number line.**

392 395 401 407

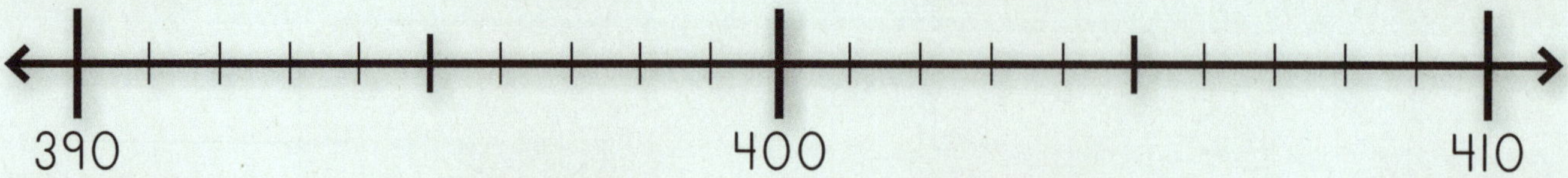


396 398 404 409

**Solve.**

Serena has 40 trading cards.
She buys 10 more.
Then, she gives 20 to her brother.
How many trading cards does she have now?

**Match.**

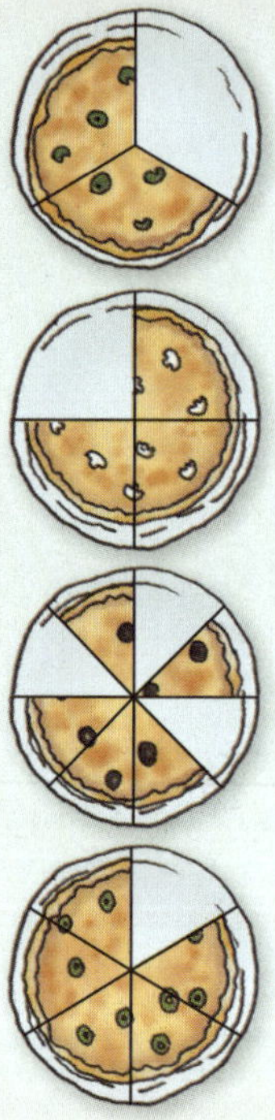

$\frac{3}{4}$

$\frac{5}{8}$

$\frac{2}{3}$

$\frac{5}{6}$

**Complete.**

$5 \times 6 =$ ___

$8 \times 2 =$ ___

$2 \times 6 =$ ___

$5 \times 9 =$ ___

$10 \times 10 =$ ___

$10 \times 2 =$ ___

$5 \times 7 =$ ___

$10 \times 4 =$ ___

$9 \times 2 =$ ___

$5 \times 8 =$ ___

## Lesson Activities

**A**

| 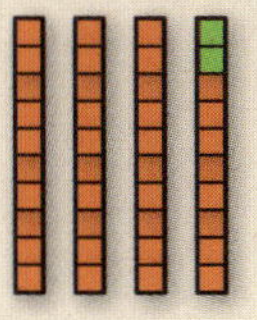 | 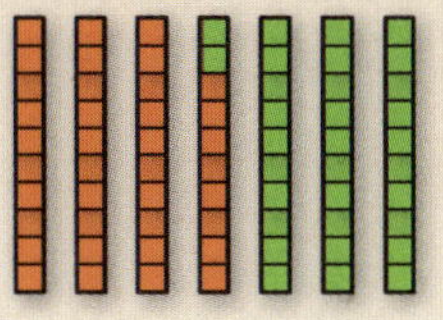 | 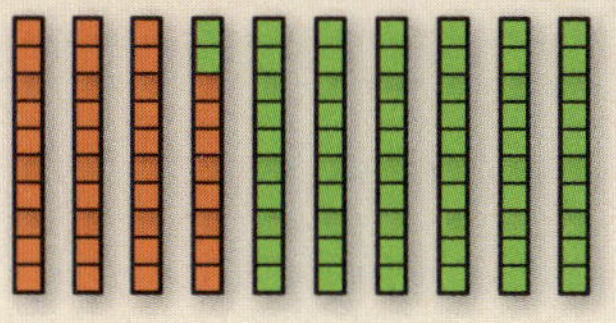 |
|---|---|---|
| $38 + \square = 40$ | $38 + \square = 70$ | $38 + \square = 100$ |

$49 + \square = 50$ $\quad$ $67 + \square = 70$ $\quad$ $52 + \square = 80$

$76 + \square = 90$ $\quad$ $85 + \square = 100$ $\quad$ $27 + \square = 100$

**B**

### Pretend Store

## Practice

**Complete.**

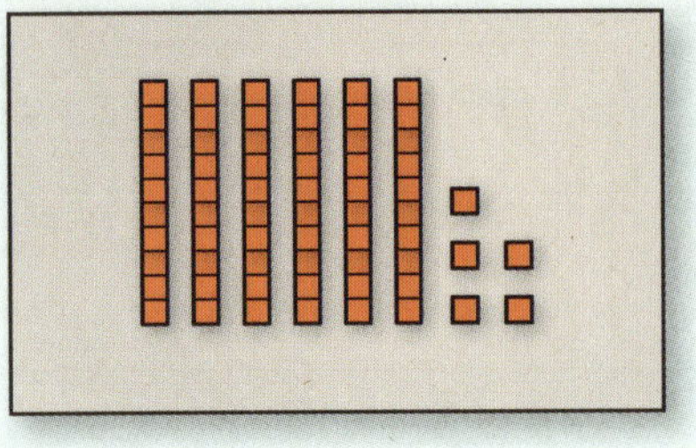

65 + ☐ = 70

65 + ☐ = 80

65 + ☐ = 90

65 + ☐ = 100

★ 65 + ☐ = 110

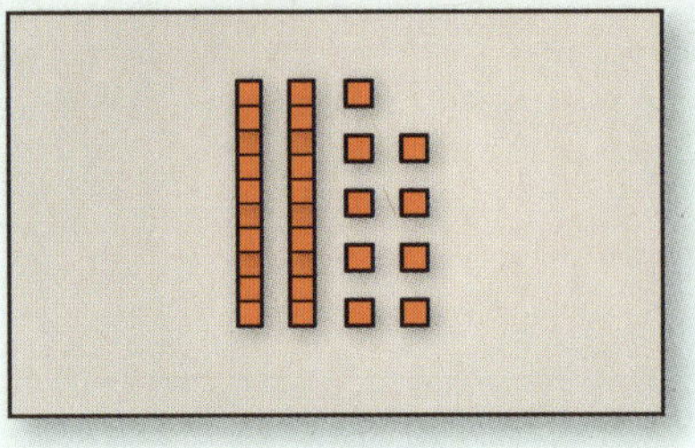

29 + ☐ = 30

29 + ☐ = 40

29 + ☐ = 70

29 + ☐ = 100

★ 29 + ☐ = 130

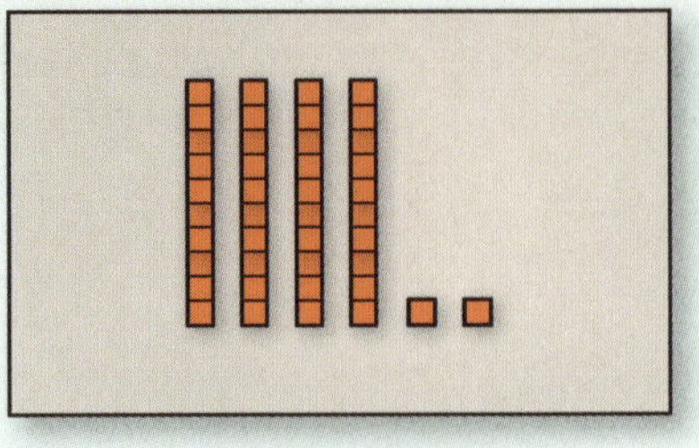

42 + ☐ = 50

42 + ☐ = 70

42 + ☐ = 80

42 + ☐ = 100

★ 42 + ☐ = 200

**Solve.**

You pay the clerk $20.
How much change do you get?

Change
$ ☐

You pay the clerk $60.
How much change do you get?

Change
$ ☐

You pay the clerk $80.
How much change do you get?

Change
$ ☐

You pay the clerk $100.
How much change do you get?

Change
$ ☐

## Review

**Complete the sequences.**

| | | | | | | | | |
|---|---|---|---|---|---|---|---|---|
| Count by 3s | 9 | | | 18 | | | | |
| Count by 4s | | 16 | 20 | | 28 | | | 40 |
| Count by 10s | 56 | 66 | | | 96 | | 116 | |

**Complete with <, >, or =.**

14 - 7 ◯ 8

10 ◯ 18 - 9

15 - 8 ◯ 7

8 ◯ 13 - 4

**Complete.**

| | | |
|---|---|---|
| | 3 | 8 |
| + | 6 | 2 |
| | | |

| | | |
|---|---|---|
| | 8 | 0 |
| - | 5 | 1 |
| | | |

**Solve. Write a multiplication problem to match.**

RJ filled 4 vases with flowers. He put 5 flowers in each vase. How many flowers did he use?

☐ × ☐ = ☐

Mia's family bought 6 ice cream cones. Each cone cost $2. How much did they pay?

☐ × ☐ = ☐

## Lesson Activities

**A**

Use Related Addition Facts

49 + 3 = ☐

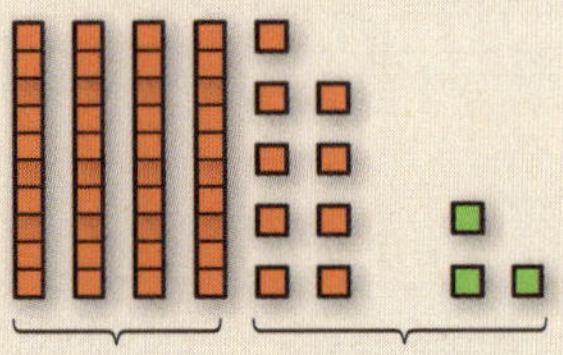

☐ ☐

Complete a 10

49 + 3 = ☐

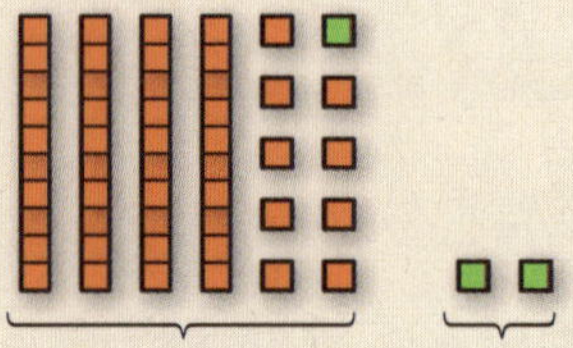

☐ ☐

68 + 5 = ☐ 77 + 4 = ☐ 97 + 6 = ☐

**B**

## Climb and Slide

## Practice

**Complete.**

99 + 5 = ___

89 + 5 = ___

39 + 5 = ___

Start 9 + 5 = ___

8 + 84 = ___

8 + 54 = ___

8 + 24 = ___

8 + 4 = ___

37 + 9 = ___

37 + 6 = ___

37 + 4 = ___

37 + 3 = ___

75 + 9 = ___

75 + 8 = ___

75 + 6 = ___

75 + 5 = ___

**Solve. Write the equations you use.**

Amara has 29 yellow stickers.
She has 8 green stickers.
How many stickers does she have in all?

Rylan has 18 blue robots.
He has 4 more green robots than blue robots.
How many green robots does he have?

3.3

## Review

Connect each number to its dot on the number line.

733 | 712 | 763 | 795 | 790

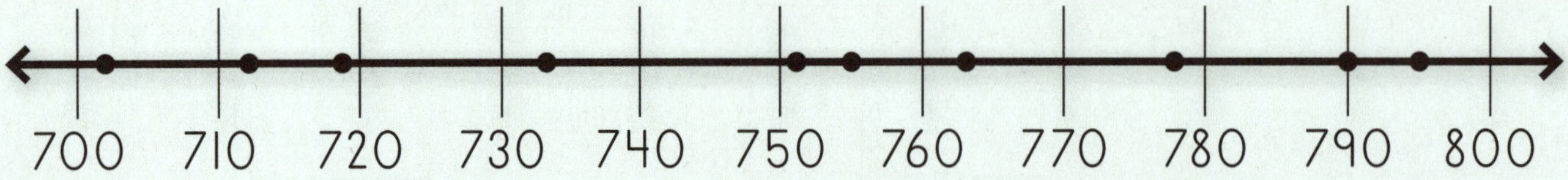


719 | 702 | 751 | 755 | 778

## Complete the sequences.

| Count by 100s | 300 | 400 | | | | | | 1,000 |
|---|---|---|---|---|---|---|---|---|
| **Count by 50s** | 300 | 350 | | | | | | 650 |
| **Count by 10s** | 300 | 310 | | | | | | 370 |

## Round each number to the nearest ten.

| | |
|---|---|
| 48 | |
| 96 | |
| 15 | |
| 9 | |
| 81 | |

## Complete.

| | |
|---|---|
| $5 \times 4 =$ ☐ | $9 \times 10 =$ ☐ |
| $2 \times 3 =$ ☐ | $6 \times 5 =$ ☐ |
| $5 \times 8 =$ ☐ | $3 \times 5 =$ ☐ |
| $5 \times 9 =$ ☐ | $4 \times 2 =$ ☐ |
| $8 \times 2 =$ ☐ | $9 \times 0 =$ ☐ |

## Lesson Activities

### A

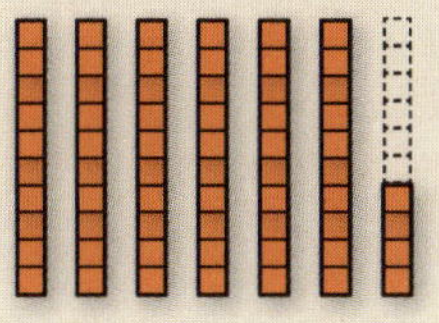

70 - 6 = ☐

80 - 5 = ☐    30 - 2 = ☐    100 - 7 = ☐

### B

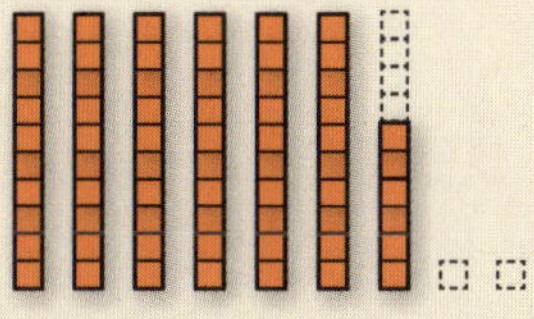

72 - 6 = ☐

91 - 5 = ☐    47 - 6 = ☐    83 - 8 = ☐

### C

## Roll and Subtract

| Player 1 | Player 2 |
|---|---|
| 82 - ☐ = ☐ | 82 - ☐ = ☐ |
| 60 - ☐ = ☐ | 60 - ☐ = ☐ |
| 41 - ☐ = ☐ | 41 - ☐ = ☐ |
| 57 - ☐ = ☐ | 57 - ☐ = ☐ |
| 100 - ☐ = ☐ | 100 - ☐ = ☐ |

## Practice

Complete.

| 70 | -7 → | | -7 → | | -7 → | | -7 → | 42 |
|---|---|---|---|---|---|---|---|---|
| 90 | -9 → | | -9 → | | -9 → | | -9 → | 54 |
| 80 | -8 → | | -8 → | | -8 → | | -8 → | 48 |

Use the clues to complete the chart.

- Piper is 4 inches shorter than Brayden.
- Leo is 7 inches taller than Piper.
- Josiah is 8 inches taller than Leo.
- Valentina is 6 inches shorter than Josiah.
- Olive is 5 inches shorter than Valentina.

| Name | Height (Inches) |
|---|---|
| Brayden | 50 |
| Piper | |
| Leo | |
| Josiah | |
| Valentina | |
| Olive | |

## Review

**Complete.**

|   | 5 |
|---|---|
| × | 6 |
|   |   |

|   | 7 |
|---|---|
| × | 2 |
|   |   |

| 1 | 0 |
|---|---|
| × | 6 |
|   |   |

|   | 5 |
|---|---|
| × | 8 |
|   |   |

|   | 3 |
|---|---|
| × | 5 |
|   |   |

**Solve.**

You pay the clerk $60.
How much change do you get?

Change
$

You pay the clerk $40.
How much change do you get?

Change
$

**Write the time.**

___ : ___

___ : ___

**Complete.**

|   | 2 | 8 |
|---|---|---|
| + | 2 | 8 |
|   |   |   |

|   | 9 | 5 |
|---|---|---|
| - | 3 | 7 |
|   |   |   |

**Write a multiplication equation to match each array.**

☐ × ☐ = ☐

☐ × ☐ = ☐

☐ × ☐ = ☐

3.5

# Lesson Activities

A

- The chess set costs $20.
- The chess set costs $5 more than the basketball.
- The harmonica costs $10 less than the basketball.
- The harmonica costs $3 more than the markers.

| Toy | Price |
|---|---|
| Chess set | |
| Basketball | |
| Harmonica | |
| Markers | |

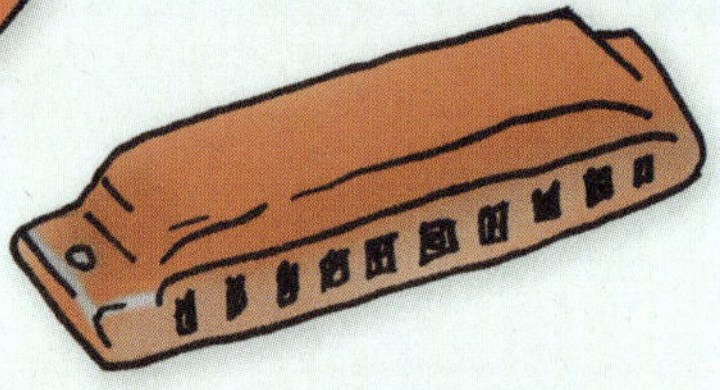

B

Brielle scored 10 points in a game.
She scored 5 fewer points than her sister.
How many points did her sister score?

Last week, Tomo checked out 12 library books.
This week, he checked out 5 fewer books than last week.
How many books did he check out this week?

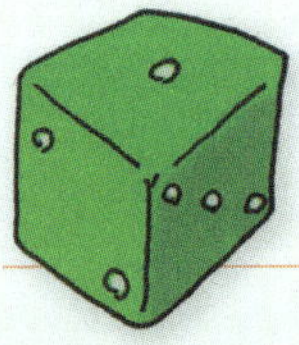

C

Kendal is 6 years old.
Preston is 7 years older than Kendal.
Grace is 10 years younger than Preston.
How old is Grace?

On Monday, Jake scored 9 points at his basketball game.
On Tuesday, he scored 4 fewer points than Monday.
How many points did he score in both games?

## Practice

**Use the clues to complete the chart.**

- Ben is 3 years older than Leena.
- Leena is 5 years younger than Seth.
- Seth is 8 years younger than Mira.

| Name | Age |
|---|---|
| Ben | 8 |
| Leena | |
| Seth | |
| Mira | |

**Solve. Write the equations you use.**

Eduardo is 10 years old.
Maria is 3 years younger than Eduardo.
Celeste is 1 year older than Maria.
How old is Celeste?

Nico collected 6 hats for the hat drive.
Cody collected 3 more hats than Nico.
How many did they collect in all?

**Complete.**

6 → +6 → ☐ → +6 → ☐ → +6 → ☐ → +6 → 30

60 → -6 → ☐ → -6 → ☐ → -6 → ☐ → -6 → 36

## Review

**Complete the sequences.**

| Count by | | | | | | | | |
|---|---|---|---|---|---|---|---|---|
| 1s | | | | | | 598 | 599 | 600 |
| 2s | | | | | | 596 | 598 | 600 |
| 10s | | | | | | 580 | 590 | 600 |

**Color the problems that match the number in the star.**

| 20 | 30 | 40 | 50 |
|---|---|---|---|
| 5 × 4 | 10 × 3 | 8 × 5 | 10 × 5 |
| 10 × 2 | 2 × 8 | 1 × 40 | 9 × 5 |
| 7 × 2 | 6 × 5 | 4 × 10 | 50 × 1 |

**Solve.**

Ramona bought 5 books.
Each book cost $5.
How much did she pay?

☐ × ☐ = ☐

**Complete.**

| | Double |
|---|---|
| 8 | 16 |
| 5 | |
| 10 | |
| 20 | |
| 50 | |
| 100 | |
| ★ 150 | |

## Lesson Activities

**A**

**Split Both Addends**

48 + 23 = ☐

40 8 20 3

40 + 20 = ☐

8 + 3 = ☐

**Split the Second Addend**

48 + 23 = ☐

20 3

48 +20 → ☐ +3 → ☐

35 + 57 = ☐

89 + 15 = ☐

**B**

4 7 + 6 1 = ☐

How close to 100? ☐

1 4 + 7 6 = ☐

How close to 100? ☐

C

# Close to 100

| Sum | Score (How close to 100?) |
|---|---|
| | |
| | |
| | |
| Player 1 Total | |

| Sum | Score (How close to 100?) |
|---|---|
| | |
| | |
| | |
| Player 2 Total | |

## Practice

**Match.**

| | | |
|---|---|---|
| 64 + 26 | 90 | 65 + 34 |
| 17 + 82 | 92 | 46 + 46 |
| 34 + 58 | 99 | 38 + 62 |
| 57 + 43 | 100 | 25 + 77 |
| 49 + 53 | 102 | 35 + 55 |

## Review

**Complete.**

| | | | | |
|---|---|---|---|---|
| 2 × 8 | 4 × 5 | 10 × 9 | 7 × 5 | 2 × 6 |
| 10 × 4 | 9 × 5 | 5 × 5 | 3 × 1 | 9 × 2 |

**Use the pictograph to complete the chart.**

| Color | Number of People |
|---|---|
| Red | |
| Yellow | |
| Green | |

**Use the key to color the shapes.**

**Key**

Triangle - Red
Quadrilateral - Orange
Pentagon - Green
Hexagon - Blue

## Lesson Activities

**A**

64 - 25 = ☐

20 5

64 −20 → ☐ −5 → ☐

90 - 17 = ☐

☐ ☐

73 - 45 = ☐

☐ ☐

**B**

## Climb and Slide

## Practice

**Complete.**

Start

$62 - 23 = \square$

$62 - 20 = \square$

$74 - 18 = \square$

$74 - 10 = \square$

$80 - 45 = \square$

$80 - 40 = \square$

$75 - 25 = \square$

$75 - 20 = \square$

$32 - 16 = \square$

$32 - 10 = \square$

$53 - 27 = \square$

$53 - 20 = \square$

$100 - 31 = \square$

$100 - 30 = \square$

$100 - 68 = \square$

$100 - 60 = \square$

★ $117 - 46 = \square$

★ $117 - 40 = \square$

**Solve. Write the equations you use.**

Jada read 75 pages on Monday and 26 pages on Tuesday. How many pages did she read in all?

Jada read 75 pages on Monday and 26 pages on Tuesday. How many more pages did she read on Monday than on Tuesday?

3.7

## Review

**Write a multiplication equation to match each array.**

☐ × ☐ = ☐

☐ × ☐ = ☐

☐ × ☐ = ☐

**Write each amount of money two ways.**

☐ ¢ $ ☐

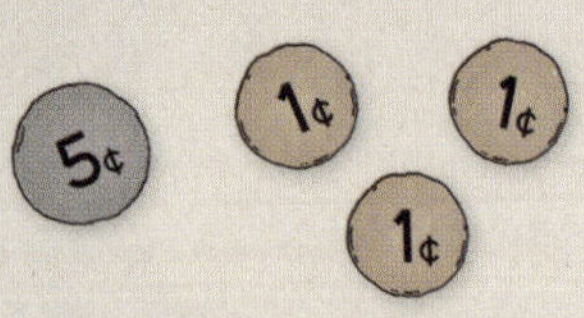


☐ ¢ $ ☐

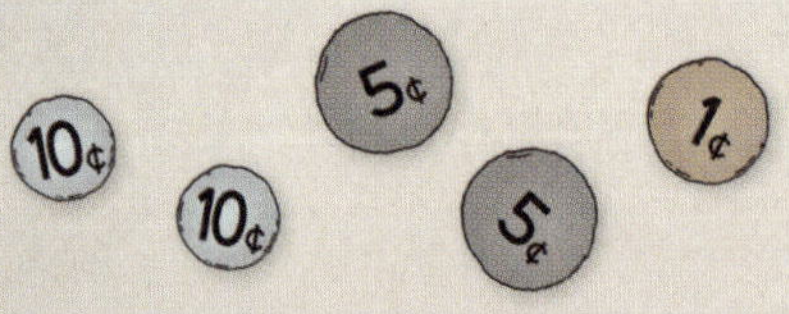


☐ ¢ $ ☐

**Write a.m. or p.m.**

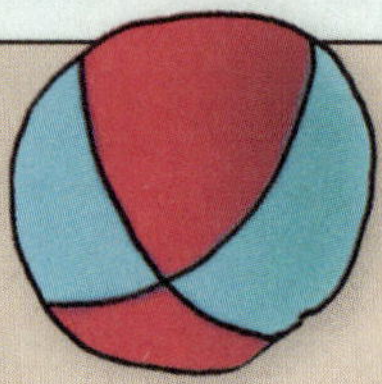

Play outside 2:00 ☐

Bedtime 8:00 ☐

Sunrise 7:00 ☐

**Complete.**

$$\begin{array}{r} 10 \\ \times\ \ 6 \\ \hline \end{array} \qquad \begin{array}{r} 2 \\ \times\ 9 \\ \hline \end{array} \qquad \begin{array}{r} 7 \\ \times\ 5 \\ \hline \end{array} \qquad \begin{array}{r} 8 \\ \times\ 2 \\ \hline \end{array} \qquad \begin{array}{r} 5 \\ \times\ 9 \\ \hline \end{array}$$

## Lesson Activities

**A**

52 - 49 = ☐

49 + ☐ = 52

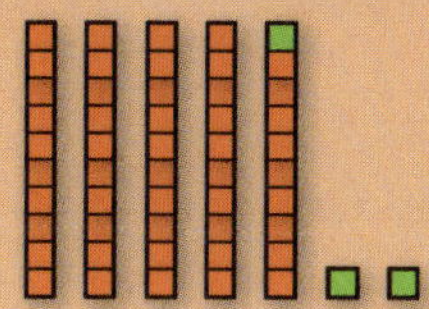

82 - 75 = ☐

75 + ☐ = 82

64 - 49 = ☐

49 + ☐ = 64

★ 104 - 88 = ☐

88 + ☐ = 104

**B**

8 9 - 6 3 = ☐

☐☐ - ☐☐ = ☐

C

# Close to Zero

| Difference | Score (How close to zero?) |
|---|---|
| | |
| | |
| | |
| Player 1 Total | |

| Difference | Score (How close to zero?) |
|---|---|
| | |
| | |
| | |
| Player 2 Total | |

## Practice

**Match.**

| | | |
|---|---|---|
| 72 - 67 | 3 | 84 - 79 |
| 43 - 39 | 4 | 54 - 50 |
| 60 - 45 | 5 | 87 - 84 |
| 91 - 88 | 14 | 72 - 57 |
| 51 - 37 | 15 | 61 - 47 |

## Review

**Complete.**

- ★ $11 \times 5 =$ ☐
- $1 \times 5 =$ ☐
- $2 \times 5 =$ ☐
- $3 \times 5 =$ ☐
- $4 \times 5 =$ ☐
- $5 \times 5 =$ ☐
- $6 \times 5 =$ ☐
- $7 \times 5 =$ ☐
- $8 \times 5 =$ ☐
- $9 \times 5 =$ ☐
- $10 \times 5 =$ ☐

**Use the chart to complete the bar graph and answer the questions.**

### Favorite Ice Cream Flavor

| Flavor | Number of People |
|---|---|
| Strawberry | 28 |
| Mint Chip | 15 |
| Cookies and Cream | 34 |

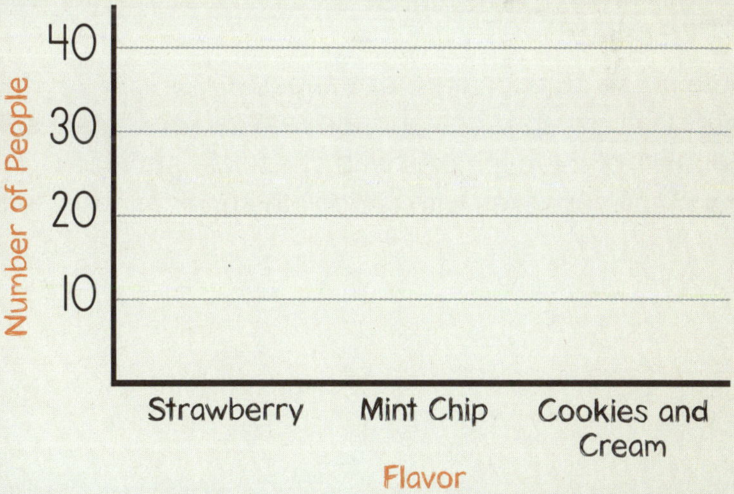


How many more people chose strawberry than mint chip?

How many fewer people chose strawberry than cookies and cream?

## Lesson Activities

A

Taylor read 9 pages on Tuesday morning and 6 pages on Tuesday afternoon.
She read 12 pages on Wednesday.
How many more pages did she read on Tuesday than Wednesday?

Jonah has $7.
He wants to buy a book that costs $6 and an action figure that costs $5.
How much more money does he need?

B

Sadie made 15 cupcakes for the party.
8 had rainbow sprinkles and the rest had chocolate sprinkles.
She ate 2 of the cupcakes with chocolate sprinkles.
How many cupcakes with chocolate sprinkles were left?

There are 14 dogs at the dog park.
9 are big, and the rest are small.
2 more small dogs arrive.
How many small dogs are there now?

## Practice

**Solve. Write the equations you use.**

Kenyana wants to collect 16 hats for the hat drive.
She collected 9 hats on Saturday and 3 hats on Sunday.
How many more hats does she need to collect to meet her goal?

Cayden planted 14 plants.
3 plants were zucchini, and the rest were tomato plants.
Then, 2 tomato plants died.
How many tomato plants were left?

August made 9 clay sculptures.
4 of the sculptures were animals, and the rest were people.
Then, he made 3 more sculptures of people.
How many sculptures of people did he make in all?

Riana painted 13 pictures this week.
She painted 4 pictures on Tuesday and 6 pictures on Friday.
She painted the rest of the pictures on Saturday.
How many pictures did she paint on Saturday?

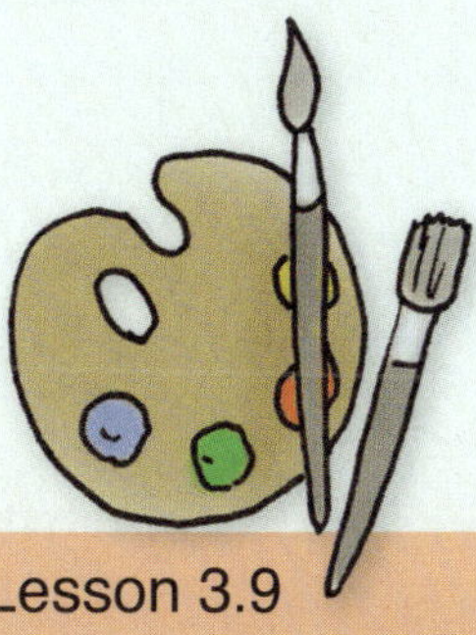

## Review

### Complete the sequences.

| Count by ☐s | | 8 | 12 | | 20 | 24 | | 32 |
|---|---|---|---|---|---|---|---|---|

| Count by ☐s | | | 9 | 12 | 15 | | 21 | |
|---|---|---|---|---|---|---|---|---|

### Write the time.

☐

☐

☐

☐

### Complete.

$ ☐

$ ☐

### Complete.

| | |
|---|---|
| 5 × 8 = ☐ | 8 × 10 = ☐ |
| 6 × 2 = ☐ | 1 × 5 = ☐ |
| 10 × 3 = ☐ | 6 × 5 = ☐ |
| 5 × 5 = ☐ | 5 × 9 = ☐ |
| 2 × 8 = ☐ | 8 × 0 = ☐ |

## Unit Wrap-Up

**Complete. Then, color each answer in black on the 100 Chart to make a picture.**

52 + 25 = ☐

65 - 6 = ☐

6 + 57 = ☐

50 - 16 = ☐

48 + 26 = ☐

62 - 25 = ☐

59 + 9 = ☐

93 - 17 = ☐

28 + 47 = ☐

61 - 9 = ☐

| | | | | | | | | | |
|---|---|---|---|---|---|---|---|---|---|
| 1 | 2 | 3 | 4 | 5 | 6 | 7 | 8 | 9 | 10 |
| 11 | 12 | 13 | 14 | 15 | 16 | 17 | 18 | 19 | 20 |
| 21 | 22 | 23 | 24 | 25 | 26 | 27 | 28 | 29 | 30 |
| 31 | 32 | 33 | 34 | 35 | 36 | 37 | 38 | 39 | 40 |
| 41 | 42 | 43 | 44 | 45 | 46 | 47 | 48 | 49 | 50 |
| 51 | 52 | 53 | 54 | 55 | 56 | 57 | 58 | 59 | 60 |
| 61 | 62 | 63 | 64 | 65 | 66 | 67 | 68 | 69 | 70 |
| 71 | 72 | 73 | 74 | 75 | 76 | 77 | 78 | 79 | 80 |
| 81 | 82 | 83 | 84 | 85 | 86 | 87 | 88 | 89 | 90 |
| 91 | 92 | 93 | 94 | 95 | 96 | 97 | 98 | 99 | 100 |

3.10

# Unit Wrap-Up

**Complete.**

10 tens = ☐

15 tens = ☐

11 tens = ☐

18 tens = ☐

**Solve.**

You pay the clerk $100.
How much change do you get?

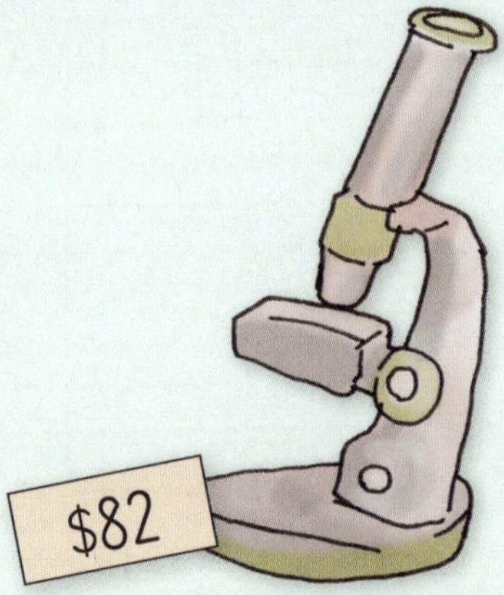


Change
$

**Solve. Write the equations you use.**

At the movie theater, popcorn costs $6.
Candy costs $3 less than popcorn.
Nachos cost $5 more than candy.
How much do nachos cost?

Mark wants to buy popcorn for $6
and a drink for $5. He has $8.
How much more money does he need?

Hannah collected 24 shells.
She collected 9 on Friday, 7 on Saturday,
and the rest on Sunday.
How many did she collect on Sunday?

Hannah collected 24 shells on the beach.
She collected 7 more shells than her sister.
How many shells did they collect in all?

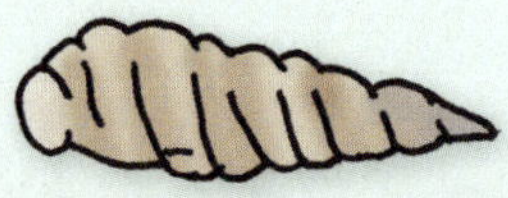

## Lesson Activities

A

3 × 1 = ☐ 3 × 6 = ☐

3 × 2 = ☐ 3 × 7 = ☐

3 × 3 = ☐ 3 × 8 = ☐

3 × 4 = ☐ 3 × 9 = ☐

3 × 5 = ☐ 3 × 10 = ☐

B

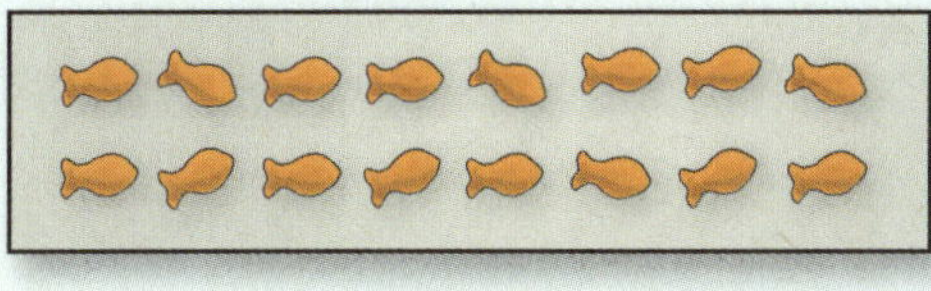

2 × 8 = ☐

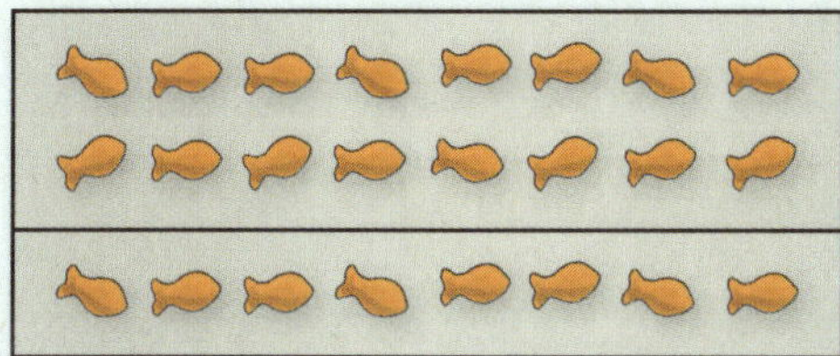

3 × 8 = ☐

3 × 7 = ☐

Start 2 × 7 = ☐

3 × 9 = ☐

2 × 9 = ☐

C

## Multiplication Cover Up

| | | | | | | | | | | |
|---|---|---|---|---|---|---|---|---|---|---|
| Player 1 | 3 | 6 | 9 | 12 | 15 | 18 | 21 | 24 | 27 | 30 |
| Player 2 | 3 | 6 | 9 | 12 | 15 | 18 | 21 | 24 | 27 | 30 |

4.1

## Practice

**Complete.**

$3 \times 5 =$ ☐

$2 \times 5 =$ ☐

$3 \times 4 =$ ☐

$2 \times 4 =$ ☐

$3 \times 6 =$ ☐

$2 \times 6 =$ ☐

$3 \times 3 =$ ☐

$2 \times 3 =$ ☐

$3 \times 8 =$ ☐

$2 \times 8 =$ ☐

$3 \times 7 =$ ☐

$2 \times 7 =$ ☐

$3 \times 10 =$ ☐

$2 \times 10 =$ ☐

$3 \times 9 =$ ☐

$2 \times 9 =$ ☐

## Review

Use the chart to complete the bar graph and answer the questions.

| Art Supply | Number |
|---|---|
| Markers | 26 |
| Colored Pencils | 35 |
| Paint Brushes | 8 |

How many markers and colored pencils are there?

How many more colored pencils than markers are there?

**Complete.**

34 + ☐ = 40

34 + ☐ = 50

34 + ☐ = 70

34 + ☐ = 90

34 + ☐ = 100

**Write the time.**

☐ : ☐ ☐ : ☐

# Lesson Activities

## A

$3 \times 5 = 15$

| | |
|---|---|
| | |

## B

| Multiples of 5 | 5 | 10 | 15 | 20 | 25 | 30 | 35 | 40 | 45 | 50 |
|---|---|---|---|---|---|---|---|---|---|---|
| Multiples of 2 | 2 | 4 | 6 | | | | | | | |
| Multiples of ☐ | 3 | 6 | 9 | 12 | 15 | | 21 | | 27 | 30 |
| Multiples of ☐ | 4 | 8 | 12 | 16 | 20 | | | 32 | | |

## C

### Tic-Tac-Toe Crash (×3)

| | | |
|---|---|---|
| 18 | 6 | 24 |
| 27 | 15 | 3 |
| 21 | 9 | 12 |

## Practice

Complete.

| | 3 |
|---|---|
| × | 3 |
| | |

| | 3 |
|---|---|
| × | 8 |
| | |

| | 3 |
|---|---|
| × | 2 |
| | |

| | 3 |
|---|---|
| × | 9 |
| | |

| | 3 |
|---|---|
| × | 4 |
| | |

| | 3 |
|---|---|
| × | 7 |
| | |

| | 3 |
|---|---|
| × | 1 |
| | |

| | 3 |
|---|---|
| × | 6 |
| | |

| | 3 |
|---|---|
| × | 5 |
| | |

| 1 | 0 |
|---|---|
| × | 3 |
| | |

Color the multiples in order from Start to End.

### Multiples of 2

| | | | | |
|---|---|---|---|---|
| Start 2 | 4 | 6 | 11 | 19 |
| 3 | 25 | 8 | 13 | 37 |
| 46 | 9 | 10 | 12 | 17 |
| 1 | 15 | 7 | 14 | 20 END |
| 5 | 28 | 41 | 16 | 18 |

### Multiples of 5

| | | | | |
|---|---|---|---|---|
| 10 | 15 | 24 | 49 | 88 |
| Start 5 | 20 | 25 | 36 | 16 |
| 14 | 22 | 30 | 35 | 37 |
| 72 | 18 | 28 | 40 | 45 |
| 54 | 32 | 21 | 42 | 50 END |

### Multiples of 3

| | | | | |
|---|---|---|---|---|
| 49 | 32 | 28 | 24 | 27 |
| 50 | 5 | 35 | 21 | 30 END |
| 8 | 14 | 20 | 18 | 35 |
| 6 | 9 | 12 | 15 | 13 |
| Start 3 | 11 | 10 | 16 | 8 |

### Multiples of 4

| | | | | |
|---|---|---|---|---|
| 21 | 18 | 44 | 36 | 40 END |
| 17 | 35 | 37 | 32 | 45 |
| 6 | 50 | 25 | 28 | 30 |
| Start 4 | 8 | 14 | 24 | 27 |
| 9 | 12 | 16 | 20 | 25 |

## Review

**Use a ruler to draw a line that matches each length.**

5 centimeters

5 inches

**Complete the sequences.**

| Count by 1s | | | | | | | | 873 |
|---|---|---|---|---|---|---|---|---|

| Count by 10s | | | | | | | | 630 |
|---|---|---|---|---|---|---|---|---|

| Count by 5s | | | | | | | | 415 |
|---|---|---|---|---|---|---|---|---|

**Complete.**

| | Double |
|---|---|
| 9 | |
| 12 | |
| 20 | |
| 24 | |
| 27 | |

**Complete.**

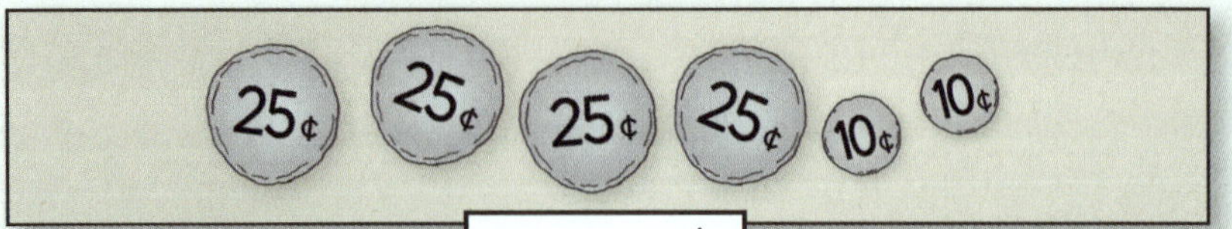


¢

¢

## Lesson Activities

**A**

$20

$2 \times 20 =$

$50

$2 \times 50 =$

$40

$2 \times 40 =$

**B**

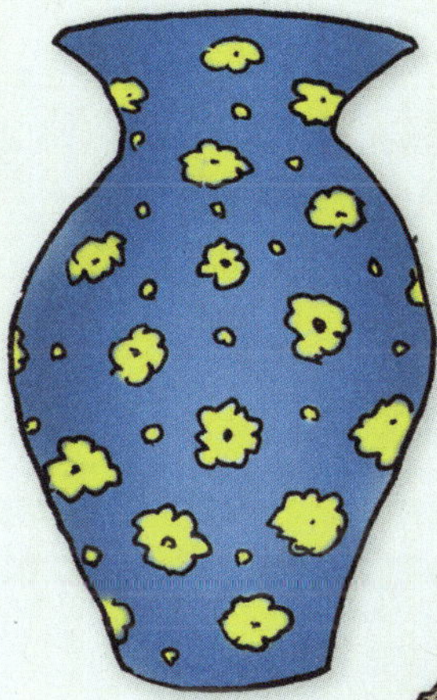

$2 \times 26 =$

20 6

$2 \times 20 =$

$2 \times 6 =$

$14

$28

$37

$59

$2 \times 14 =$

$2 \times 28 =$

$2 \times 37 =$

★ $2 \times 59 =$

4.3

## Practice

**Complete.**

$2 \times 12 = \square$

$2 \times 16 = \square$

$2 \times 24 = \square$

$2 \times 29 = \square$

$2 \times 33 = \square$

$2 \times 45 = \square$

★ $2 \times 200 = \square$

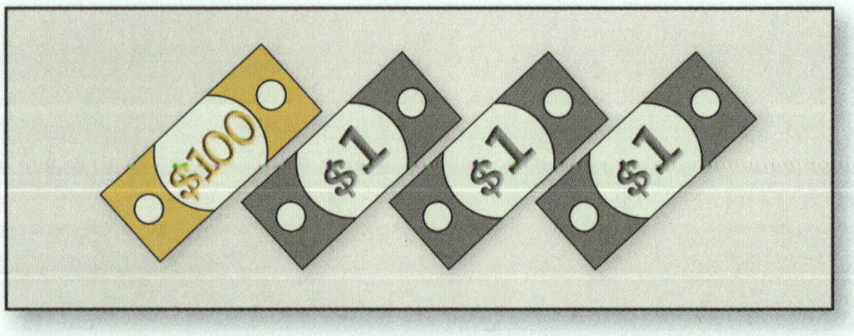


★ $2 \times 103 = \square$

## Review

**Use the pictograph to complete the chart.**

### Books I've Read

| Type of Book | Number |
|---|---|
| Mystery | |
| Fantasy | |
| Science | |

**Write the time.**

:

:

:

:

**Solve.**

You pay the clerk $60.
How much change do you get?

Change
$

**Complete the sequences.**

| Count by 4s | 4 | | | | | | | 32 |
|---|---|---|---|---|---|---|---|---|
| **Count by 6s** | 6 | | | | | 36 | | |

## Lesson Activities

### A

$4 \times 1 =$ □

$4 \times 2 =$ □

$4 \times 3 =$ □

$4 \times 4 =$ □

$4 \times 5 =$ □

$4 \times 6 =$ □

$4 \times 7 =$ □

$4 \times 8 =$ □

$4 \times 9 =$ □

$4 \times 10 =$ □

### B

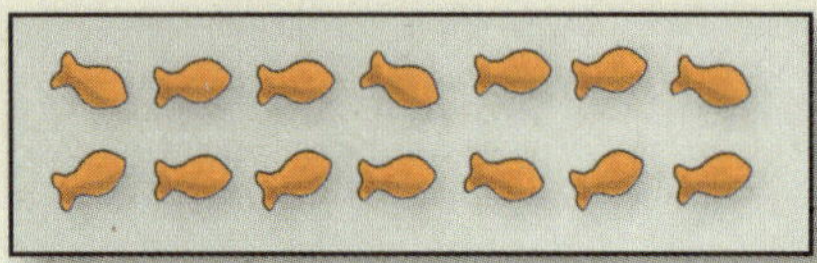

$2 \times 7 =$ □

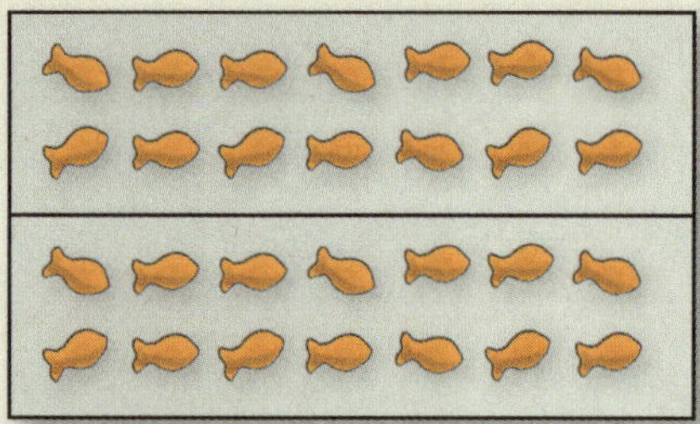

$4 \times 7 =$ □

Start

$2 \times 6 =$ □

$4 \times 6 =$ □

$2 \times 9 =$ □

$4 \times 9 =$ □

### C

## Multiplication Crash

| 4 | 8 | 12 | 16 | 20 |
|---|---|---|---|---|
| 24 | 28 | 32 | 36 | 40 |

## Practice

**Complete.**

$4 \times 2 =$ ☐

$4 \times 3 =$ ☐

$4 \times 5 =$ ☐

$4 \times 8 =$ ☐

$4 \times 9 =$ ☐

$4 \times 6 =$ ☐

$4 \times 4 =$ ☐

$4 \times 7 =$ ☐

## Review

**Complete.**

| | 6 | 8 |
|---|---|---|
| + | 5 | 9 |
| | | |

| | 7 | 4 |
|---|---|---|
| - | 2 | 8 |
| | | |

**Copy the shapes.**

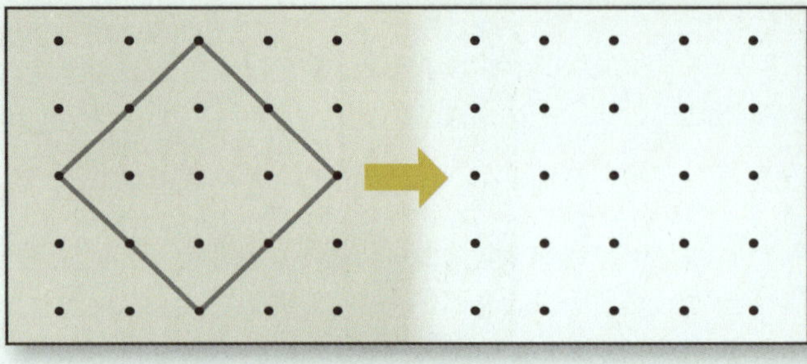

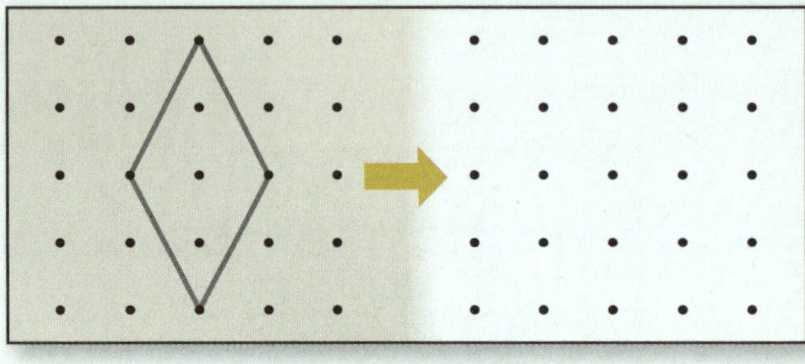

**Complete.**

1 minute = ☐ seconds

1 hour = ☐ minutes

1 day = ☐ hours

1 week = ☐ days

**Complete.**

$ ______

$ ______

**Circle the sandwiches that are split in half. X the sandwiches that are not split in half.**

## Lesson Activities

**A**

# Multiplication Undercover

| Player 1 | 4 | 8 | 12 | 16 | 20 | 24 | 28 | 32 | 36 | 40 |
|---|---|---|---|---|---|---|---|---|---|---|
| Player 2 | 4 | 8 | 12 | 16 | 20 | 24 | 28 | 32 | 36 | 40 |

**B**

| Day | Multiplication Problem | Number of Donuts |
|---|---|---|
| Friday | | |
| Saturday | | |
| Sunday | | |

**C**

| Day | Multiplication Problem | Number of Tickets |
|---|---|---|
| Friday | | |
| Saturday | | |
| Sunday | | |

## Practice

**Use the pictograph to answer the questions. Write a multiplication equation for each question.**

How many pumpkins were sold on Friday?

☐ × ☐ = ☐

How many pumpkins were sold on Saturday?

☐ × ☐ = ☐

How many pumpkins were sold on Sunday?

☐ × ☐ = ☐

**Complete.**

| | | | | |
|---|---|---|---|---|
| 4 × 3 = ☐ | 10 × 4 = ☐ | 4 × 9 = ☐ | 2 × 4 = ☐ | 4 × 6 = ☐ |
| 5 × 4 = ☐ | 4 × 8 = ☐ | 0 × 4 = ☐ | 4 × 4 = ☐ | 7 × 4 = ☐ |
| 3 × 6 = ☐ | 9 × 3 = ☐ | 3 × 7 = ☐ | 8 × 3 = ☐ | 3 × 0 = ☐ |

## Review

**Complete.**

| | 2 | 9 |
|---|---|---|
| + | 4 | 8 |
| | | |

| | 6 | 5 |
|---|---|---|
| + | 3 | 5 |
| | | |

| | 4 | 2 |
|---|---|---|
| - | 1 | 6 |
| | | |

| | 8 | 0 |
|---|---|---|
| - | 2 | 7 |
| | | |

**Write the time.**

:

:

:

:

**Complete.**

17 tens = ☐

14 tens = ☐

☐ tens = 150

☐ tens = 190

★ ☐ tens = 560

★ 38 tens = ☐

**Solve. Write the equations you use.**

The sum of 2 numbers is 20.
One of the numbers is 11.
What is the other number?

★ The sum of 3 numbers is 24.
One of the numbers is 8.
Another one of the numbers is 7.
What is the other number?

## Lesson Activities

A

# Dice Tic-Tac-Toe

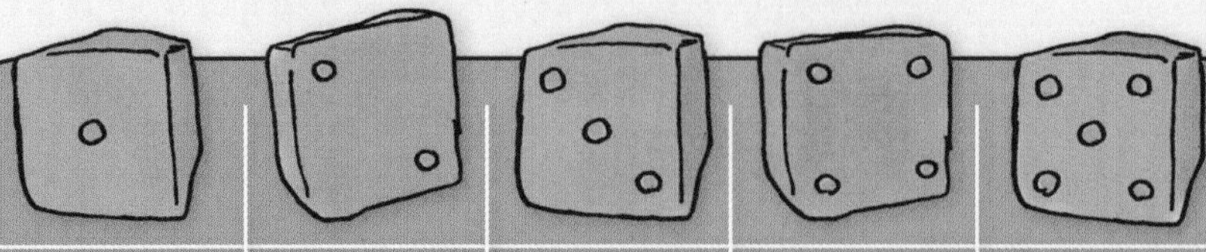

| | | | | |
|---|---|---|---|---|
| 8 × 2 | 9 × 5 | 4 × 4 | 6 × 0 | 6 × 4 |
| 5 × 3 | 8 × 4 | 7 × 2 | 7 × 3 | 8 × 5 |
| 9 × 4 | 5 × 5 | 8 × 3 | 6 × 5 | 7 × 4 |
| 7 × 5 | 9 × 3 | 7 × 10 | 5 × 4 | 6 × 5 |
| 8 × 1 | 3 × 4 | 3 × 3 | 9 × 2 | 6 × 3 |

B

| × | 1 | 2 | 3 | 4 | 5 | 6 | 7 | 8 | 9 | 10 |
|---|---|---|---|---|---|---|---|---|---|---|
| 1 | 1 | 2 | 3 | 4 | 5 | 6 | 7 | | 9 | 10 |
| 2 | 2 | 4 | 6 | 8 | 10 | | 14 | 16 | 18 | 20 |
| 3 | 3 | | 9 | 12 | 15 | 18 | 21 | 24 | | 30 |
| 4 | 4 | 8 | 12 | 16 | | 24 | 28 | 32 | 36 | 40 |
| 5 | 5 | 10 | 15 | 20 | 25 | 30 | 35 | 40 | 45 | 50 |
| 6 | 6 | 12 | 18 | 24 | 30 | 36 | 42 | 48 | 54 | 60 |
| 7 | 7 | 14 | 21 | 28 | | 42 | 49 | 56 | 63 | 70 |
| 8 | 8 | | 24 | 32 | 40 | 48 | 56 | 64 | 72 | |
| 9 | 9 | 18 | 27 | | 45 | 54 | 63 | 72 | 81 | 90 |
| 10 | 10 | 20 | 30 | 40 | 50 | 60 | 70 | | 90 | 100 |

## Practice

**Complete.**

| | | |
|---|---|---|
| $3 \times 5 = \square$ | $4 \times 5 = \square$ | $3 \times 6 = \square$ |
| $4 \times 3 = \square$ | $3 \times 7 = \square$ | $4 \times 4 = \square$ |
| $3 \times 9 = \square$ | $10 \times 3 = \square$ | $3 \times 8 = \square$ |
| $6 \times 4 = \square$ | $7 \times 5 = \square$ | $4 \times 10 = \square$ |
| $5 \times 9 = \square$ | $4 \times 9 = \square$ | $5 \times 6 = \square$ |
| $8 \times 4 = \square$ | $5 \times 5 = \square$ | $7 \times 4 = \square$ |

**Solve. Write a multiplication equation to match.**

Xavier made 4 treat bags for a party.
Each treat bag had 3 lollipops.
How many lollipops did he use?

$\square \times \square = \square$

Lauren bought 3 pumpkins.
Each pumpkin cost $6.
How much did the pumpkins cost in all?

$\square \times \square = \square$

## Review

**Use the numbers to complete the blanks. You will use each number once.**

| 10 | 20 | 30 | 40 | 50 | 60 | 70 | 80 | 90 |
|---|---|---|---|---|---|---|---|---|

| | | |
|---|---|---|
| 30 + ☐ = 50 | ☐ - 40 = 20 | 100 = ☐ + 60 |
| 90 - ☐ = 10 | ☐ + 50 = 60 | 40 = ☐ - 30 |
| 50 + ☐ = 80 | ☐ - 20 = 70 | 60 = ☐ + 10 |

**Complete.**

1 foot = ☐ inches

1 yard = ☐ feet

1 yard = ☐ inches

1 meter = ☐ centimeters

**Solve. Write the equation you use.**

Ben had $90. Then, he spent $67.
How much money did he have left?

**Complete.**

Start

47 - 7 = ☐

47 - 9 = ☐

53 - 20 = ☐

53 - 26 = ☐

60 - 4 = ☐

60 - 24 = ☐

## Unit Wrap-Up

**Complete.**

| | | | | |
|---|---|---|---|---|
| 4 × 10 = ___ | 3 × 5 = ___ | 4 × 7 = ___ | 6 × 3 = ___ | 3 × 4 = ___ |
| 7 × 3 = ___ | 9 × 4 = ___ | 3 × 8 = ___ | 4 × 5 = ___ | 10 × 3 = ___ |
| 4 × 4 = ___ | 3 × 9 = ___ | 4 × 8 = ___ | 4 × 3 = ___ | 4 × 6 = ___ |

**Complete the multiples in order.**

| | | | | | | | | | | |
|---|---|---|---|---|---|---|---|---|---|---|
| **Multiples of 2** | 2 | 4 | | | 10 | | | 16 | | |
| **Multiples of 5** | | 10 | 15 | | | 30 | | | | |

**Use the words in the word bank to complete the sentences.**

2 × 7 = 14

Word bank: factors ∘ product

14 is the ______________________.

2 and 7 are the ______________________.

## Unit Wrap-Up

**Use the pictograph to answer the questions. Write a multiplication equation to match each question.**

How many minutes did Isabella practice on Monday?

☐ × ☐ = ☐

How many minutes did Isabella practice on Tuesday?

☐ × ☐ = ☐

How many minutes did Isabella practice on Wednesday?

☐ × ☐ = ☐

**Complete.**

Start

$2 \times 30 =$ ☐

$2 \times 31 =$ ☐

$2 \times 35 =$ ☐

$2 \times 40 =$ ☐

$2 \times 45 =$ ☐

$2 \times 46 =$ ☐

**Solve. Write the equations you use.**

Ellie has 6 bags of candy.
Each bag has 4 pieces of candy.
How many pieces of candy does she have?

Joey wants to make 3 spider crafts.
Each spider uses 8 craft sticks.
How many craft sticks does Joey need?

## Lesson Activities

### A

**Number Riddles**

217 · 450 · 699 · 864 · 8 · 603 · 271 · 99 · 701 · 630 · 1,000 · 375

### B

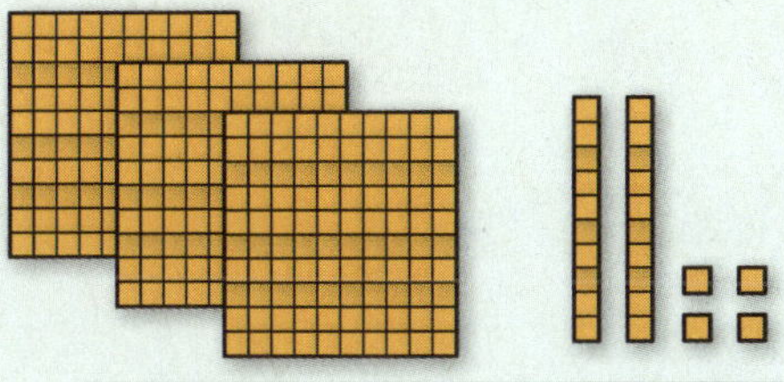

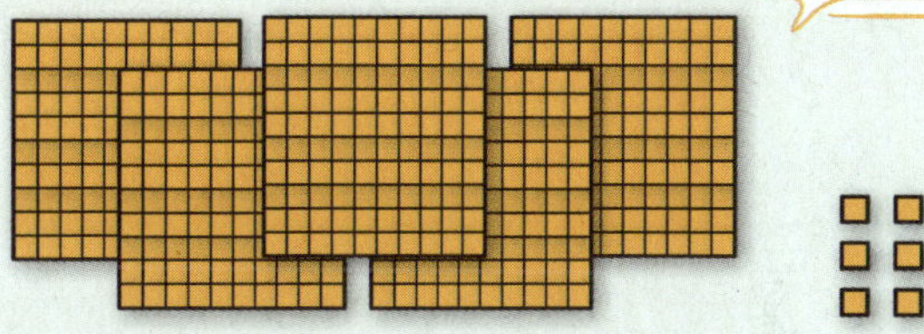

324 = ☐  506 = ☐

### C

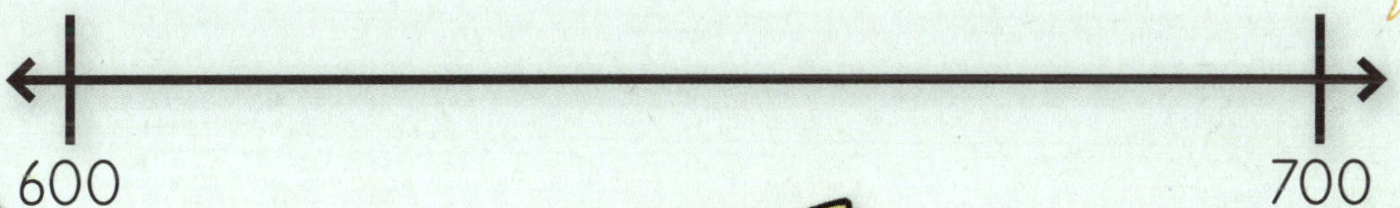

About ☐ cotton balls

About ☐ dollars

About ☐ kilometers

### D

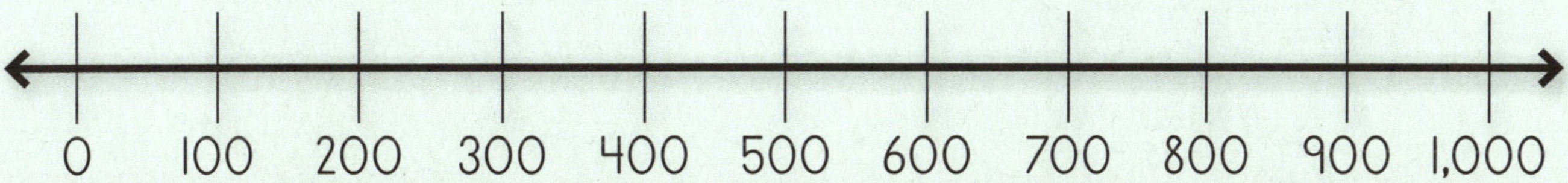


| 482 | 249 | 301 | 532 | 299 | 850 | 940 | 984 |
|---|---|---|---|---|---|---|---|
| | | | | | | | |

## Practice

Connect each number to its dot on the number line.

248 260 325 372 398

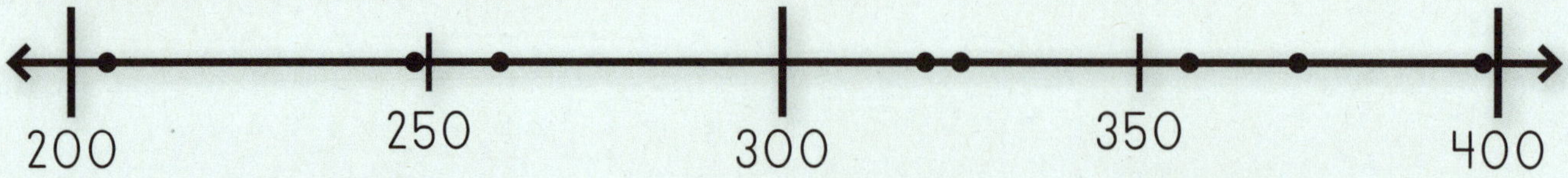


205 320 357

Round each number to the nearest hundred. Use the number line to help.

| 325 | 248 | 260 | 205 | 372 | 357 | 398 | 320 |
|---|---|---|---|---|---|---|---|
| | | | | | | | |

Round each number to the nearest hundred.

About ☐ blocks

About ☐ stickers

About ☐ rubber bands

About ☐ paper clips

## Review

**Match pairs that equal 100.**

| 50 | 55 | 60 | 65 | 70 |
|---|---|---|---|---|
| 45 | 30 | 50 | 35 | 40 |

**Complete.**

| Expanded Form | Number |
|---|---|
| 300 + 20 + 5 | 325 |
| 600 + 80 + 9 | |
| 100 + 40 + 6 | |
| | 299 |
| 700 + 4 | |
| | 980 |

**Complete.**

$ ______

$ ______

**Complete with <, >, or =.**

400 + 50 ◯ 449

900 - 600 ◯ 400

560 ◯ 500 + 6

705 ◯ 700 + 5

**Complete.**

94 + ☐ = 100

32 + ☐ = 40

71 + ☐ = 80

85 + ☐ = 100

## Lesson Activities

### A

You have saved $280.
How much more money do you need?

280 + ___ = 300

80 + ___ = 100

650 + ___ = 700

460 + ___ = 500

### B

You have saved $680.
How much more money do you need?

680 + ___ = 1,000

680 + ___ → 700 + ___ → 1,000

450 + ___ = 1,000

450 + ___ → 500 + ___ → 1,000

790 + ___ = 1,000

790 + ___ → 800 + ___ → 1,000

## Practice

**Match pairs that equal 1,000.**

| | |
|---|---|
| 900 | 300 |
| 700 | 50 |
| 800 | 100 |
| 950 | 250 |
| 750 | 200 |
| 850 | 150 |

**Complete.**

890 + ☐ = 900
790 + ☐ = 800
490 + ☐ = 500

270 + ☐ = 500
270 + ☐ = 400
270 + ☐ = 300

660 + ☐ = 1,000
660 + ☐ = 800
660 + ☐ = 700

★ 565 + ☐ = 1,000
★ 565 + ☐ = 600
★ 565 + ☐ = 570

## Review

**Color the problems that match the number in the star.**

| 12 | 16 | 18 | 20 |
|---|---|---|---|
| 4 × 3 | 8 × 2 | 2 × 9 | 4 × 5 |
| 2 × 9 | 4 × 4 | 5 × 4 | 7 × 1 |
| 2 × 6 | 6 × 0 | 3 × 6 | 10 × 2 |

| 24 | 28 | 32 | 40 |
|---|---|---|---|
| 6 × 4 | 2 × 14 | 3 × 9 | 2 × 20 |
| 2 × 12 | 7 × 4 | 4 × 8 | 8 × 5 |
| 8 × 3 | 5 × 5 | 2 × 16 | 3 × 10 |

**Solve. Write a multiplication equation to match.**

Chloe arranged her stickers
in 4 rows and 5 columns.
How many stickers did she use?

☐ × ☐ = ☐

Diego planted 3 rows of flowers.
Each row had 6 flowers.
How many flowers did he plant?

☐ × ☐ = ☐

## Lesson Activities

**A**

# Multiplication Crash

| 4 | 8 | 12 | 16 | 20 |
|---|---|---|---|---|
| 24 | 28 | 32 | 36 | 40 |

**B**

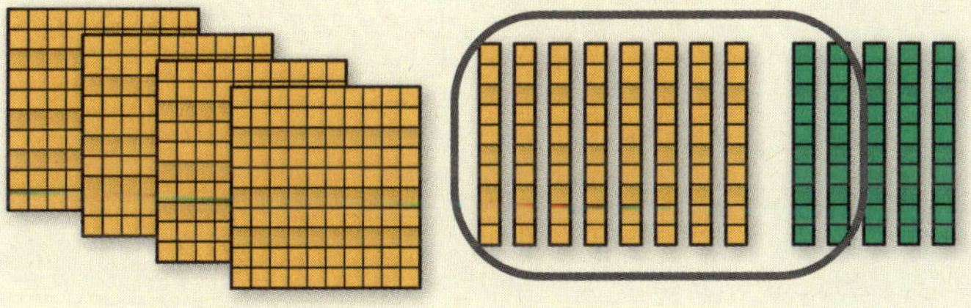

480 + 50 = ☐

480 +20 ☐ +30 ☐

290 + 30 = ☐

760 + 70 = ☐

180 + 80 = ☐

370 + 40 = ☐

**C**

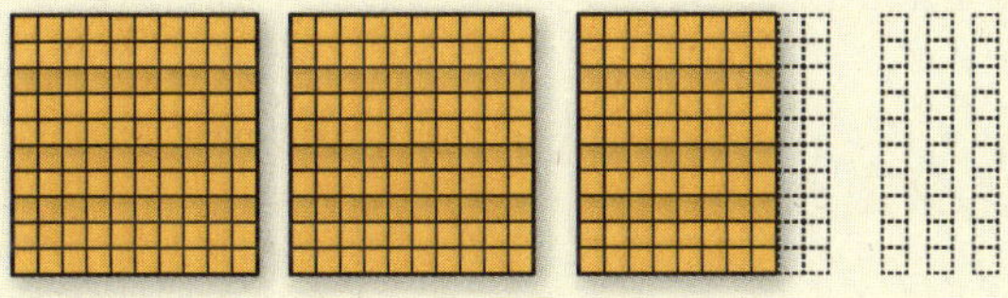

330 - 50 = ☐

330 -30 ☐ -20 ☐

210 - 40 = ☐

550 - 60 = ☐

430 - 50 = ☐

820 - 90 = ☐

# 5.3

## Practice

**Complete.**

250 + 30 =

250 + 50 =

250 + 60 =

250 + 90 =

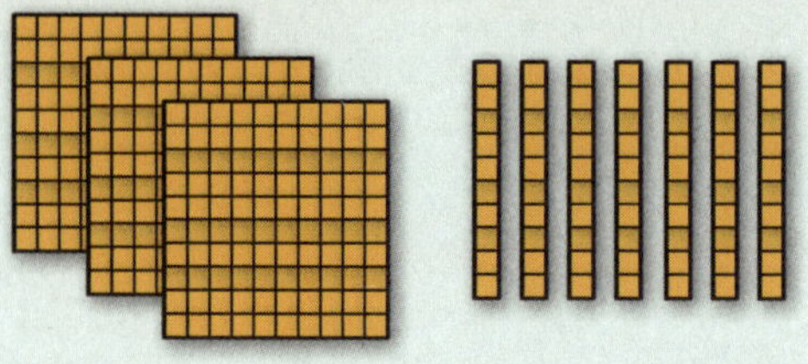

370 + 20 =

370 + 30 =

370 + 50 =

370 + 80 =

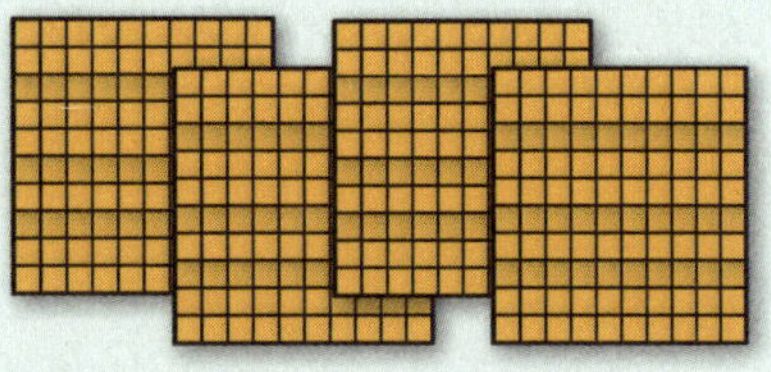

400 - 10 =

400 - 40 =

400 - 70 =

400 - 90 =

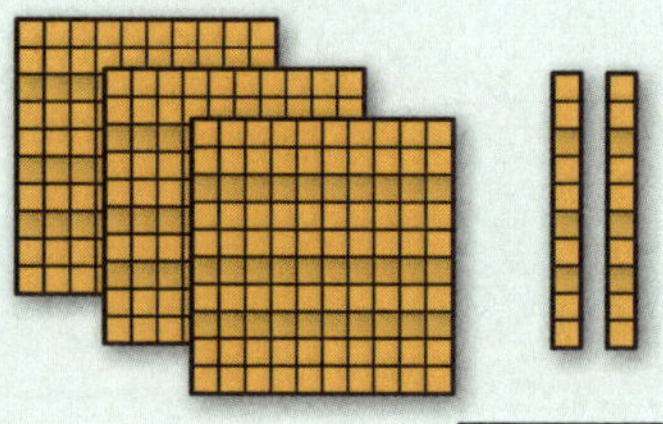

320 - 20 =

320 - 30 =

320 - 40 =

320 - 70 =

**Solve. Write the equations you use.**

Gabriella read 150 pages on Monday.
She read 80 pages on Tuesday.
How many pages did she read in all?

Gabriella read 150 pages on Monday.
She read 80 pages on Tuesday.
How many more pages did she read on Monday than on Tuesday?

## Review

### Write each number in its expanded form.

717 = ______

707 = ______

770 = ______

### Complete.

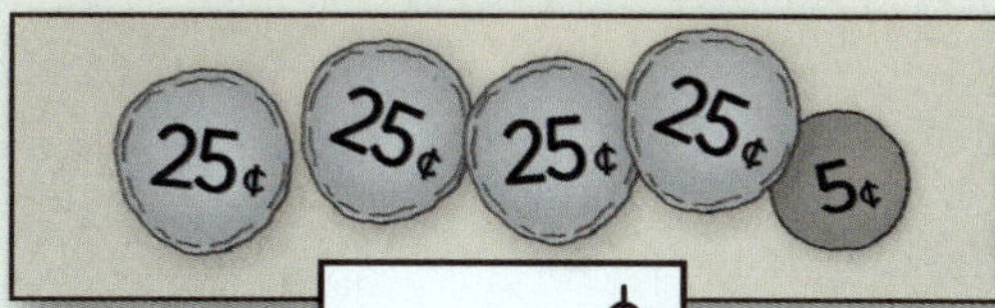


______ ¢

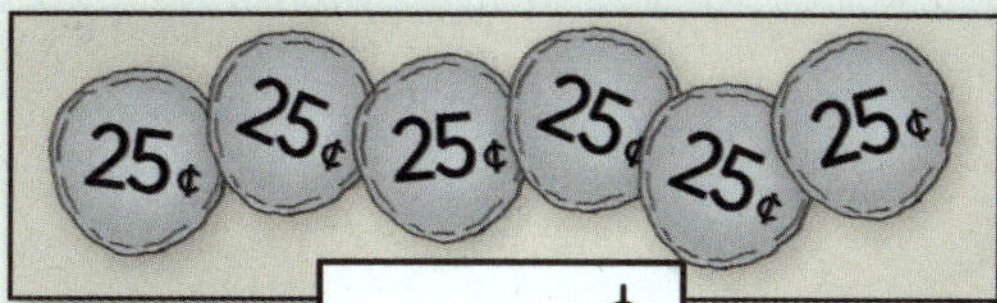


______ ¢

### Connect each number to its dot on the number line.

625 612 658 682 690

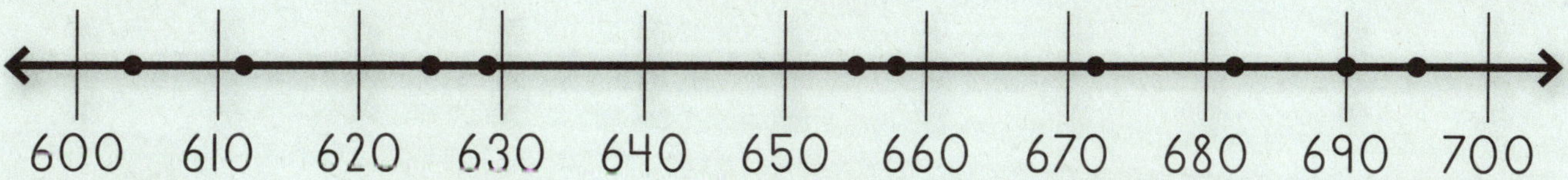


604 629 655 672 695

### Write the time.

___ : ___

___ : ___

___ : ___

___ : ___

### Complete.

|   | 7 | 4 |
|---|---|---|
| + | 2 | 9 |
|   |   |   |

|   | 8 | 8 |
|---|---|---|
| + | 8 | 8 |
|   |   |   |

## Lesson Activities

A

|   | 2 | 8 | 7 |
|---|---|---|---|
| + | 4 | 3 | 6 |
|   |   |   |   |

|   | 1 | 5 | 8 |
|---|---|---|---|
| + | 5 | 9 | 3 |
|   |   |   |   |

### The Addition Algorithm

*** Start with the ones-place.

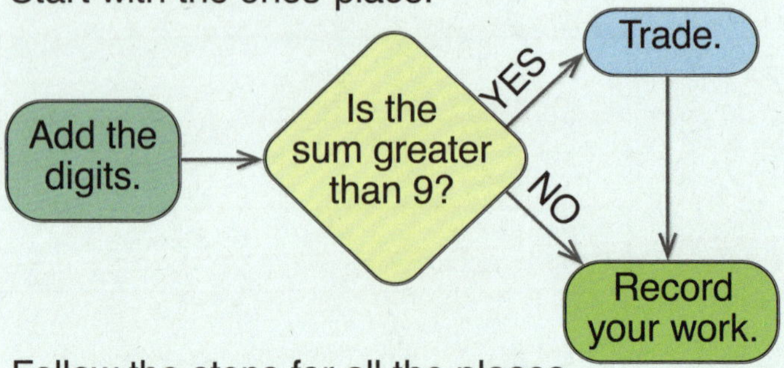


*** Follow the steps for all the places.

B

### Leaf Fight

| Player 1 | Player 2 |
|---|---|
| + | + |
| + | + |
| + | + |

## Practice

**Complete.**

| | 2 | 9 | 5 |
|---|---|---|---|
| + | 3 | 4 | 7 |
| | | | |

| | 5 | 6 | 1 |
|---|---|---|---|
| + | 2 | 3 | 8 |
| | | | |

| | 4 | 4 | 6 |
|---|---|---|---|
| + | 3 | 5 | 4 |
| | | | |

**Solve. Write the equations you use.**

Zari's family drove 275 miles in the morning and 148 miles in the afternoon. How far did they drive that day?

Charlie's family drove 362 miles to his grandparents' house. Then, they drove 362 miles back to their home. How far did they drive in all?

## Review

**Write the multiples in order.**

| Multiples of 3 | 3 | 6 | | 12 | | 18 | | 24 | | |
|---|---|---|---|---|---|---|---|---|---|---|
| Multiples of 4 | 4 | | | 16 | 20 | | 28 | | | |

**Round to the nearest hundred.**

| 401 | 682 | 949 | 951 | 550 | 234 |
|---|---|---|---|---|---|
| | | | | | |

## Lesson Activities

A

How much does it cost to buy a tire swing and a spiral slide?

Estimate

+

How much does it cost to buy a climbing net and a tire swing?

Estimate

+

How much does it cost to buy a regular slide and a spiral slide?

Estimate

+

Choose 3 items you would like to have in a playset. How much would it cost to buy all 3?

Estimate

+

## Practice

**Complete.**

| | 3 | 6 | 9 |
|---|---|---|---|
| + | 2 | 4 | 0 |
| | | | |

| | 6 | 0 | 5 |
|---|---|---|---|
| + | 3 | 9 | 4 |
| | | | |

| | 4 | 9 | 5 |
|---|---|---|---|
| + | 1 | 7 | 5 |
| | | | |

**Clara solved these problems, but she made some mistakes. Estimate the sum for each problem and check her work. Mark whether each answer is correct or incorrect.**

| | 1 | 1 | |
|---|---|---|---|
| | 2 | 9 | 6 |
| + | 3 | 8 | 7 |
| | 6 | 8 | 3 |

Estimate

  ____
+ ____

☐ Correct ☐ Incorrect

| | | 1 | |
|---|---|---|---|
| | 5 | 1 | 7 |
| + | 2 | 2 | 7 |
| | 8 | 4 | 4 |

Estimate

  ____
+ ____

☐ Correct ☐ Incorrect

| | 6 | 0 | 5 |
|---|---|---|---|
| + | | 9 | 4 |
| | 6 | 9 | 9 |

Estimate

  ____
+ ____

☐ Correct ☐ Incorrect

| | | 1 | |
|---|---|---|---|
| | 4 | 6 | 8 |
| + | 3 | 2 | 9 |
| | 6 | 9 | 7 |

Estimate

  ____
+ ____

☐ Correct ☐ Incorrect

| | 1 | | |
|---|---|---|---|
| | 6 | 5 | 7 |
| + | 1 | 5 | 3 |
| | 7 | 0 | 0 |

Estimate

  ____
+ ____

☐ Correct ☐ Incorrect

| | 8 | 7 | 3 |
|---|---|---|---|
| + | 1 | 0 | 2 |
| | 6 | 7 | 1 |

Estimate

  ____
+ ____

☐ Correct ☐ Incorrect

## Review

**Complete.**

$$\begin{array}{r} 4 \\ \times\ 6 \\ \hline \end{array} \quad \begin{array}{r} 3 \\ \times\ 7 \\ \hline \end{array} \quad \begin{array}{r} 5 \\ \times\ 6 \\ \hline \end{array} \quad \begin{array}{r} 10 \\ \times\ 7 \\ \hline \end{array} \quad \begin{array}{r} 4 \\ \times\ 8 \\ \hline \end{array}$$

$$\begin{array}{r} 4 \\ \times\ 7 \\ \hline \end{array} \quad \begin{array}{r} 3 \\ \times\ 8 \\ \hline \end{array} \quad \begin{array}{r} 4 \\ \times\ 9 \\ \hline \end{array} \quad \begin{array}{r} 3 \\ \times\ 5 \\ \hline \end{array} \quad \begin{array}{r} 7 \\ \times\ 5 \\ \hline \end{array}$$

**Maya made a pictograph to show how long she exercised. Use the pictograph to answer the questions. Write a multiplication equation for each question.**

How many minutes did Maya exercise on Tuesday?

☐ × ☐ = ☐

How many minutes did Maya exercise on Wednesday?

☐ × ☐ = ☐

How many minutes did Maya exercise on Thursday?

☐ × ☐ = ☐

**Complete.**

$$\begin{array}{r} 47 \\ -\ 21 \\ \hline \end{array} \quad \begin{array}{r} 41 \\ -\ 27 \\ \hline \end{array}$$

**Solve.**

You pay the clerk $80.
How much change do you get?

Change
$

## Lesson Activities

A

| | 4 | 3 | 2 |
|---|---|---|---|
| - | 2 | 8 | 7 |
| | | | |

| | 6 | 4 | 3 |
|---|---|---|---|
| - | 3 | 9 | 5 |
| | | | |

### The Subtraction Algorithm

*** Start with the ones-place.

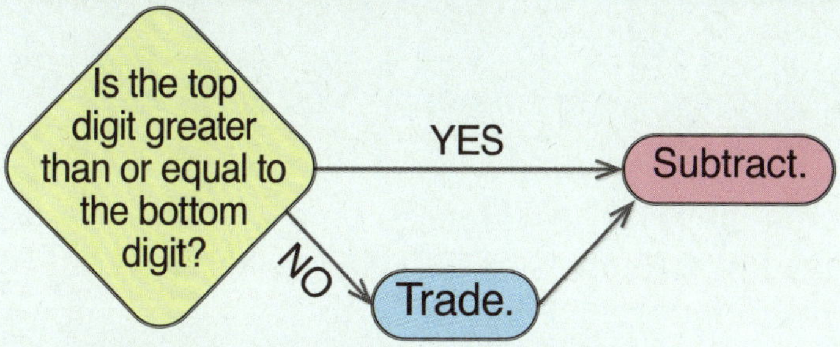


*** Follow the steps for all the places.

B

## SPIN TO WIN!

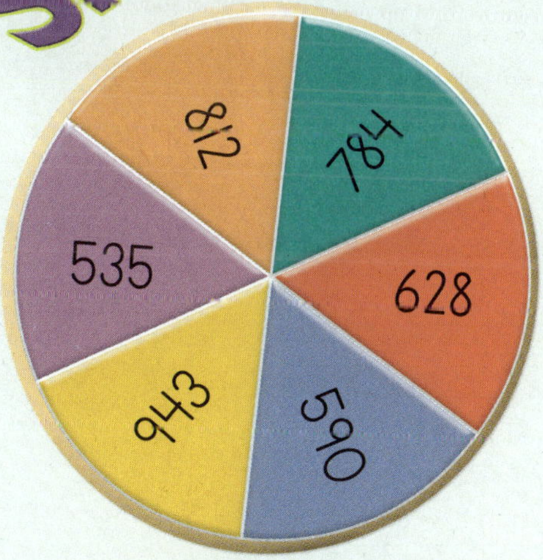


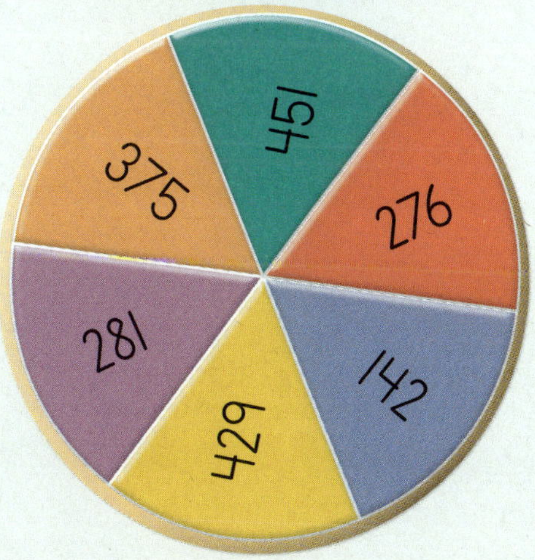


| Player 1 | Player 2 |
|---|---|
| - | - |
| - | - |
| - | - |

# 5.6

## Practice

Complete.

| | 9 | 4 | 7 |
|---|---|---|---|
| - | 6 | 8 | 2 |
| | | | |

| | 3 | 5 | 1 |
|---|---|---|---|
| - | 1 | 2 | 6 |
| | | | |

| | 8 | 3 | 0 |
|---|---|---|---|
| - | 4 | 5 | 8 |
| | | | |

Solve. Write the equations you use.

Jaydan's family drove 447 miles on Monday and 375 miles on Tuesday. How much further did they drive on Monday than Tuesday?

Daniela's cousin lives 550 miles away. After her family drives 236 miles, how much further do they need to drive to get to her cousins' house?

## Review

Complete the missing numbers.

| × | 1 | 2 | 3 | 4 | 5 | 6 | 7 | 8 | 9 | 10 |
|---|---|---|---|---|---|---|---|---|---|---|
| 1 | 1 | 2 | 3 | 4 | 5 | 6 | 7 | 8 | 9 | 10 |
| 2 | 2 | 4 | 6 | 8 | 10 | 12 | | 16 | 18 | 20 |
| 3 | 3 | 6 | 9 | 12 | 15 | | 21 | 24 | 27 | 30 |
| 4 | 4 | 8 | | 16 | 20 | 24 | | 32 | | 40 |
| 5 | 5 | | 15 | 20 | | 30 | 35 | 40 | 45 | 50 |
| 6 | 6 | 12 | 18 | 24 | 30 | 36 | 42 | 48 | 54 | |
| 7 | 7 | 14 | | 28 | 35 | 42 | 49 | 56 | 63 | 70 |
| 8 | | 16 | 24 | | 40 | 48 | 56 | 64 | 72 | 80 |
| 9 | 9 | 18 | | 36 | 45 | 54 | 63 | 72 | 81 | 90 |
| 10 | 10 | | 30 | 40 | 50 | 60 | 70 | 80 | 90 | |

## Lesson Activities

**A**

|   | 7 | 0 | 4 |
|---|---|---|---|
| - | 3 | 2 | 6 |
|   |   |   |   |

|   | 5 | 0 | 0 |
|---|---|---|---|
| - | 1 | 7 | 4 |
|   |   |   |   |

### The Subtraction Algorithm

*** Start with the ones-place.

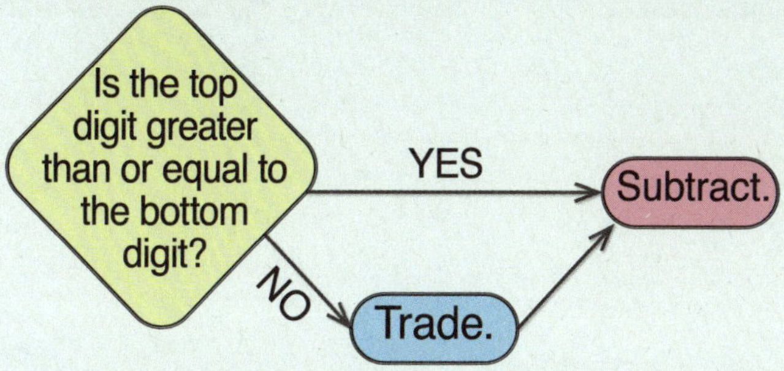


*** Follow the steps for all the places.

**B**

### Design Your OWN PLAYSET!

Tire swing .................. $235
Swing .......................... $73
Climbing net ............... $226
Slide ........................... $358
Spiral slide ................. $467

How much more does a spiral slide cost than a climbing net?

|   |   |   |   |
|---|---|---|---|
| - |   |   |   |
|   |   |   |   |

Estimate

−

You have $600. Then, you buy a climbing net. How much money do you have left?

|   |   |   |   |
|---|---|---|---|
| - |   |   |   |
|   |   |   |   |

Estimate

−

You have $300. Then, you buy a regular swing. How much money do you have left?

|   |   |   |   |
|---|---|---|---|
| - |   |   |   |
|   |   |   |   |

Estimate

−

## Practice

Complete.

| | 5 | 6 | 0 |
|---|---|---|---|
| - | 3 | 1 | 2 |
| | | | |

| | 4 | 0 | 0 |
|---|---|---|---|
| - | 2 | 8 | 3 |
| | | | |

| | 6 | 0 | 3 |
|---|---|---|---|
| - | 2 | 4 | 9 |
| | | | |

**Xander solved these problems, but he made some mistakes. Estimate the difference for each problem and check his work. Mark whether each answer is correct or incorrect.**

| | 7 | 12 | 12 |
|---|---|---|---|
| | 8 | 3 | 2 |
| – | 2 | 9 | 4 |
| | 5 | 3 | 8 |

Estimate

– ________

☐ Correct ☐ Incorrect

| | 6 | 10 | |
|---|---|---|---|
| | 7 | 0 | 8 |
| – | 3 | 1 | 5 |
| | 3 | 9 | 3 |

Estimate

– ________

☐ Correct ☐ Incorrect

| | 6 | 10 | |
|---|---|---|---|
| | 7 | 0 | 0 |
| – | 4 | 7 | 0 |
| | 2 | 3 | 0 |

Estimate

– ________

☐ Correct ☐ Incorrect

| | | 3 | 12 |
|---|---|---|---|
| | 6 | 4 | 2 |
| – | 1 | 2 | 6 |
| | 6 | 1 | 6 |

Estimate

– ________

☐ Correct ☐ Incorrect

| | 1 | | |
|---|---|---|---|
| | 4 | 6 | 2 |
| – | 2 | 9 | 5 |
| | 7 | 5 | 7 |

Estimate

– ________

☐ Correct ☐ Incorrect

| | | 9 | |
|---|---|---|---|
| | 3 | 10 | 10 |
| | 4 | 0 | 0 |
| – | 1 | 8 | 4 |
| | | 1 | 6 |

Estimate

– ________

☐ Correct ☐ Incorrect

## Review

Use the key to color the leaves.

### Complete.

9 × 5 = ☐  4 × 7 = ☐

8 × 4 = ☐  3 × 9 = ☐

3 × 7 = ☐  2 × 8 = ☐

6 × 4 = ☐  10 × 7 = ☐

5 × 5 = ☐  4 × 9 = ☐

### Write each money amount two ways.

$ ☐  ☐ ¢

$ ☐  ☐ ¢

### Solve.

You want to buy a bike that costs $300.
You have $260.
How much more money do you need?

### Complete.

9 tens = ☐

10 tens = ☐

11 tens = ☐

15 tens = ☐

18 tens = ☐

## Lesson Activities

A

### Roll and Multiply

| | | Score |
|---|---|---|
| 6 × | | |
| 7 × | | |
| 8 × | | |
| 9 × | | |
| Player 1 Total | | |

| | | Score |
|---|---|---|
| 6 × | | |
| 7 × | | |
| 8 × | | |
| 9 × | | |
| Player 2 Total | | |

B

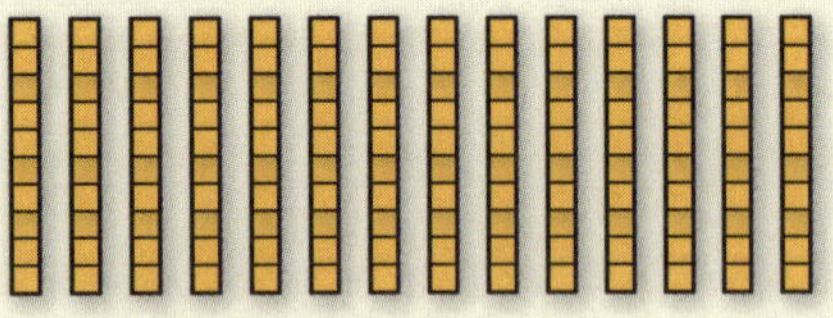

14 × 10 = ☐

14 tens = ☐

23 × 10 = ☐  46 × 10 = ☐  58 × 10 = ☐

C

### Shopping List

16 bags of oranges

☐ × ☐ = ☐ oranges

24 boxes of granola bars

☐ × ☐ = ☐ granola bars

30 cases of water

☐ × ☐ = ☐ bottles of water

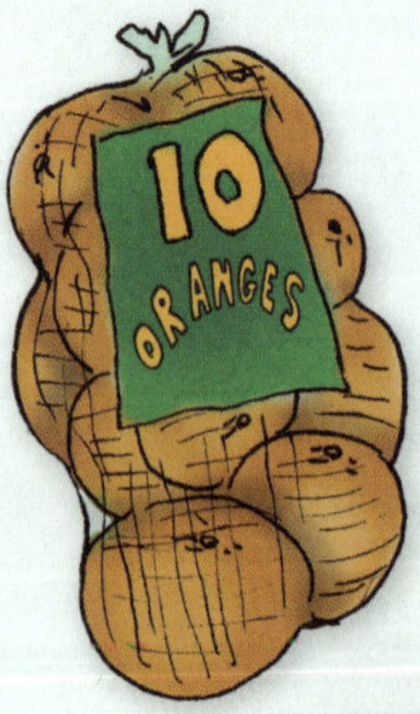

## Practice

**Complete.**

$14 \times 10 =$ ☐

$12 \times 10 =$ ☐

$10 \times 10 =$ ☐

$39 \times 10 =$ ☐

$36 \times 10 =$ ☐

$30 \times 10 =$ ☐

$70 \times 10 =$ ☐

$65 \times 10 =$ ☐

$60 \times 10 =$ ☐

$82 \times 10 =$ ☐

$81 \times 10 =$ ☐

$80 \times 10 =$ ☐

**Solve. Write the equations you use.**

Movie tickets cost $10.
How much do 34 tickets cost?

The theater has 25 rows.
Each row has 10 chairs.
How many chairs are there?

There are 10 paper plates in each pack.
Zahra buys 18 packs.
How many paper plates does she get?

Benjamin's mom drives 10 miles for work every day.
How many miles does she drive in 30 work days?

## Review

**Match pairs that equal 800.**

750 770 775 799 790

50 25 30 10 1

**Match.**

| | |
|---|---|
| 5 × 9 | 21 |
| 4 × 8 | 30 |
| 7 × 3 | 45 |
| 5 × 6 | 32 |
| 3 × 8 | 24 |

| | |
|---|---|
| 7 × 4 | 24 |
| 9 × 3 | 28 |
| 4 × 6 | 27 |
| 3 × 6 | 35 |
| 5 × 7 | 18 |

**Solve. Write the equations you use.**

The choir sold 148 adult tickets and 94 child tickets for the concert.
How many more adult tickets than child tickets did they sell?

The choir sold 148 adult tickets and 94 child tickets for the concert.
How many tickets did they sell in all?

## Lesson Activities

A

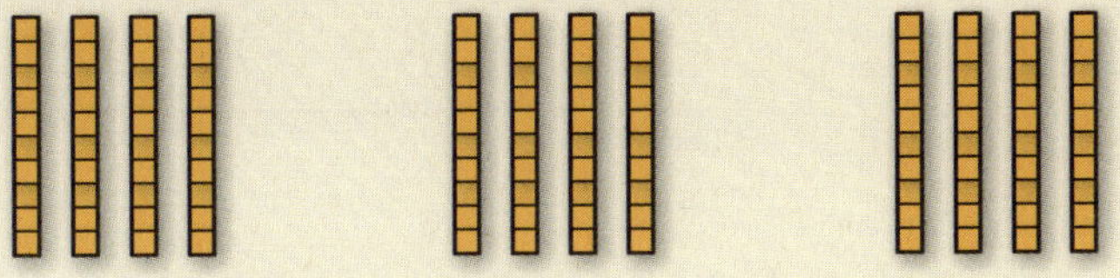

$3 \times 40 =$ ☐

$3 \times 4$ tens = ☐ tens

$2 \times 90 =$ ☐

$2 \times 9$ tens = ☐ tens

$8 \times 20 =$ ☐

$8 \times 2$ tens = ☐ tens

$5 \times 60 =$ ☐

$5 \times 6$ tens = ☐ tens

B

# Four in a Row

| | | | | |
|---|---|---|---|---|
| 3×70 | 200 | 5×50 | 160 | 4×80 |
| 100 | 270 | 160 | 150 | 10×20 |
| 120 | 500 | 320 | 2×50 | 50×10 |
| 8×20 | 200 | 210 | 200 | 4×40 |
| 6×20 | 250 | 4×50 | 9×30 | 5×30 |

## Practice

**Match.**

| | | |
|---|---|---|
| 2 × 50 | 160 | 18 × 10 |
| 4 × 40 | 180 | 4 × 30 |
| 20 × 10 | 100 | 2 × 80 |
| 6 × 20 | 200 | 5 × 20 |
| 2 × 90 | 120 | 5 × 40 |

**Solve. Write the equations you use.**

Tiana's parents buy 4 concert tickets.
Each ticket costs $70.
How much do the tickets cost in all?

Jackson likes to make crafts with yarn.
He uses 50 inches of yarn for each craft.
How much yarn does he need to make 4 crafts?

The theater has 5 sections.
Each section has 80 seats.
How many seats are in the theater?

★ There are 60 minutes in 1 hour.
How many minutes are in 4 hours?

## Review

**Draw a shape to match.**

| Triangle | Rectangle | Square |
|---|---|---|

**Complete.**

|   | 5 | 6 | 7 |
|---|---|---|---|
| + | 3 | 3 | 3 |
|   |   |   |   |

|   | 7 | 0 | 0 |
|---|---|---|---|
| - | 4 | 8 | 1 |
|   |   |   |   |

**Match.**

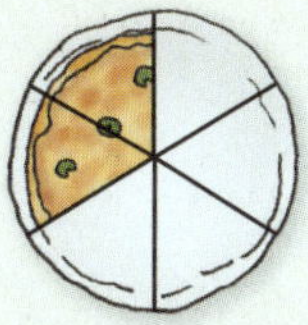

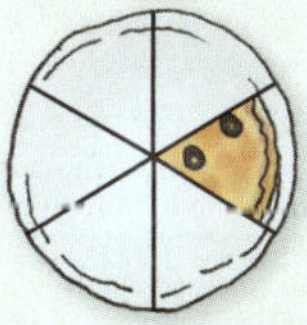

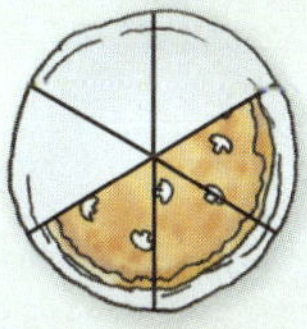

$\frac{1}{6}$

$\frac{2}{6}$

$\frac{3}{6}$

$\frac{4}{6}$

**Complete the sequences.**

5.10

## Unit Wrap-Up

**Complete.**

380 + ☐ = 400

590 + ☐ = 600

750 + ☐ = 800

750 + ☐ = 1,000

**Complete.**

| | +40 |
|---|---|
| 600 | |
| 460 | |
| 590 | |
| 750 | |
| 880 | |
| 370 | |

**Match.**

| | | |
|---|---|---|
| 570 + 30 | 580 | 650 - 60 |
| 550 + 40 | 590 | 640 - 30 |
| 580 + 30 | 600 | 620 - 40 |
| 510 + 70 | 610 | 630 - 30 |
| 590 + 30 | 620 | 700 - 80 |

## Unit Wrap-Up

**Estimate the answer to each problem. Then, find the exact answer.**

| | 6 | 2 | 5 |
|---|---|---|---|
| + | 2 | 8 | 7 |
| | | | |

Estimate: ___ + ___ = ___

| | 6 | 2 | 5 |
|---|---|---|---|
| - | 2 | 8 | 7 |
| | | | |

Estimate: ___ - ___ = ___

| | 3 | 0 | 9 |
|---|---|---|---|
| + | 4 | 8 | 3 |
| | | | |

Estimate: ___ + ___ = ___

| | 4 | 0 | 0 |
|---|---|---|---|
| - | 2 | 5 | 1 |
| | | | |

Estimate: ___ - ___ = ___

**Color the problems that equal the number in the star.**

| 200 | 240 | 280 | 400 |
|---|---|---|---|
| 4 × 50 | 60 × 4 | 4 × 70 | 40 × 10 |
| 20 × 10 | 40 × 6 | 8 × 40 | 20 × 4 |
| 30 × 6 | 70 × 3 | 28 × 10 | 8 × 50 |

**Solve. Write the equations you use.**

The ballet school sold 356 tickets to the performance. 149 were child tickets, and the rest were adult tickets. How many were adult tickets?

Makayla's mom bought 22 tickets to the ballet performance. Each ticket cost $10. How much did she pay for the tickets?

## Lesson Activities

A

# Escape the Maze (×3)

B

C

Halves | Thirds | Fourths | Sixths

D

## Practice

Circle the shapes that are split into thirds.
X the shapes that are not split into thirds.

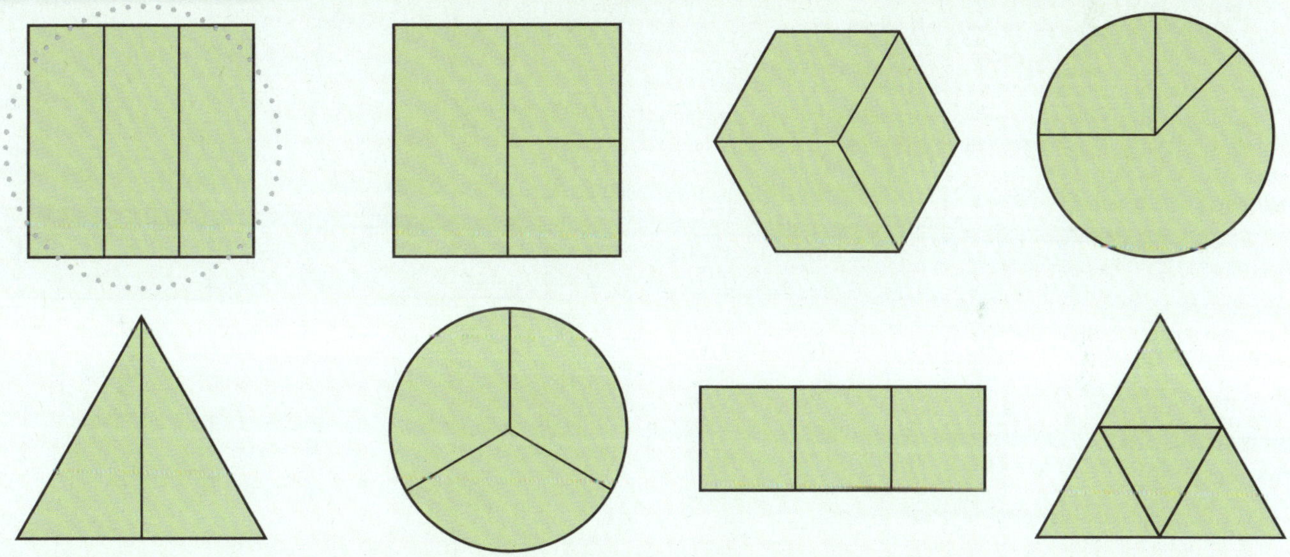

Circle the shapes that are cut into sixths. X the shapes that are not cut into sixths.

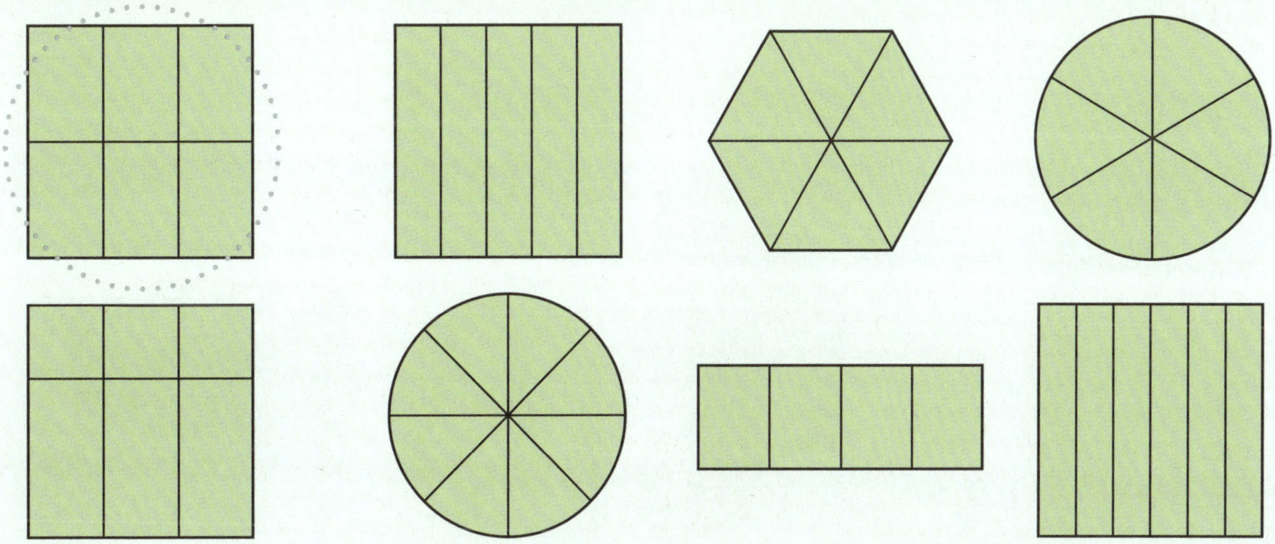

## Review

**Complete.**

560 + 80 = ☐

560 + 50 = ☐

560 + 40 = ☐

740 - 80 = ☐

740 - 50 = ☐

740 - 40 = ☐

**Complete.**

|   | 3 | 8 | 5 |
|---|---|---|---|
| + | 2 | 4 | 5 |
|   |   |   |   |

|   | 6 | 0 | 0 |
|---|---|---|---|
| - | 3 | 2 | 6 |
|   |   |   |   |

**Write the time.**

☐ : ☐

☐ : ☐

☐ : ☐

☐ : ☐

**Solve. Write a multiplication equation.**

Max bought 3 packs of pencils.
Each pack had 20 pencils.
How many pencils did he buy?

☐ × ☐ = ☐

Viv bought 4 boxes of paper clips.
Each box had 50 paper clips.
How many paper clips did she buy?

☐ × ☐ = ☐

## Lesson Activities

**A**

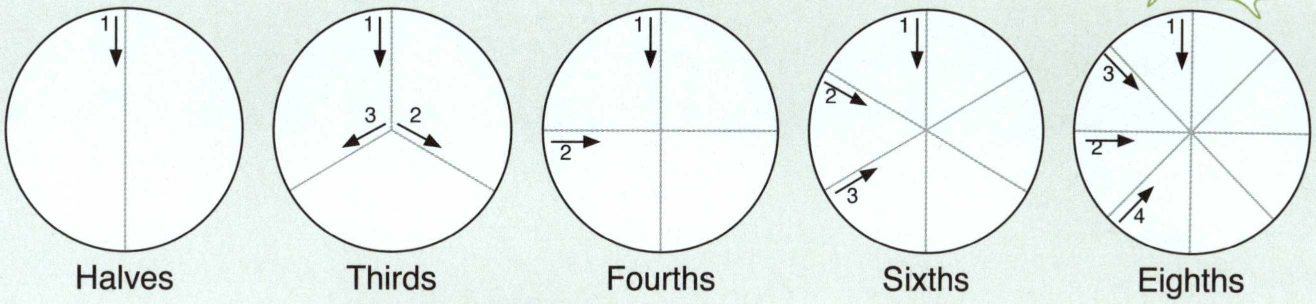


**B**

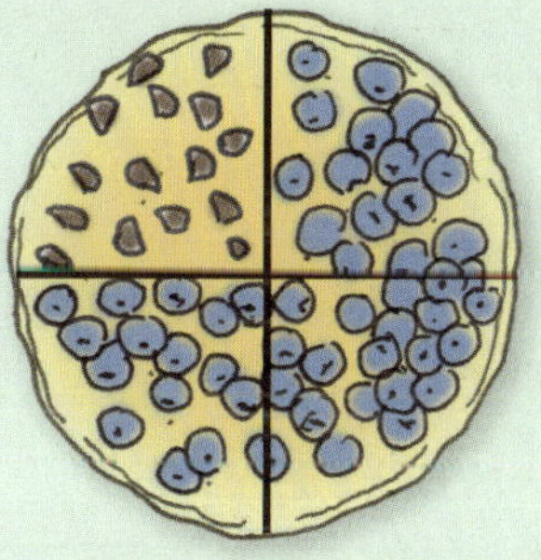

**Guest Check**

| | |
|---|---|
| Chocolate Chips | $\frac{1}{4}$ |
| Blueberries | $\frac{3}{4}$ |

$\frac{1}{4}$

- 1 → **Numerator** Number of parts
- 4 → **Denominator** How many equal parts the whole was split into

**C**

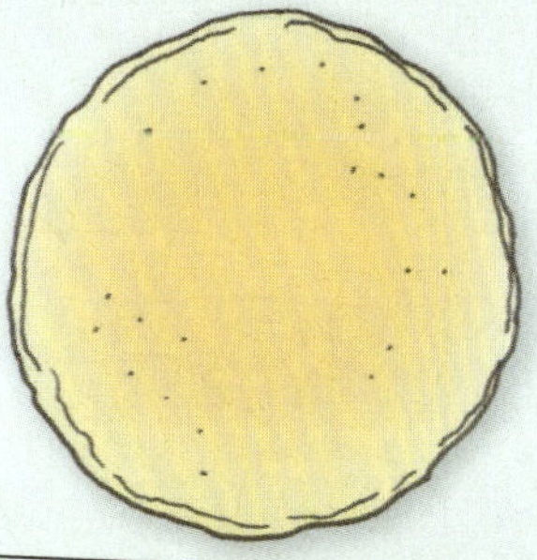

| | |
|---|---|
| Strawberries | $\frac{1}{8}$ |
| Chocolate Chips | $\frac{7}{8}$ |

| | |
|---|---|
| Bananas | $\frac{1}{3}$ |
| Blueberries | $\frac{2}{3}$ |

| | |
|---|---|
| Strawberries | $\frac{5}{6}$ |
| Bananas | $\frac{1}{6}$ |

D

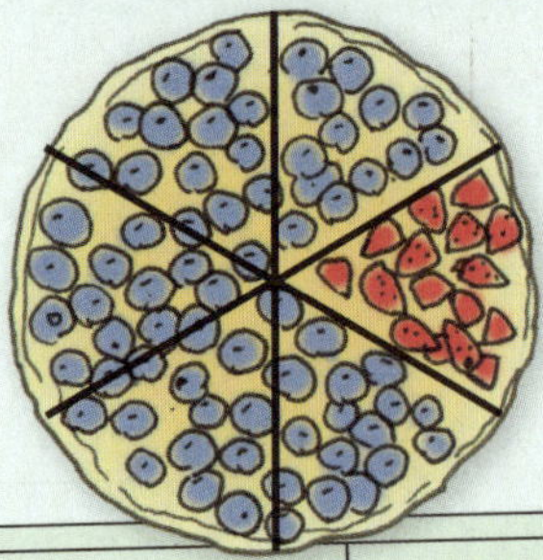

| Blueberries | — |
|---|---|
| Strawberries | — |

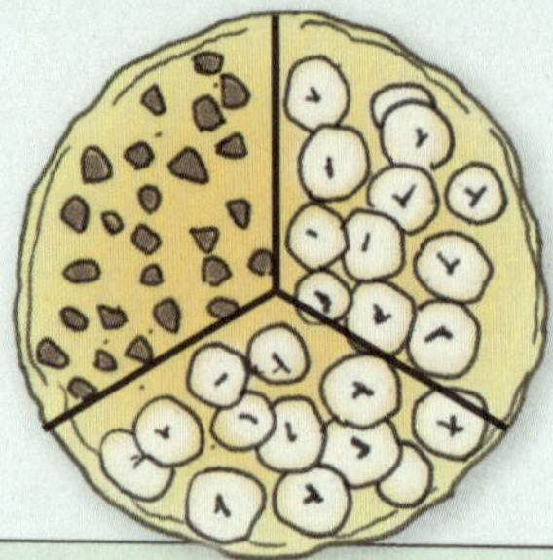

| Chocolate Chips | — |
|---|---|
| Bananas | — |

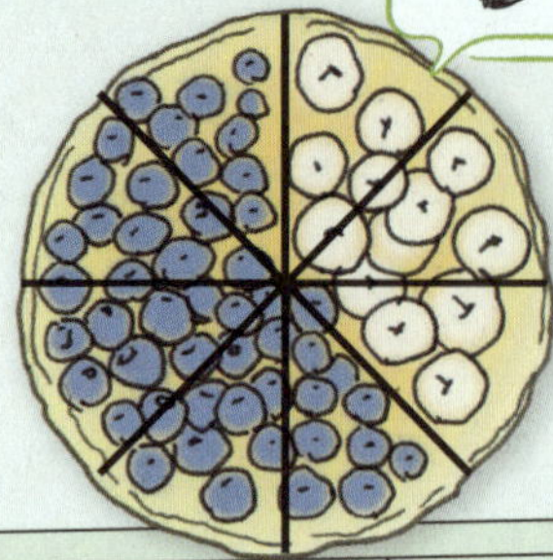

| Blueberries | — |
|---|---|
| Bananas | — |

## Practice

**Write fractions to match the waffle toppings.**

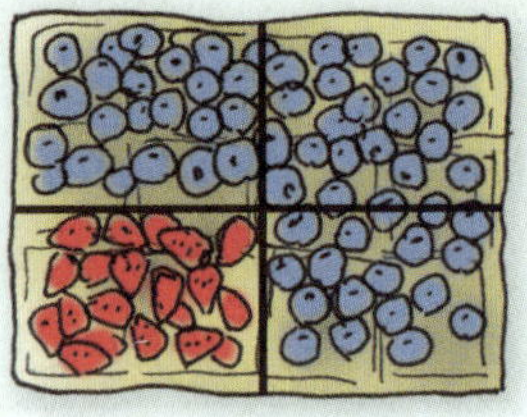

Blueberries —

Strawberries —

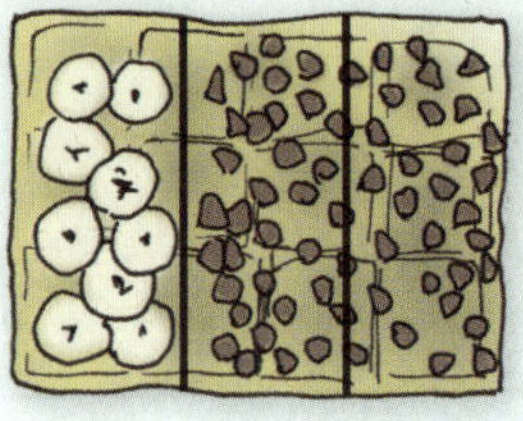

Bananas —

Chocolate Chips —

Chocolate Chips —

Strawberries —

Bananas —

Chocolate Chips —

Strawberries —

Bananas —

Strawberries —

Bananas —

## Review

Match pairs that equal 1,000.

| 800 | 700 | 600 | 750 | 650 |
|---|---|---|---|---|
| 300 | 250 | 200 | 350 | 400 |

Complete.

$4 \times 6 = \square$ $7 \times 2 = \square$ $5 \times 8 = \square$

$3 \times 3 = \square$ $8 \times 3 = \square$ $1 \times 6 = \square$

$5 \times 7 = \square$ $2 \times 9 = \square$ $3 \times 7 = \square$

$0 \times 6 = \square$ $6 \times 5 = \square$ $4 \times 4 = \square$

$8 \times 2 = \square$ $7 \times 4 = \square$ $9 \times 3 = \square$

Round to the nearest hundred.

| 895 | |
|---|---|
| 536 | |
| 450 | |
| 707 | |
| 619 | |
| 244 | |

Copy the shapes.

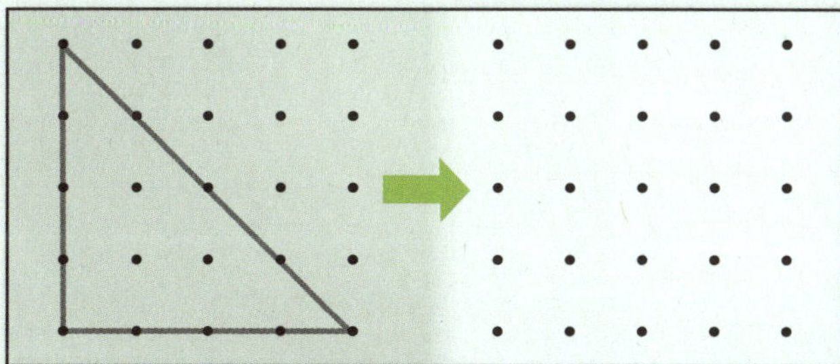

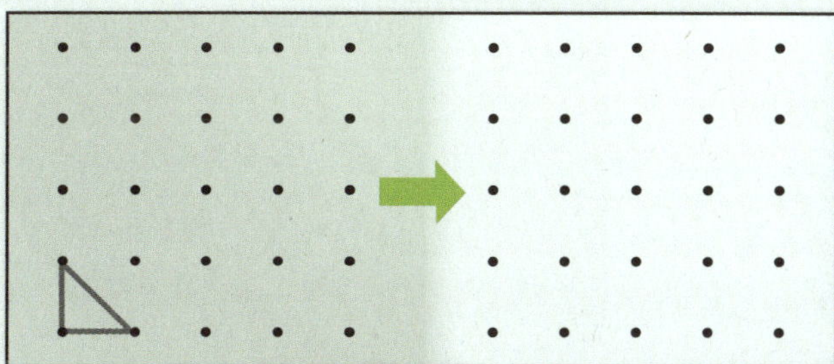

## Lesson Activities

A

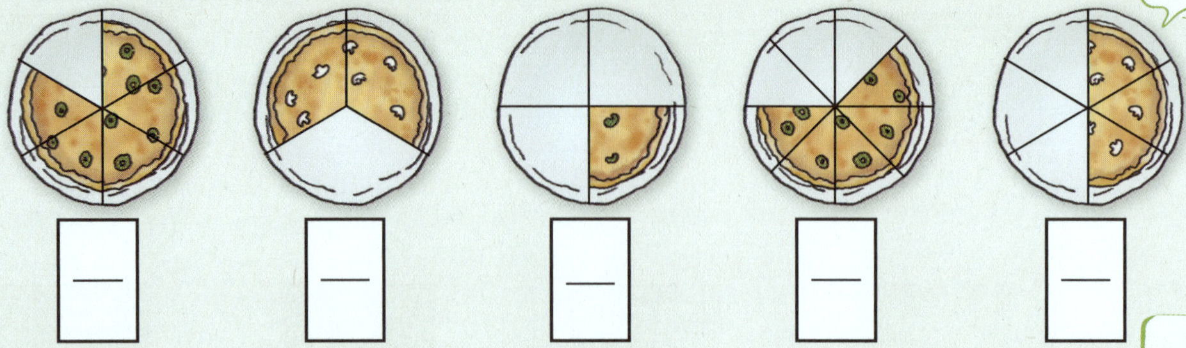

B

C

# Fraction Four in a Row

| | | | | |
|---|---|---|---|---|
| $\frac{5}{8}$ | $\frac{7}{8}$ | $\frac{0}{8}$ | $\frac{1}{2}$ | $\frac{1}{4}$ |
| $\frac{2}{8}$ | $\frac{5}{6}$ | $\frac{4}{6}$ | $\frac{2}{3}$ | $\frac{3}{6}$ |
| $\frac{3}{6}$ | $\frac{2}{4}$ | $\frac{3}{8}$ | $\frac{4}{4}$ | $\frac{1}{6}$ |
| $\frac{1}{3}$ | $\frac{8}{8}$ | $\frac{1}{2}$ | $\frac{6}{8}$ | $\frac{2}{6}$ |
| $\frac{3}{4}$ | $\frac{5}{6}$ | $\frac{0}{4}$ | $\frac{2}{4}$ | $\frac{1}{8}$ |

## Practice

**Complete the fractions to match the toppings.**

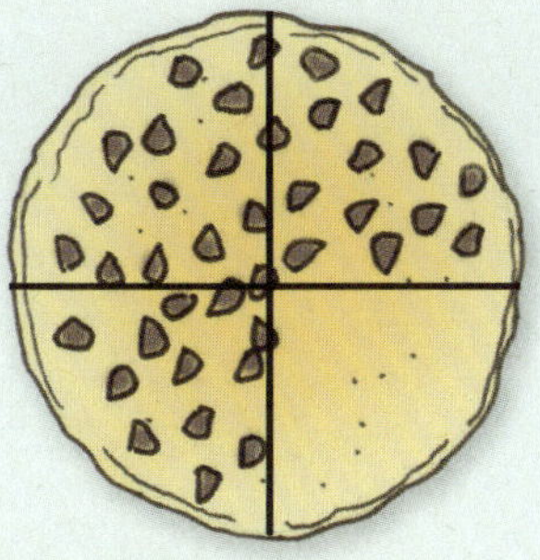

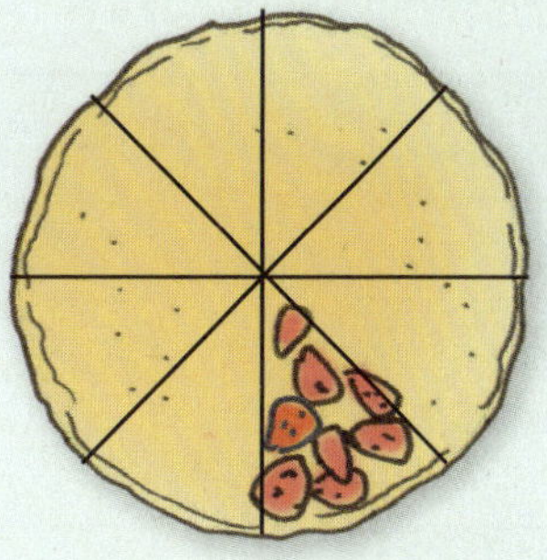

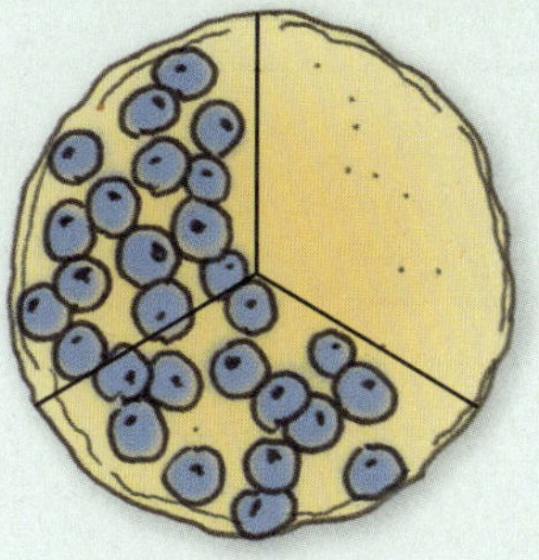

| Chocolate Chips | — |
|---|---|
| Plain | — |

| Strawberries | — |
|---|---|
| Plain | — |

| Blueberries | — |
|---|---|
| Plain | — |

**Match pairs of fractions that equal one whole.**

$\frac{1}{6}$ $\frac{1}{8}$ $\frac{1}{3}$ $\frac{1}{4}$ $\frac{1}{2}$

$\frac{2}{3}$ $\frac{5}{6}$ $\frac{7}{8}$ $\frac{1}{2}$ $\frac{3}{4}$

**Solve.**

Gabe's family ate $\frac{3}{8}$ of this pie.

What fraction of the pie did they have left?

$\frac{\square}{\square}$

Aria put strawberries on $\frac{1}{6}$ of her waffle.

She left the rest plain.

What fraction of the waffle was plain?

$\frac{\square}{\square}$

6.3

## Review

**Match.**

| | |
|---|---|
| 4 × 7 | 28 |
| 4 × 10 | 36 |
| 4 × 9 | 24 |
| 4 × 6 | 40 |
| 4 × 8 | 32 |

| | |
|---|---|
| 3 × 8 | 18 |
| 3 × 9 | 30 |
| 3 × 7 | 24 |
| 3 × 10 | 27 |
| 3 × 6 | 21 |

**Complete.**

5 × 30 = ☐

4 × 20 = ☐

2 × 30 = ☐

2 × 35 = ☐

**Write the time.**

☐ : ☐

☐ : ☐

**Solve. Write the equations you use.**

Samuel's bookshelf has 3 shelves.
There are 9 books on each shelf.
How many books are on the bookshelf?

Samuel's book has 319 pages.
He has already read 184 pages.
How many pages does he have left to read?

## Lesson Activities

**A**

1 apple + 2 apples = ☐ apples

1 fourth + 2 fourths = ☐ fourths

$\frac{1}{4} + \frac{2}{4} = \frac{\square}{\square}$

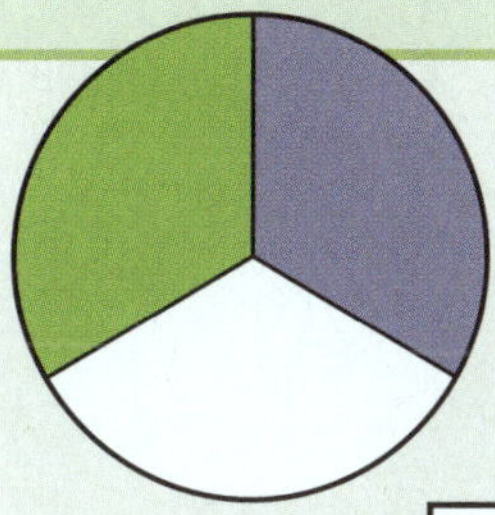

$\frac{1}{3} + \frac{1}{3} = \frac{\square}{\square}$

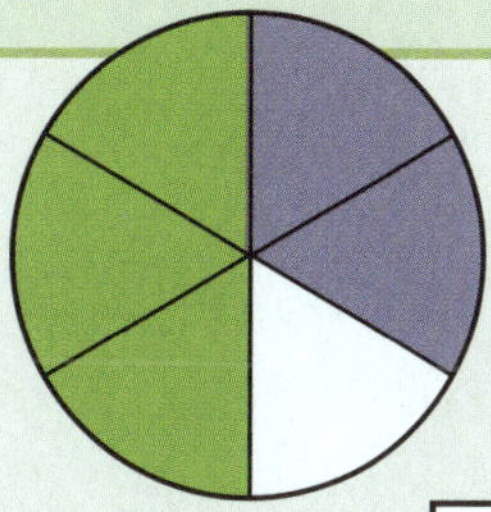

$\frac{3}{6} + \frac{2}{6} = \frac{\square}{\square}$

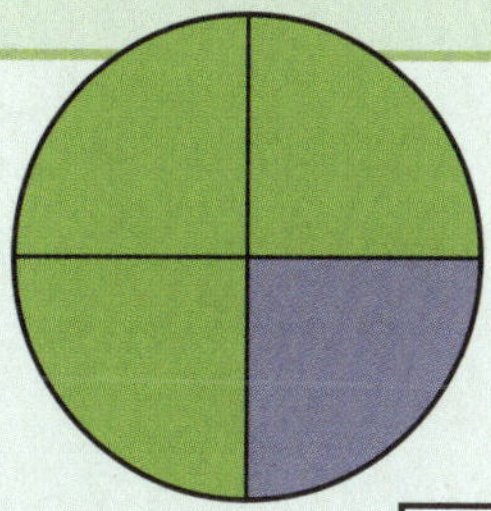

$\frac{3}{4} + \frac{1}{4} = \frac{\square}{\square}$

**B**

| Player 1 | Player 2 |
|---|---|
| $\frac{\square}{\square} + \frac{\square}{\square} = \frac{\square}{\square}$ | $\frac{\square}{\square} + \frac{\square}{\square} = \frac{\square}{\square}$ |
| $\frac{\square}{\square} + \frac{\square}{\square} = \frac{\square}{\square}$ | $\frac{\square}{\square} + \frac{\square}{\square} = \frac{\square}{\square}$ |
| $\frac{\square}{\square} + \frac{\square}{\square} = \frac{\square}{\square}$ | $\frac{\square}{\square} + \frac{\square}{\square} = \frac{\square}{\square}$ |
| $\frac{\square}{\square} + \frac{\square}{\square} = \frac{\square}{\square}$ | $\frac{\square}{\square} + \frac{\square}{\square} = \frac{\square}{\square}$ |
| $\frac{\square}{\square} + \frac{\square}{\square} = \frac{\square}{\square}$ | $\frac{\square}{\square} + \frac{\square}{\square} = \frac{\square}{\square}$ |

# 6.4

## Practice

**Complete.**

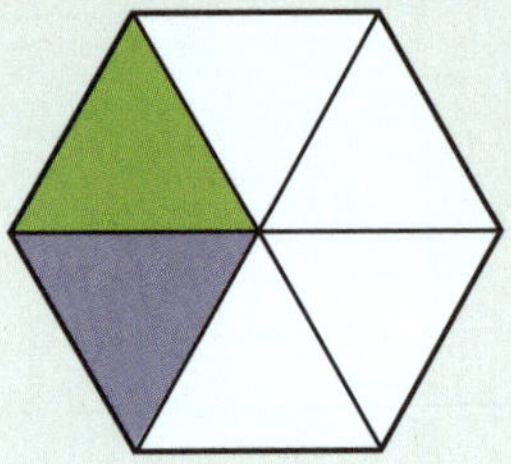

$\frac{1}{6} + \frac{1}{6} = \frac{\square}{\square}$

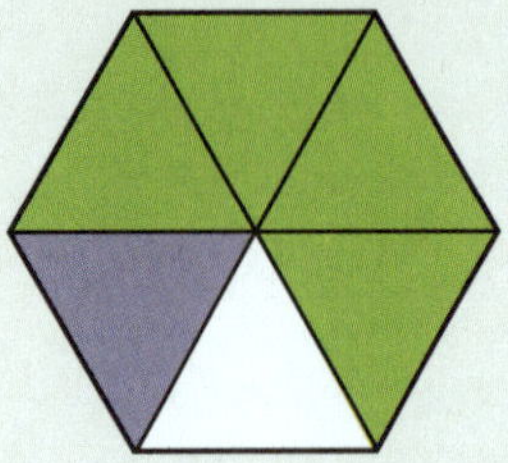

$\frac{4}{6} + \frac{1}{6} = \frac{\square}{\square}$

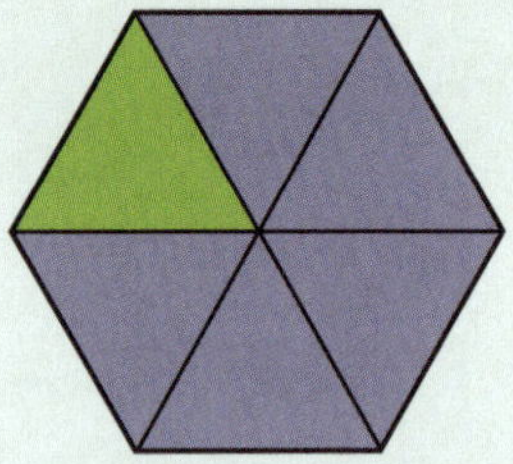

$\frac{1}{6} + \frac{\square}{\square} = \frac{6}{6}$

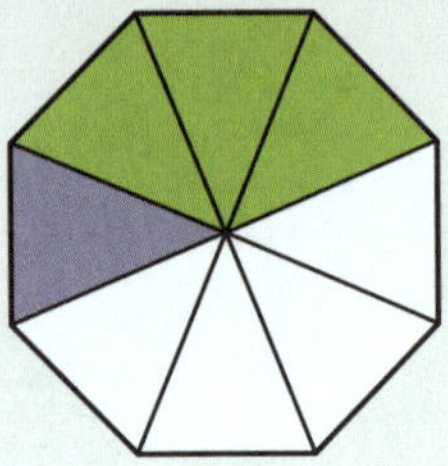

$\frac{1}{8} + \frac{3}{8} = \frac{\square}{\square}$

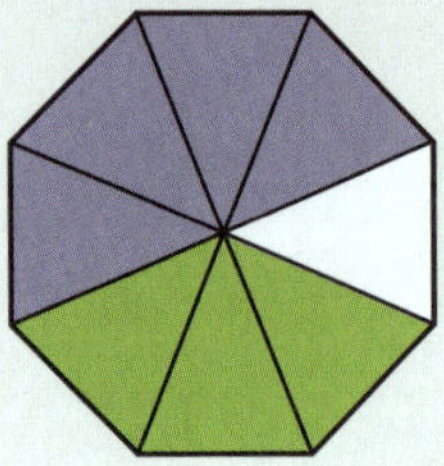

$\frac{4}{8} + \frac{3}{8} = \frac{\square}{\square}$

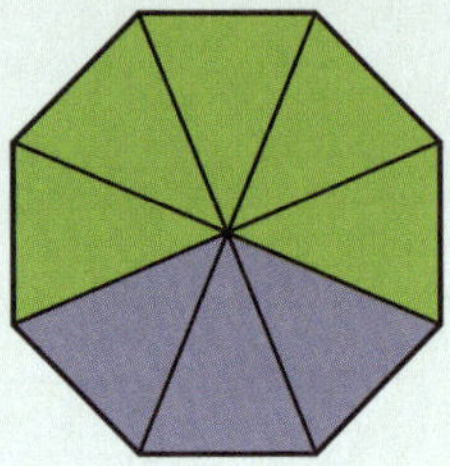

$\frac{5}{8} + \frac{\square}{\square} = \frac{8}{8}$

**Solve. Write an equation to match.**

Henry ate $\frac{1}{8}$ of a pizza.

Then, he ate $\frac{2}{8}$ of the pizza.

What fraction of the pizza did he eat?

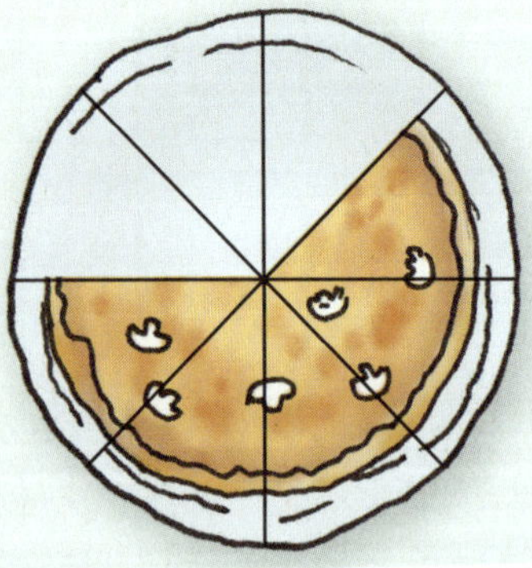

$\frac{\square}{\square} + \frac{\square}{\square} = \frac{\square}{\square}$

Elizabeth put green frosting on $\frac{2}{6}$ of the cake.

She put blue frosting on $\frac{3}{6}$ of the cake.

She left the rest plain.

What fraction of the cake has frosting?

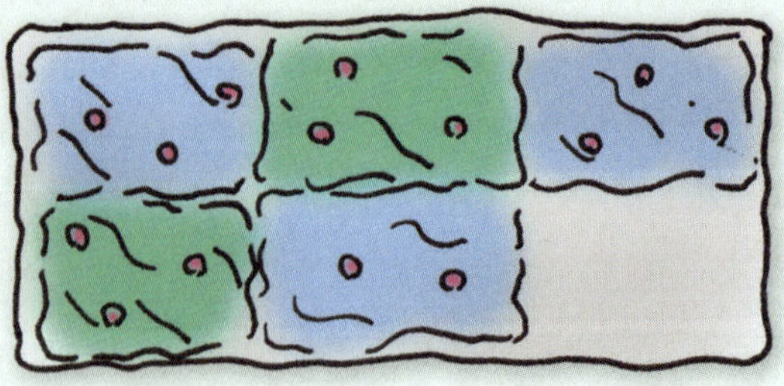

$\frac{\square}{\square} + \frac{\square}{\square} = \frac{\square}{\square}$

## Review

Complete.

$2 \times 27 =$ ☐

$2 \times 25 =$ ☐

$2 \times 20 =$ ☐

$2 \times 48 =$ ☐

$2 \times 43 =$ ☐

$2 \times 40 =$ ☐

$7 \times 30 =$ ☐

$6 \times 30 =$ ☐

$5 \times 30 =$ ☐

★ $5 \times 41 =$ ☐

$5 \times 40 =$ ☐

$4 \times 40 =$ ☐

Aaron made a pictograph about raking leaves.
Use the pictograph to complete the chart and answer the questions.

### Time Spent Raking Leaves

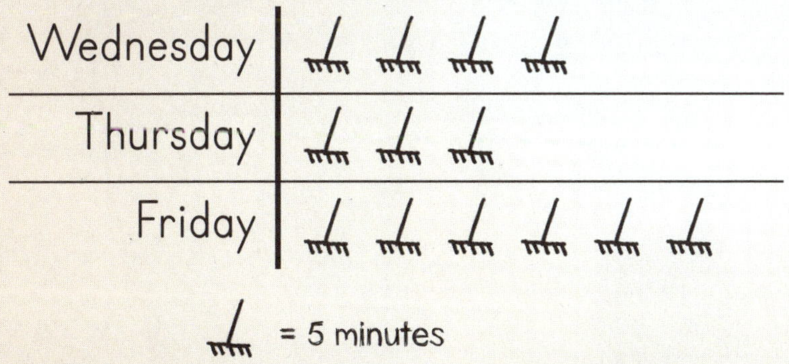


| Day | Minutes |
|---|---|
| Wed. | |
| Thur. | |
| Fri. | |

How much more time did he spend raking leaves on Friday than Thursday?

How much time did he spend raking leaves in all?

## Lesson Activities

### A

3 apples – 1 apple = ☐ apples

3 fourths – 1 fourth = ☐ fourths

$\frac{3}{4} - \frac{1}{4} = \frac{\square}{\square}$

$\frac{5}{8} - \frac{3}{8} = \frac{\square}{\square}$

$\frac{2}{3} - \frac{1}{3} = \frac{\square}{\square}$

$\frac{4}{6} - \frac{2}{6} = \frac{\square}{\square}$

### B

## Practice

**Complete. X out the pizza slices to match each equation.**

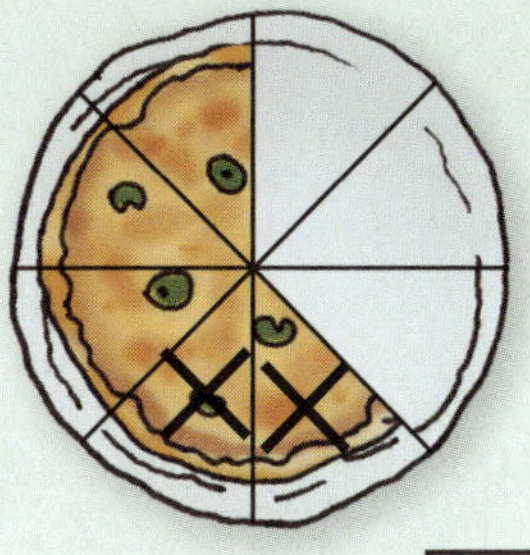

$\frac{5}{8} - \frac{2}{8} = \frac{\square}{\square}$

$\frac{3}{6} - \frac{1}{6} = \frac{\square}{\square}$

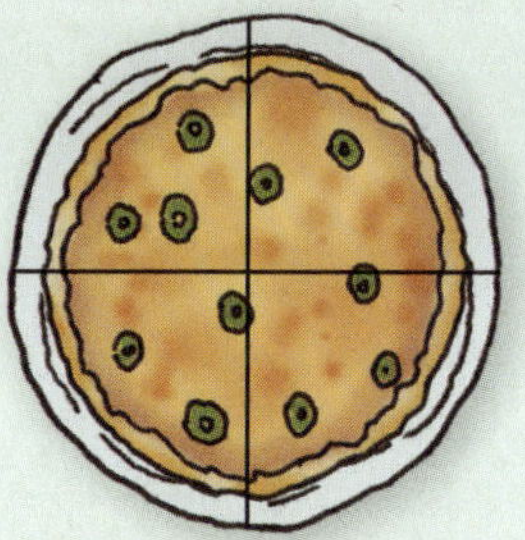

★ $\frac{4}{4} - \frac{1}{4} = \frac{\square}{\square}$

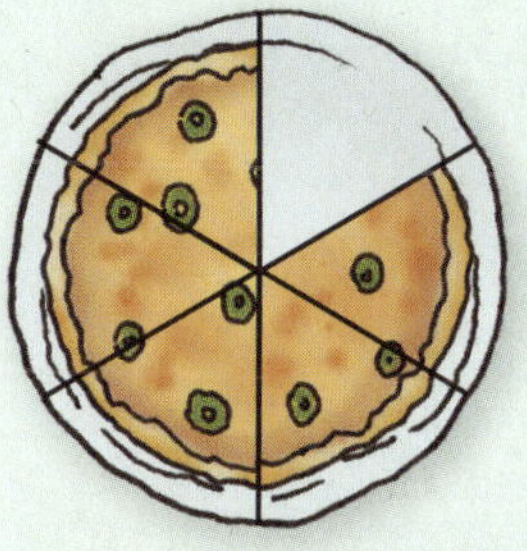

$\frac{5}{6} - \frac{4}{6} = \frac{\square}{\square}$

$\frac{7}{8} - \frac{4}{8} = \frac{\square}{\square}$

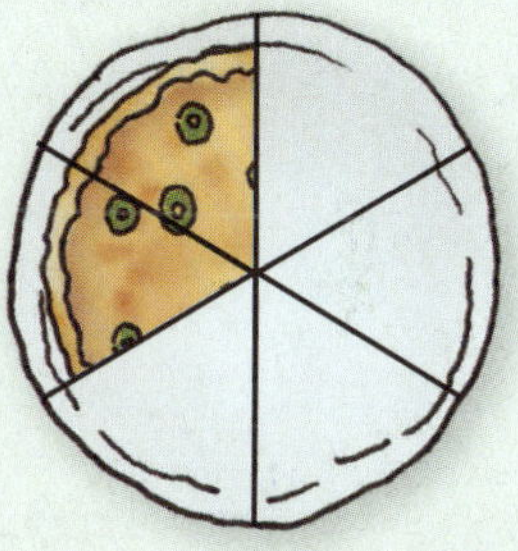

★ $\frac{2}{6} - \frac{0}{6} = \frac{\square}{\square}$

**Solve. Write an equation to mach.**

Hudson's family has $\frac{7}{8}$ of a pan of brownies.
They eat $\frac{5}{8}$ of the pan.
What fraction of the pan is left?

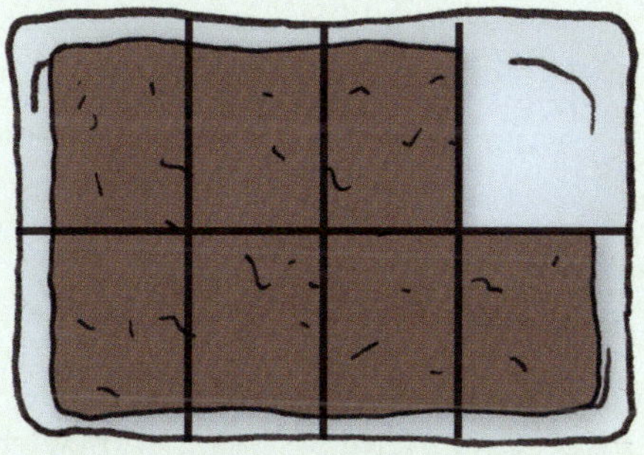

$\frac{\square}{\square} - \frac{\square}{\square} = \frac{\square}{\square}$

Bella's family has $\frac{5}{8}$ of a pizza.
Bella eats $\frac{2}{8}$ of the pizza.
What fraction of the whole pizza is left?

$\frac{\square}{\square} - \frac{\square}{\square} = \frac{\square}{\square}$

## Review

**Complete.**

| × | 1 | 2 | 3 | 4 | 5 | 6 | 7 | 8 | 9 | 10 |
|---|---|---|---|---|---|---|---|---|---|---|
| 1 | 1 | 2 | 3 | 4 | 5 | 6 | 7 | 8 | 9 | 10 |
| 2 | 2 | 4 | 6 | 8 | 10 | 12 | 14 | 16 | 18 | 20 |
| 3 | 3 | 6 | 9 | 12 | | 18 | | 24 | | 30 |
| 4 | 4 | 8 | 12 | 16 | 20 | | 28 | | 36 | 40 |
| 5 | 5 | 10 | | 20 | 25 | 30 | 35 | 40 | 45 | 50 |
| 6 | 6 | 12 | 18 | | 30 | 36 | 42 | 48 | 54 | 60 |
| 7 | 7 | 14 | | 28 | 35 | 42 | 49 | 56 | 63 | 70 |
| 8 | 8 | 16 | 24 | | 40 | 48 | 56 | 64 | 72 | 80 |
| 9 | 9 | 18 | | 36 | 45 | 54 | 63 | 72 | 81 | 90 |
| 10 | 10 | 20 | 30 | 40 | 50 | 60 | 70 | 80 | 90 | 100 |

**Complete.**

1 foot = ☐ inches

1 yard = ☐ feet

1 yard = ☐ inches

1 meter = ☐ centimeters

1 minute = ☐ seconds

1 hour = ☐ minutes

1 day = ☐ hours

1 week = ☐ days

**Use a ruler to measure the sticks.**

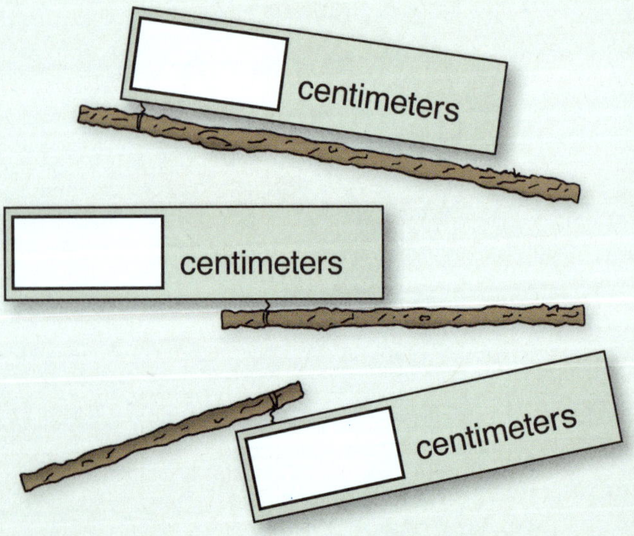


**Write each number in its expanded form.**

396 = 300 + 90 + 6

475 = ☐

808 = ☐

880 = ☐

## Lesson Activities

**A**

# Multiplication Crash (×4)

| 12 | 24 | 36 | 8 | 40 |
|---|---|---|---|---|
| 28 | 4 | 32 | 20 | 16 |

**B**

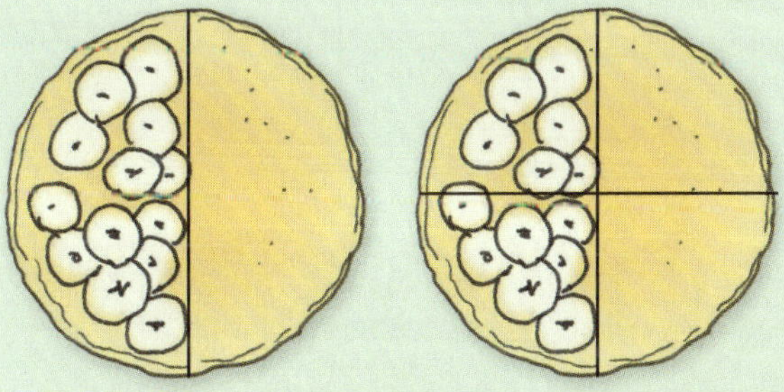

— = —

**Equivalent Fractions**
have the same value but have different numerators and denominators.

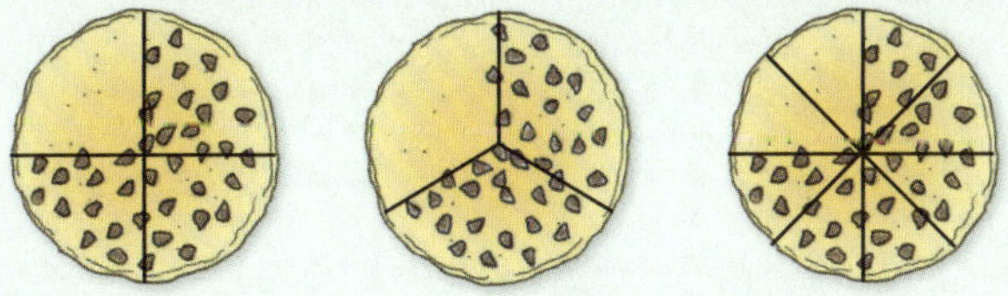

— = —

— = —

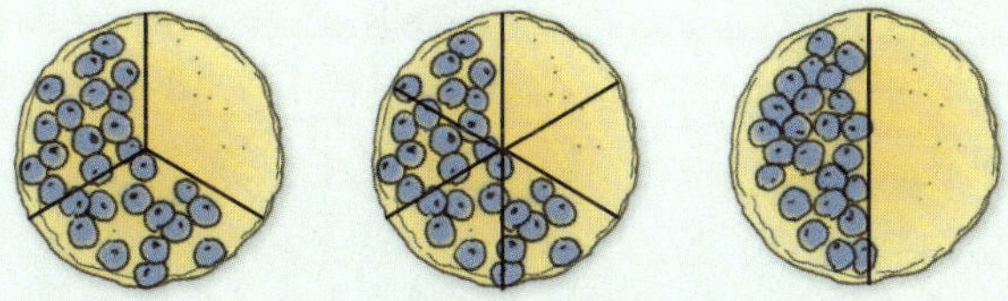

— = —

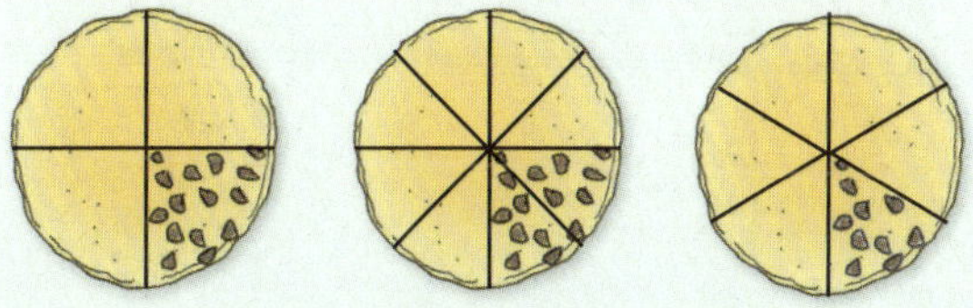

— = —

## Practice

**Complete the equivalent fractions to match the pancakes.**

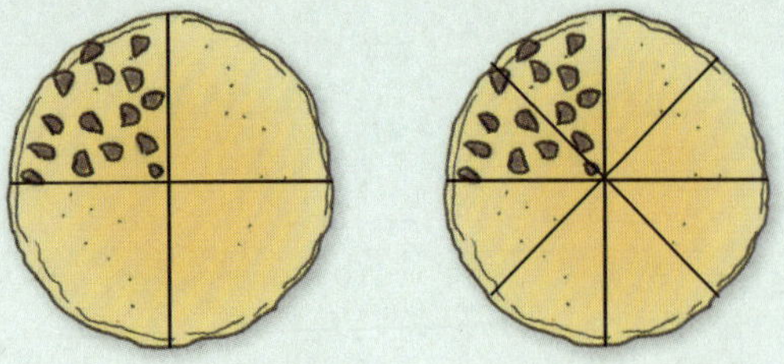

___ = ___

___ = ___

___ = ___

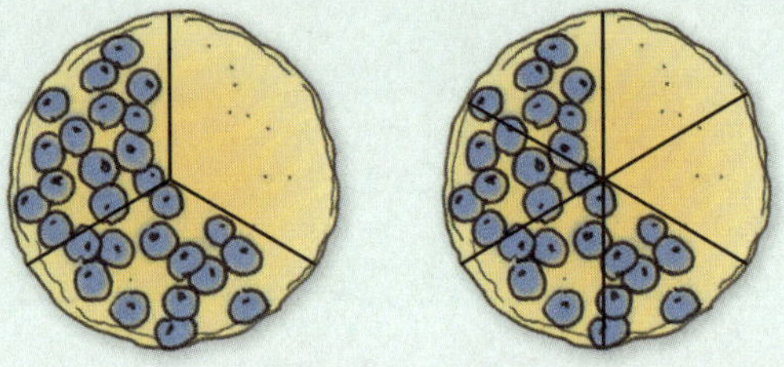

___ = ___

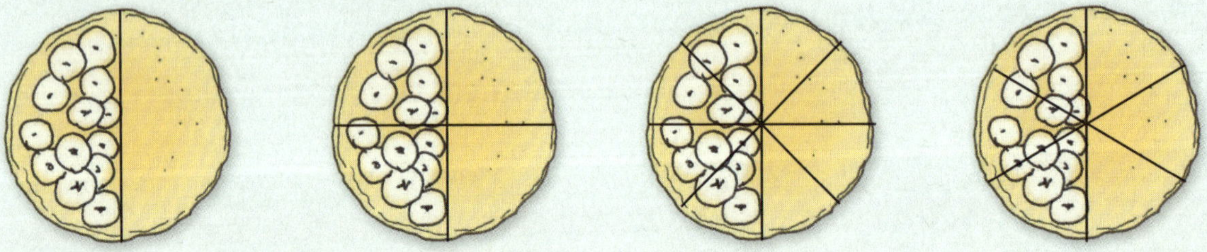

___ = ___ = ___ = ___

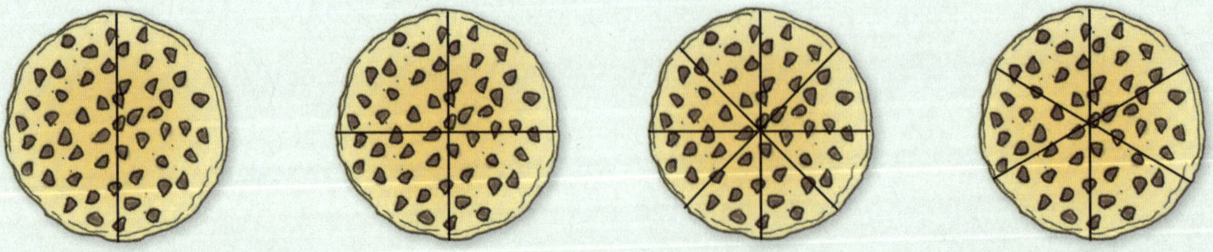

___ = ___ = ___ = ___

## Review

**Complete the fractions to match the pictures.**

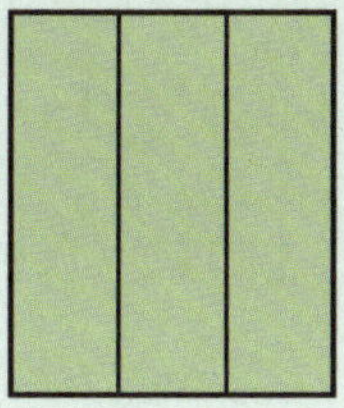

1 whole = $\frac{\square}{\square}$

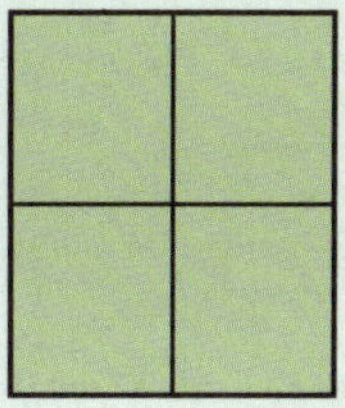

1 whole = $\frac{\square}{\square}$

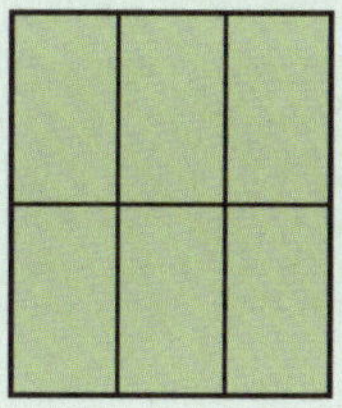

1 whole = $\frac{\square}{\square}$

**Complete.**

| | | | | |
|---|---|---|---|---|
| 5 × 7 = | 8 × 3 = | 7 × 4 = | 4 × 1 = | 3 × 3 = |
| 3 × 9 = | 5 × 5 = | 4 × 2 = | 3 × 4 = | 9 × 4 = |

**Complete.**

70 - 38 = ☐

70 - 18 = ☐

70 - 8 = ☐

★ 380 + 130 = ☐

380 + 30 = ☐

380 + 20 = ☐

★ 410 - 150 = ☐

410 - 50 = ☐

410 - 10 = ☐

2 × 36 = ☐

2 × 33 = ☐

2 × 30 = ☐

## Lesson Activities

### A

$\frac{1}{2} = \frac{\phantom{0}}{\phantom{0}}$

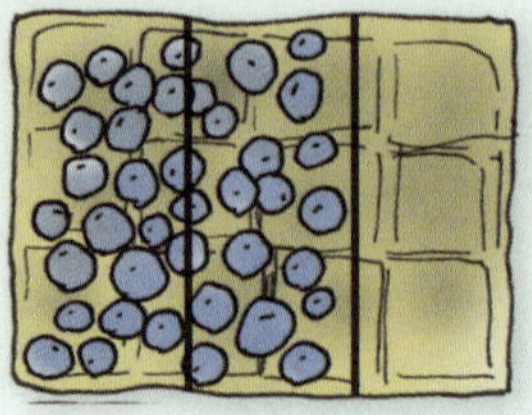

$\frac{2}{3} = \frac{\phantom{0}}{\phantom{0}}$

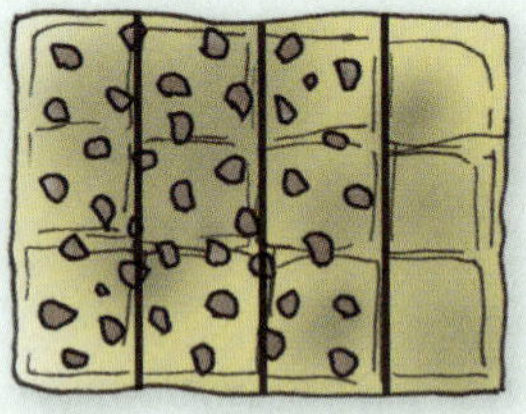

$\frac{3}{4} = \frac{\phantom{0}}{\phantom{0}}$

$\frac{1}{2} = \frac{\phantom{0}}{\phantom{0}}$

### B

## Roll and Cover

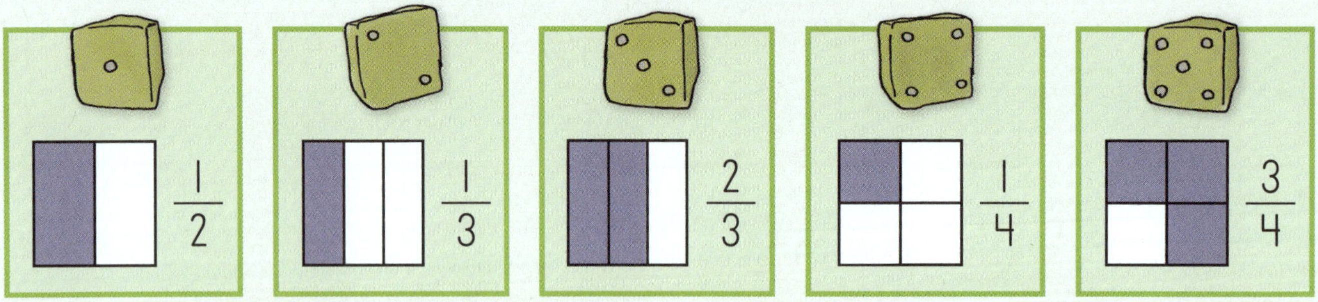


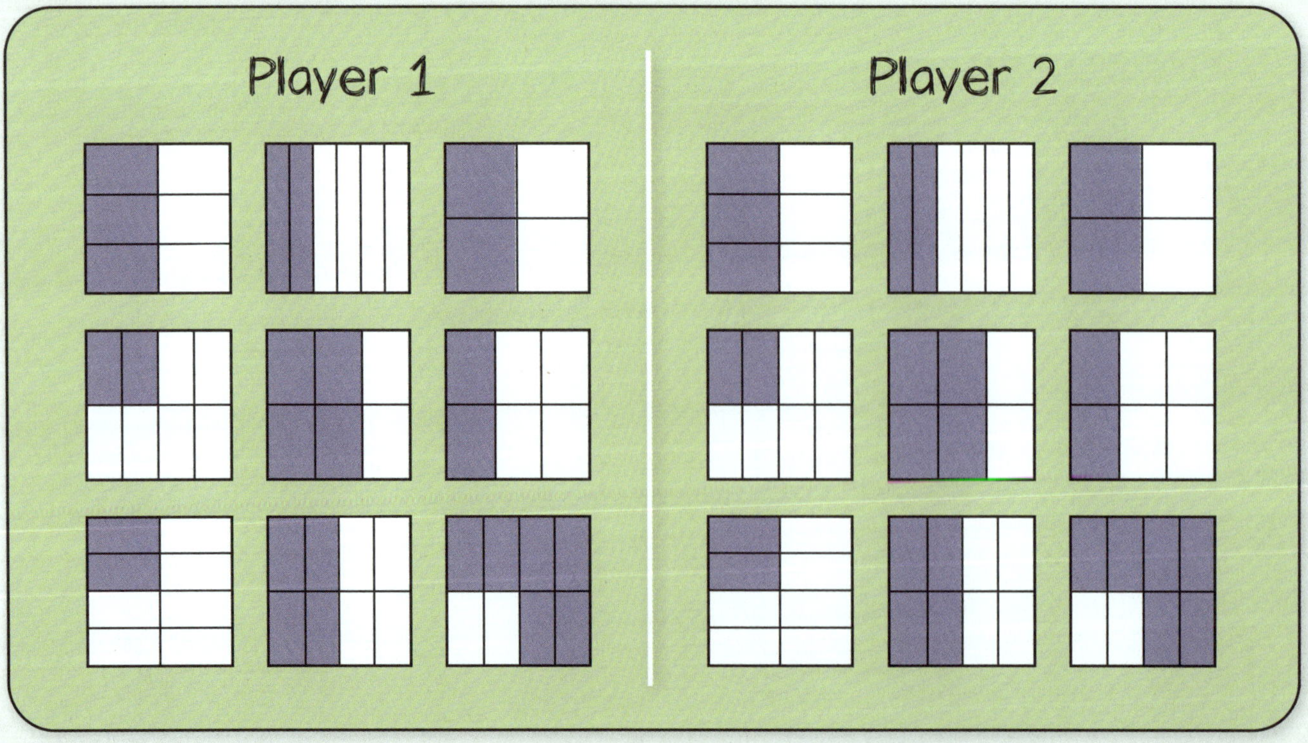

## Practice

**Color the second shape in each pair to match the first shape. Then, complete the fraction.**

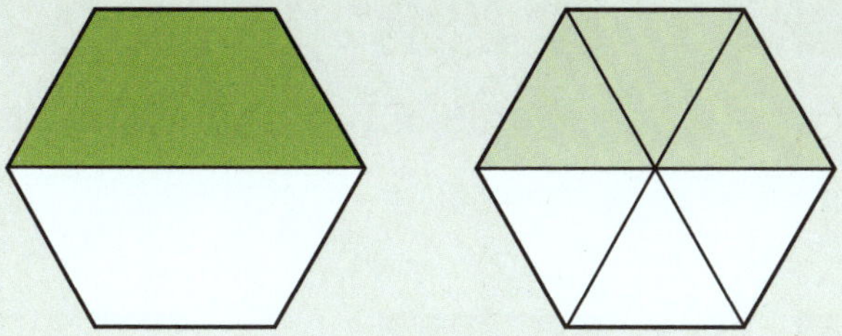

$\frac{1}{2} = \frac{3}{6}$

$\frac{2}{3} = \frac{\phantom{0}}{\phantom{0}}$

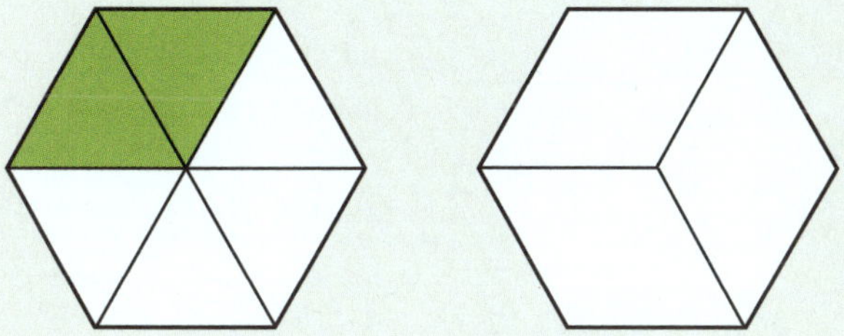

$\frac{2}{6} = \frac{\phantom{0}}{\phantom{0}}$

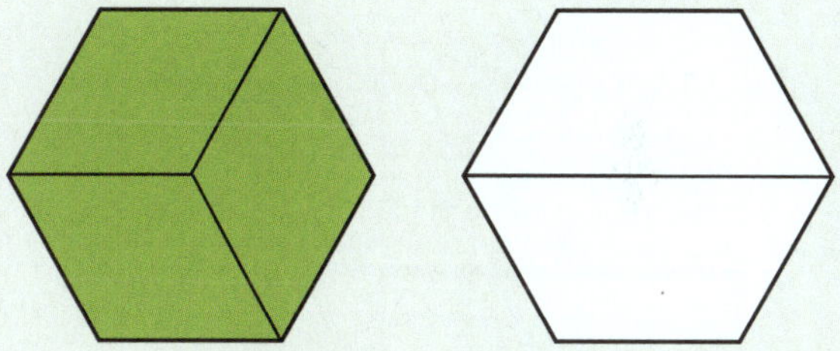

$\frac{3}{3} = \frac{\phantom{0}}{\phantom{0}}$

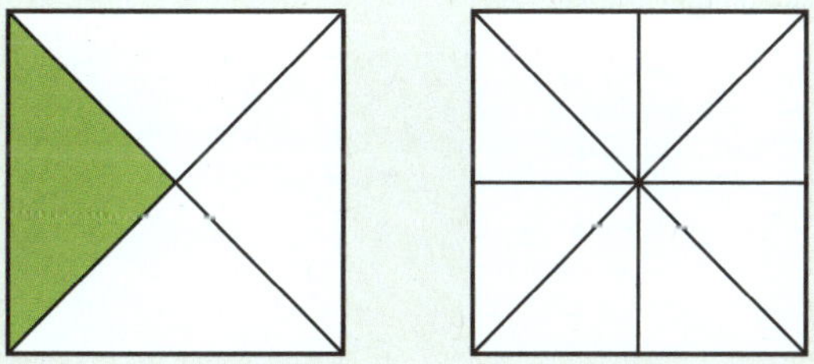

$\frac{1}{4} = \frac{\phantom{0}}{\phantom{0}}$

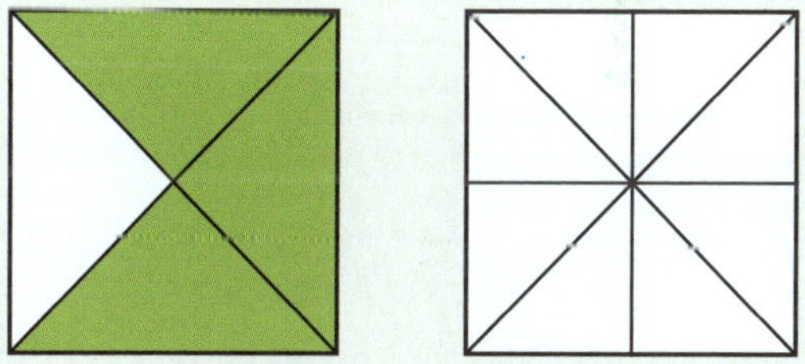

$\frac{3}{4} = \frac{\phantom{0}}{\phantom{0}}$

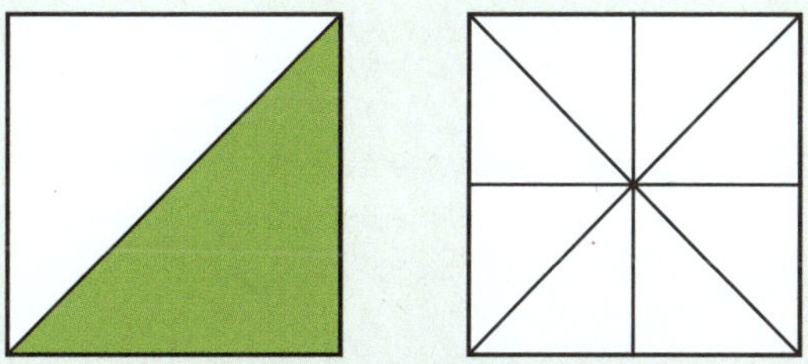

$\frac{1}{2} = \frac{\phantom{0}}{\phantom{0}}$

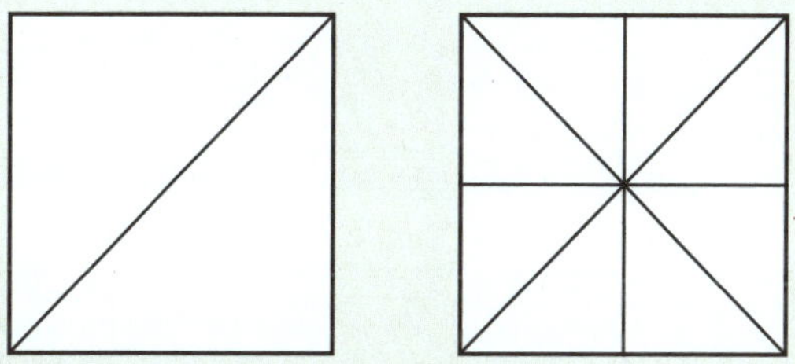

★ $\frac{0}{2} = \frac{\phantom{0}}{\phantom{0}}$

## 6.7

### Review

**Match pairs that equal 1,000.**

| 860 | 560 | 760 | 460 | 660 |
|---|---|---|---|---|
| 240 | 140 | 440 | 340 | 540 |

**Complete.**

| | 4 | 3 | 8 |
|---|---|---|---|
| + | 3 | 7 | 9 |
| | | | |

| | 4 | 3 | 8 |
|---|---|---|---|
| - | 3 | 7 | 9 |
| | | | |

**Complete.**

300 + ☐ = 330

600 - ☐ = 400

☐ + 75 = 575

☐ - 200 = 500

☐ - 1 = 399

**Solve. Write the equations you use.**

Makayla had $32. She earned $18.
Then, she spent $9.
How much money did she have left?

Makayla jumped rope for 16 minutes on Friday, 27 minutes on Saturday, and 8 minutes on Sunday. How many minutes did she jump rope in all?

## Lesson Activities

**A**

$\frac{1}{3} \bigcirc \frac{2}{3}$

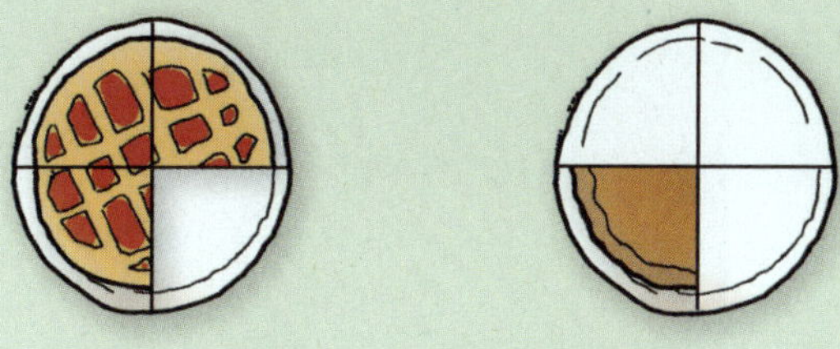

$\frac{3}{4} \bigcirc \frac{1}{4}$

$\frac{1}{8} \bigcirc \frac{5}{8}$ $\frac{3}{6} \bigcirc \frac{2}{6}$ $\frac{3}{6} \bigcirc \frac{1}{6}$

**B**

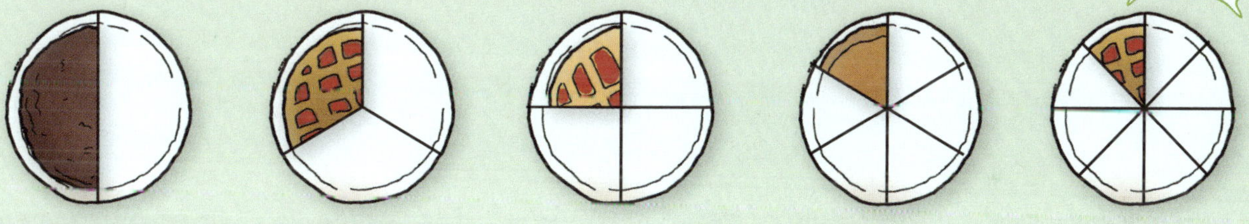

$\frac{\square}{\square}$ $\frac{\square}{\square}$ $\frac{\square}{\square}$ $\frac{\square}{\square}$ $\frac{\square}{\square}$

$\frac{1}{2} \bigcirc \frac{1}{8}$ $\frac{1}{4} \bigcirc \frac{1}{3}$ $\frac{1}{6} \bigcirc \frac{1}{8}$

**C**

$\frac{1}{8} \bigcirc \frac{1}{3}$ $\frac{1}{4} \bigcirc \frac{1}{6}$ $\frac{1}{6} \bigcirc \frac{1}{8}$

$\frac{2}{8} \bigcirc \frac{2}{3}$ $\frac{2}{4} \bigcirc \frac{2}{6}$ $\frac{3}{6} \bigcirc \frac{3}{8}$

$\frac{3}{8} \bigcirc \frac{3}{3}$ $\frac{3}{4} \bigcirc \frac{3}{6}$ $\frac{5}{6} \bigcirc \frac{5}{8}$

## Practice

Write <, >, or =. Use the pictures to help.

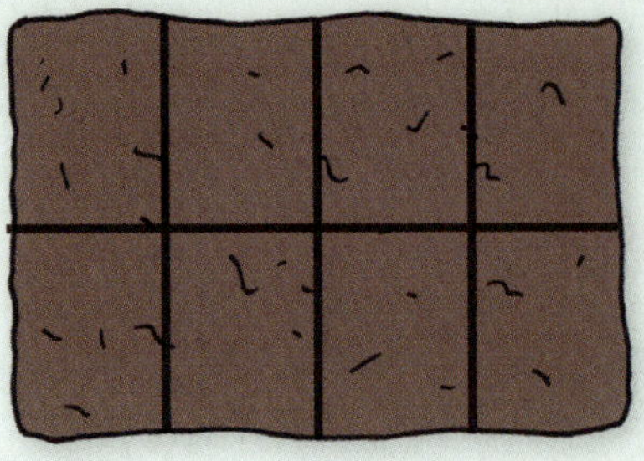

$\frac{2}{8} \bigcirc \frac{5}{8}$

$\frac{3}{8} \bigcirc \frac{7}{8}$

$\frac{8}{8} \bigcirc \frac{4}{8}$

$\frac{1}{8} \bigcirc \frac{6}{8}$

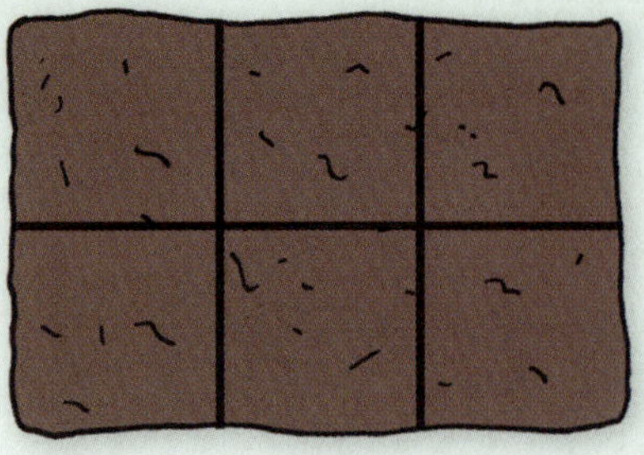

$\frac{3}{6} \bigcirc \frac{1}{6}$

$\frac{4}{6} \bigcirc \frac{5}{6}$

$\frac{2}{6} \bigcirc \frac{2}{6}$

$\frac{6}{6} \bigcirc \frac{5}{6}$

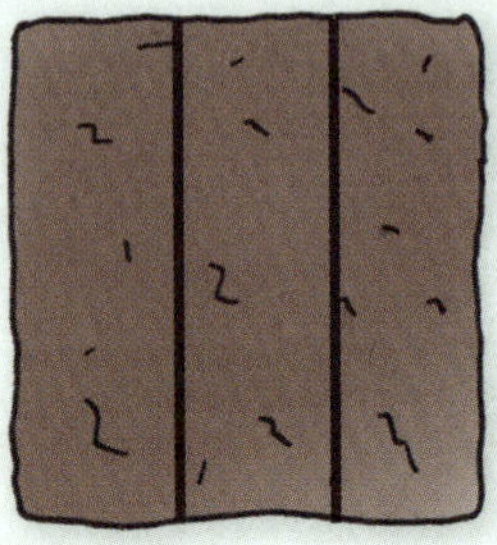

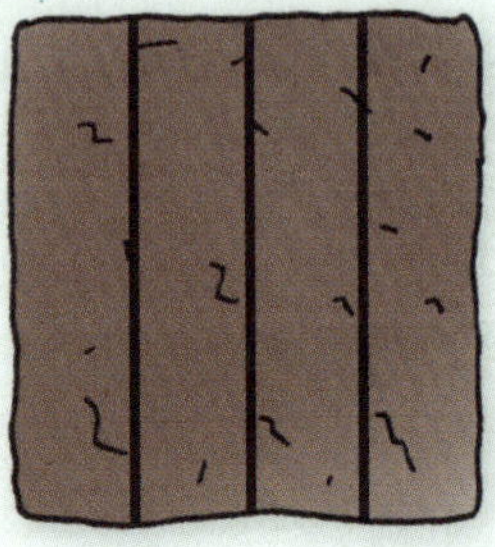

$\frac{1}{3} \bigcirc \frac{1}{4}$

$\frac{2}{3} \bigcirc \frac{2}{4}$

$\frac{3}{3} \bigcirc \frac{3}{4}$

$\frac{3}{3} \bigcirc \frac{4}{4}$

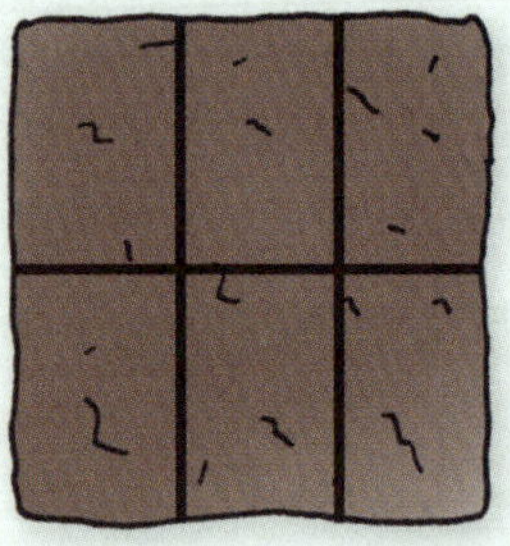

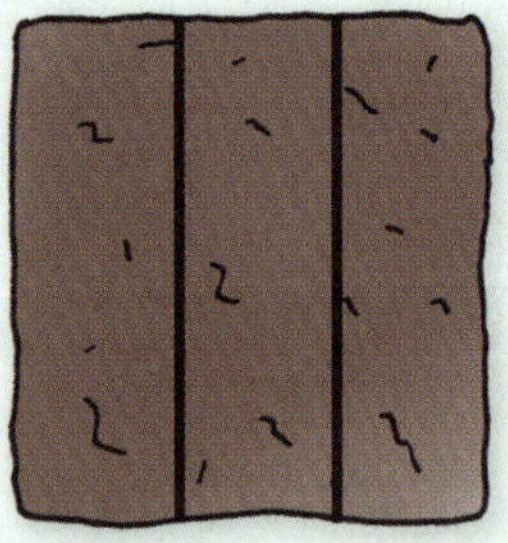

$\frac{1}{6} \bigcirc \frac{1}{3}$

$\frac{2}{6} \bigcirc \frac{2}{3}$

$\frac{3}{6} \bigcirc \frac{3}{3}$

$\frac{6}{6} \bigcirc \frac{3}{3}$

## Review

**Complete.**

$\begin{array}{r} 3 \\ \times\ 6 \\ \hline \end{array}$ $\begin{array}{r} 4 \\ \times\ 9 \\ \hline \end{array}$ $\begin{array}{r} 5 \\ \times\ 5 \\ \hline \end{array}$ $\begin{array}{r} 4 \\ \times\ 8 \\ \hline \end{array}$ $\begin{array}{r} 7 \\ \times\ 1 \\ \hline \end{array}$

$\begin{array}{r} 4 \\ \times\ 7 \\ \hline \end{array}$ $\begin{array}{r} 3 \\ \times\ 8 \\ \hline \end{array}$ $\begin{array}{r} 6 \\ \times\ 2 \\ \hline \end{array}$ $\begin{array}{r} 9 \\ \times\ 5 \\ \hline \end{array}$ $\begin{array}{r} 10 \\ \times\ 9 \\ \hline \end{array}$

**Complete.**

$\frac{3}{8} + \frac{3}{8} = \frac{\square}{\square}$

$\frac{7}{8} - \frac{1}{8} = \frac{\square}{\square}$

$\frac{3}{6} + \frac{1}{6} = \frac{\square}{\square}$

$\frac{3}{4} - \frac{1}{4} = \frac{\square}{\square}$

**Complete.**

$\begin{array}{r} 459 \\ +\ 186 \\ \hline \end{array}$

$\begin{array}{r} 307 \\ -\ 174 \\ \hline \end{array}$

**Complete.**

$ ____

$ ____

## Lesson Activities

A

| Less than $\frac{1}{2}$ | Equal to $\frac{1}{2}$ | Greater than $\frac{1}{2}$ |
|---|---|---|
| | | |

$\frac{2}{6}$ $\frac{3}{6}$ $\frac{7}{8}$ $\frac{2}{3}$ $\frac{1}{4}$ $\frac{1}{8}$ $\frac{3}{4}$ $\frac{5}{6}$

$\frac{4}{6}$ $\frac{4}{8}$ $\frac{1}{3}$ $\frac{6}{8}$ $\frac{2}{4}$ $\frac{3}{8}$ $\frac{1}{6}$ $\frac{5}{8}$

B

$\frac{5}{8}$ ◯ $\frac{1}{3}$

$\frac{3}{6}$ ◯ $\frac{4}{8}$

$\frac{1}{3}$ ◯ $\frac{3}{4}$

$\frac{1}{8}$ ◯ $\frac{3}{6}$

$\frac{2}{4}$ ◯ $\frac{5}{8}$

$\frac{5}{6}$ ◯ $\frac{3}{8}$

## Practice

**Write fractions to match each shape.**
**Then, write the fractions in order from least to greatest.**

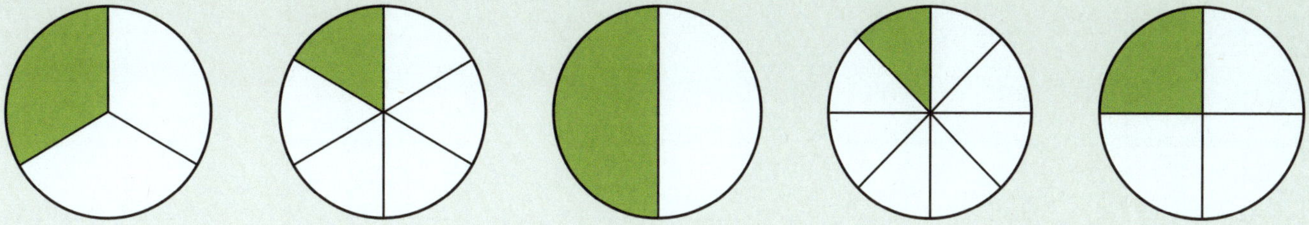

LEAST → ☐ ☐ ☐ ☐ ☐ ← GREATEST

LEAST → ☐ ☐ ☐ ☐ ☐ ← GREATEST

## Review

**Complete.**

$$\begin{array}{r} 7 \\ \times\ 4 \\ \hline \end{array} \quad \begin{array}{r} 9 \\ \times\ 3 \\ \hline \end{array} \quad \begin{array}{r} 3 \\ \times\ 4 \\ \hline \end{array} \quad \begin{array}{r} 5 \\ \times\ 6 \\ \hline \end{array} \quad \begin{array}{r} 10 \\ \times\ 4 \\ \hline \end{array}$$

$$\begin{array}{r} 4 \\ \times\ 4 \\ \hline \end{array} \quad \begin{array}{r} 2 \\ \times\ 7 \\ \hline \end{array} \quad \begin{array}{r} 9 \\ \times\ 4 \\ \hline \end{array} \quad \begin{array}{r} 8 \\ \times\ 3 \\ \hline \end{array} \quad \begin{array}{r} 3 \\ \times\ 7 \\ \hline \end{array}$$

**Write each money amount two ways.**

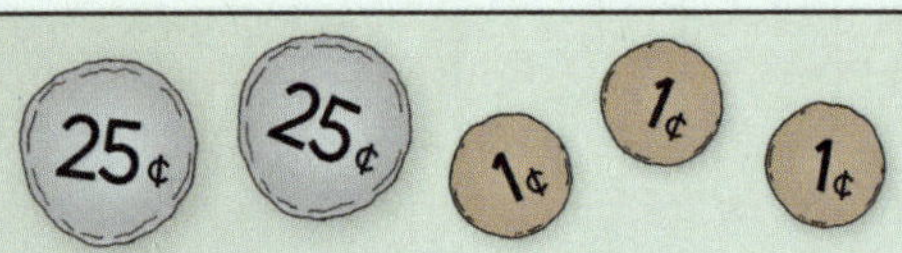


$ ______ ______ ¢

$ ______ ______ ¢

**Complete.**

$10 \times 10 =$ ______

$16 \times 10 =$ ______

$18 \times 10 =$ ______

$3 \times 50 =$ ______

$4 \times 30 =$ ______

$6 \times 20 =$ ______

**Solve. Write the equations you use.**

Isaac's mom is 35. His dad is 3 years older than his mom. What is the sum of his mom's age and his dad's age?

Isaac is 8. His sister is 2 years younger than him. His brother is 3 years older than him. What is the sum of all 3 children's ages?

## Lesson Activities

**A**

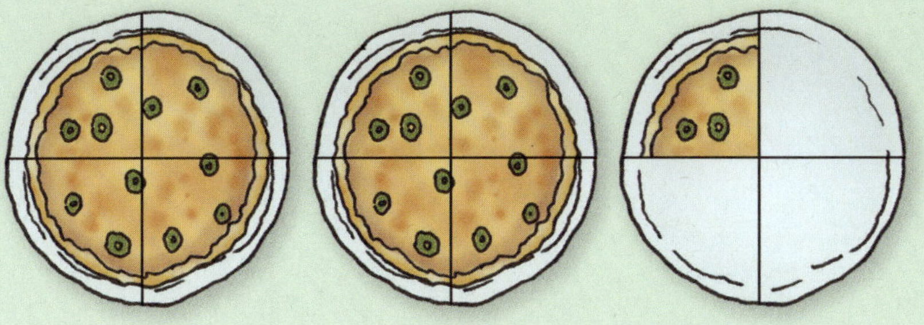

Mixed Number

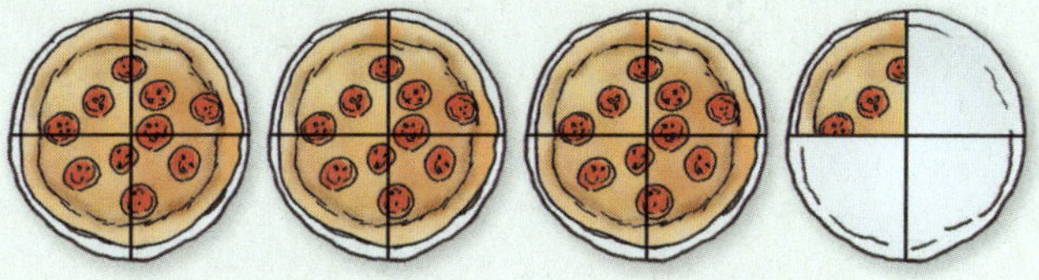

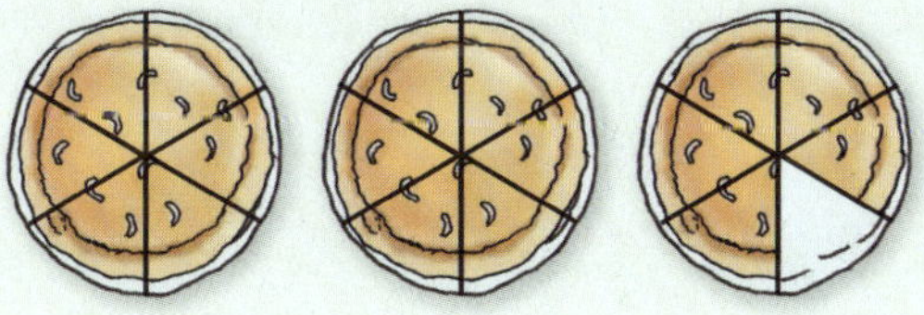

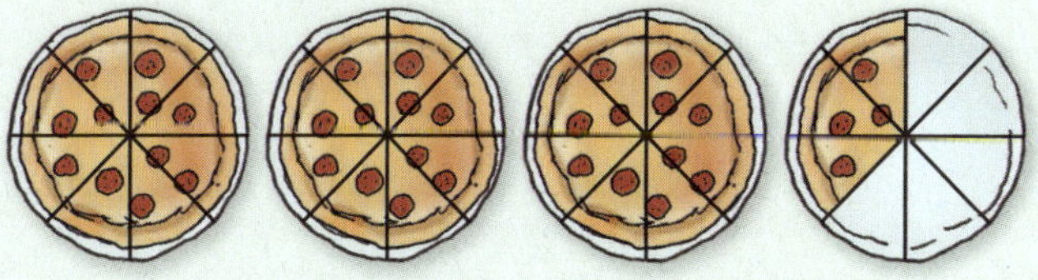

**B**

### PUMPKIN BREAD INGREDIENTS

$1\frac{1}{3}$ cups sugar
$1\frac{1}{4}$ cups canned pumpkin puree
$\frac{3}{4}$ cup vegetable oil
$1\frac{1}{2}$ cups flour
$\frac{1}{2}$ cup chocolate chips
$\frac{2}{3}$ cup chopped walnuts

## Practice

**Write a mixed number to match each picture.**

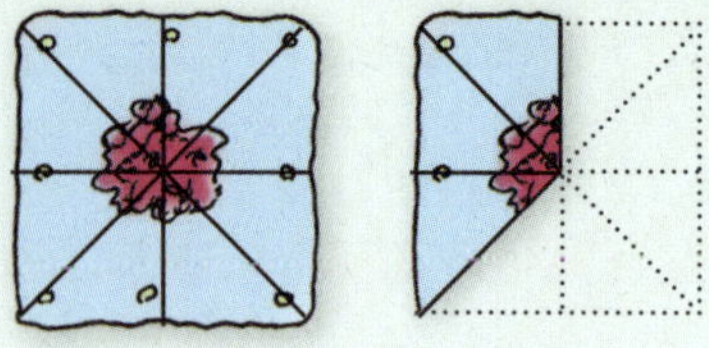

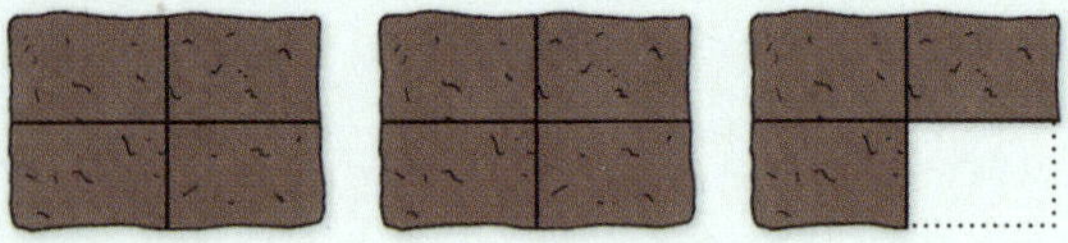

**Solve.**

Oliver's dad has 3 pizzas.
He cuts each pizza into eighths.
How many slices does he get?

☐ slices

★ Jenna's mom has 2 cakes. She wants to serve the cakes to 12 people.
What fractional part should she cut each cake into?

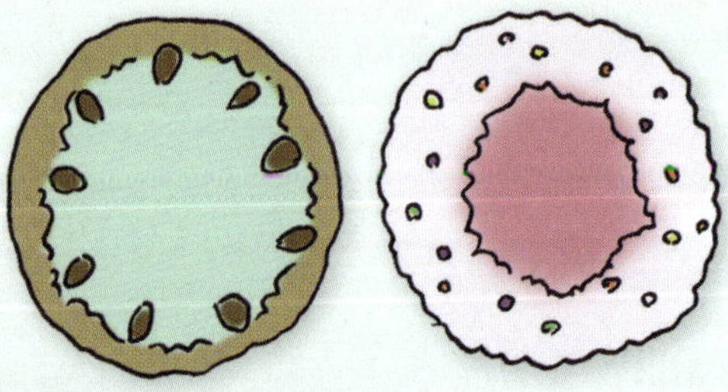

She should cut each cake into ☐ .

## Review

**Complete the equivalent fractions.**

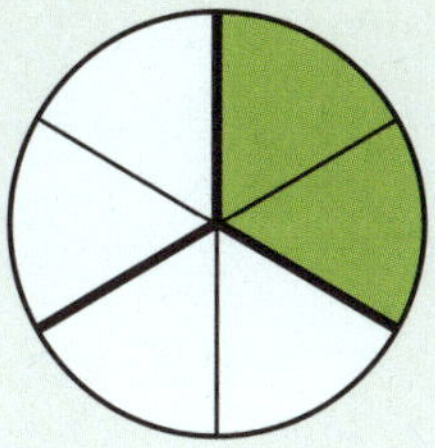

$\frac{1}{3} = \frac{\square}{6}$

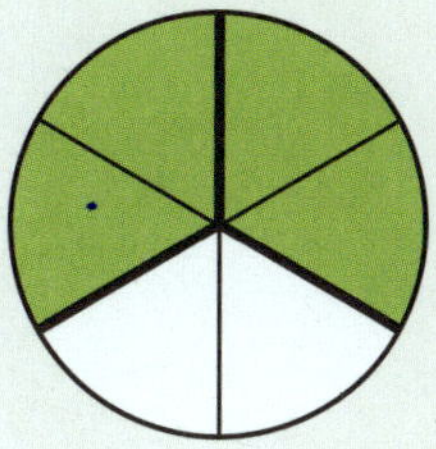

$\frac{2}{3} = \frac{\square}{6}$

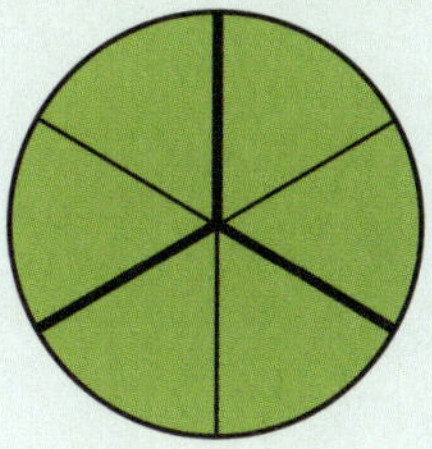

$\frac{3}{3} = \frac{\square}{6}$

**Complete.**

| | | |
|---|---|---|
| $10 \times 4 = \square$ | $7 \times 3 = \square$ | $5 \times 4 = \square$ |
| $2 \times 3 = \square$ | $4 \times 6 = \square$ | $3 \times 6 = \square$ |
| $8 \times 4 = \square$ | $1 \times 3 = \square$ | $4 \times 4 = \square$ |
| $4 \times 3 = \square$ | $3 \times 5 = \square$ | $3 \times 10 = \square$ |

**Solve. Write the equations you use.**

The game costs $27.
Hazel gives the clerk $40.
How much change does she get?

Hazel scored 285 points in the game.
Lauren scored 315 points.
How many more points did Lauren score than Hazel?

6.11

## Unit Wrap-Up

Use the words in the word bank to complete the blanks.

| equivalent fractions | denominator | mixed numbers | numerator |
|---|---|---|---|

$\frac{1}{3}$

The top number is the ______________________.

It tells how many parts.

The bottom number is the ______________________.

It tells how many equal parts the whole was split into.

$\frac{1}{3} = \frac{2}{6}$

Fractions that look different but have the same value are called ______________________.

$2\frac{1}{2}$

Numbers with a whole number and a fraction are called ______________________.

### Use the key to color the fractions.

$\frac{5}{6}$ $\frac{1}{3}$ $\frac{1}{6}$ $\frac{1}{4}$ $\frac{6}{6}$ $\frac{2}{4}$ $\frac{2}{6}$ $\frac{4}{6}$ $\frac{3}{4}$

**Key**

Less than $\frac{1}{2}$ - Green

Equal to $\frac{1}{2}$ - Blue

Greater than $\frac{1}{2}$ - Purple

## Unit Wrap-Up

**Write <, >, or =.**

$\frac{1}{6} \bigcirc \frac{4}{6}$

$\frac{1}{4} \bigcirc \frac{1}{8}$

$\frac{3}{8} \bigcirc \frac{3}{4}$

$\frac{7}{8} \bigcirc \frac{1}{6}$

**Complete.**

$\frac{5}{6} - \frac{2}{6} = \frac{\square}{\square}$

$\frac{3}{8} + \frac{4}{8} = \frac{\square}{\square}$

$\frac{8}{8} - \frac{1}{8} = \frac{\square}{\square}$

$\frac{7}{8} + \frac{1}{8} = \frac{\square}{\square}$

**Complete the equivalent fractions.**

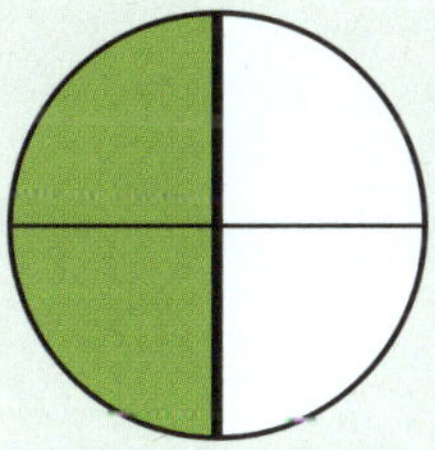

$\frac{1}{2} = \frac{\square}{4}$

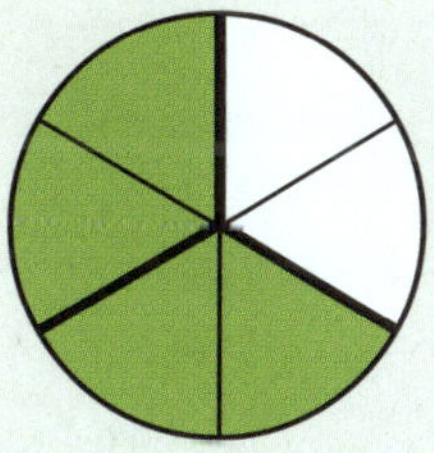

$\frac{2}{3} = \frac{\square}{6}$

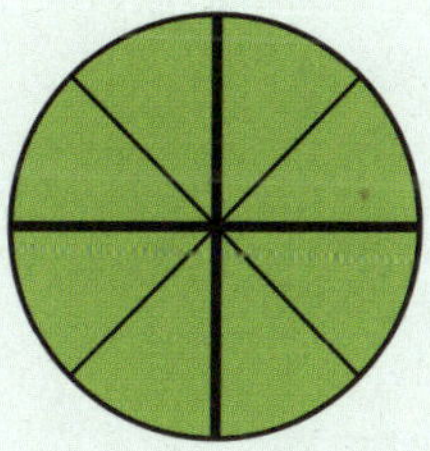

$\frac{4}{4} = \frac{\square}{8}$

**Write a mixed number to match each picture.**

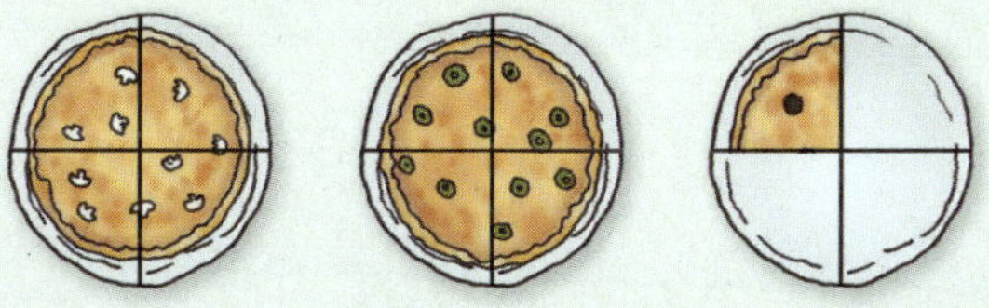

$\square \frac{\square}{\square}$

$\square \frac{\square}{\square}$

7.1

## Lesson Activities

A

B

| Cereal | Almonds | Broccoli | Grapes | Cucumber | Apple |
|---|---|---|---|---|---|
| | | | | | |

C

## Practice

**Round each price to the nearest dollar.**

| \$2.09 | \$2.19 | \$2.49 | \$2.59 | \$2.79 | \$2.89 |
|---|---|---|---|---|---|
| \$2 | | | | | |

| \$3.17 | \$6.94 | \$8.50 | \$12.64 | \$38.07 | \$46.39 |
|---|---|---|---|---|---|
| | | | | | |

**Complete with <, >, or =.**

\$2.47 ◯ \$2.74

\$2.40 ◯ \$2.04

\$2.00 ◯ \$2

\$0.02 ◯ \$0.20

\$2.02 ◯ \$2.00

**Complete. Use a dollar sign and decimal point for each amount.**

| Coins | Value |
|---|---|
| 4 pennies | \$ |
| 4 nickels | |
| 4 dimes | |
| 4 quarters | |

**Solve.**

Gabe has 4 dimes and 6 pennies.
Sarah has 3 dimes and 3 nickels.
Who has more money? How much more?

Gisele has 3 quarters.
Eli has 5 dimes, 4 nickels, and 2 pennies.
Who has more money? How much more?

## Review

**Write mixed numbers to match the shapes.**

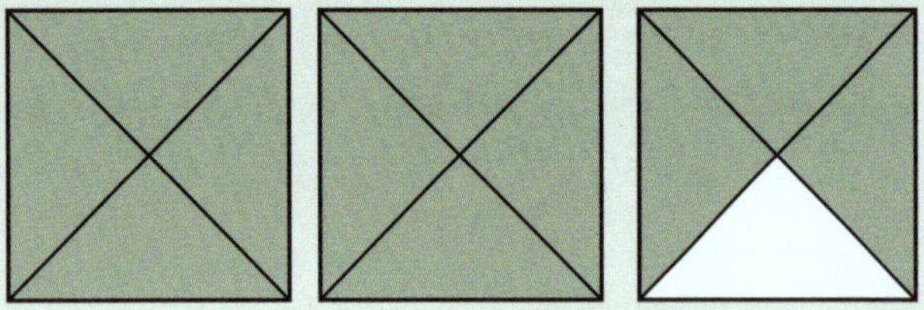

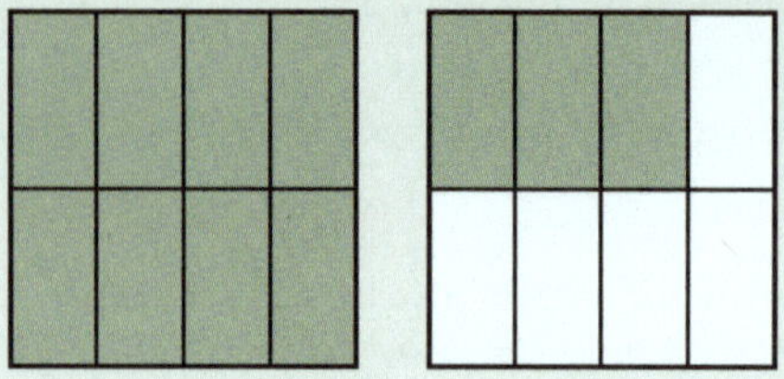

**Complete.**

36 → +6 → ☐ → +6 → ☐ → +6 → ☐ → +6 → 60

42 → +7 → ☐ → +7 → ☐ → +7 → ☐ → +7 → 70

48 → +8 → ☐ → +8 → ☐ → +8 → ☐ → +8 → 80

**Complete.**

25 + 50 = ☐

75 + 25 = ☐

150 + 25 = ☐

50 + 150 = ☐

200 + 250 = ☐

**Match pairs that equal 100.**

| | |
|---|---|
| 38 | 72 |
| 48 | 82 |
| 28 | 52 |
| 18 | 62 |

## Lesson Activities

### A

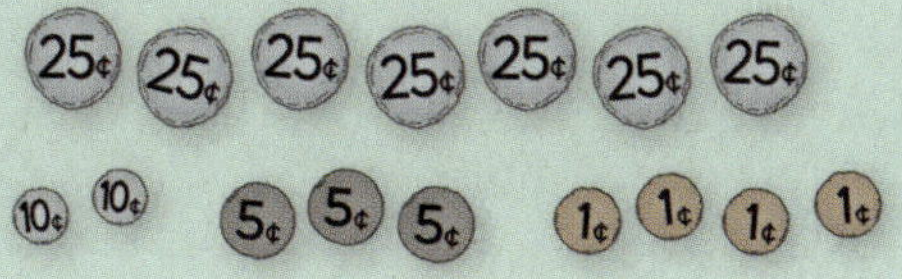

214 ¢ = $ ____

139 ¢ = $ ____

201 ¢ = $ ____

400 ¢ = $ ____

445 ¢ = $ ____

### B

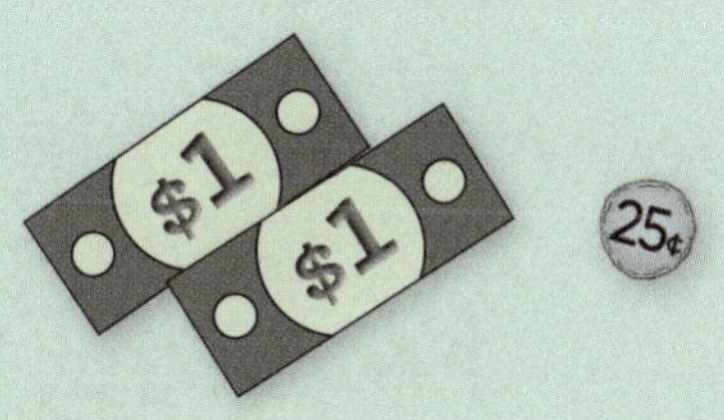

$2.25 = ____ ¢

$3.50 = ____ ¢

$3.79 = ____ ¢

$5.00 = ____ ¢

$5.07 = ____ ¢

### C

$0.80 + $0.40 = $ ____

80 ¢ + 40 ¢ = ____ ¢

$1.30 − $0.60 = $ ____

130 ¢ − 60 ¢ = ____ ¢

### D

## Roll and Add

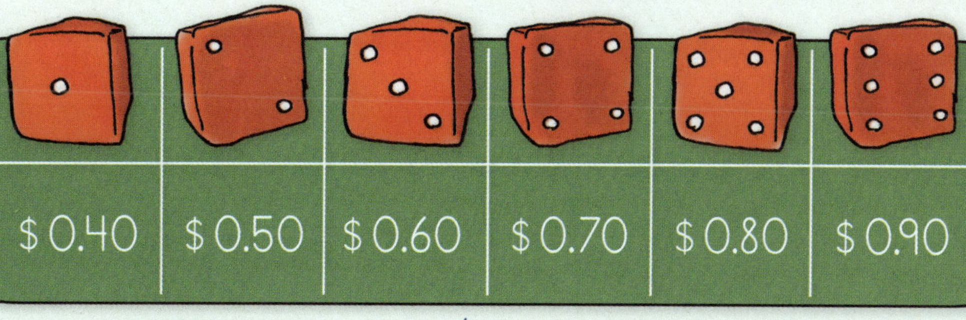

| | | | | | |
|---|---|---|---|---|---|
| $0.40 | $0.50 | $0.60 | $0.70 | $0.80 | $0.90 |

# 7.2

## Practice

**Complete.**

| $ | ¢ |
|---|---|
| $2.00 | 200 ¢ |
| $2.09 | |
| $2.45 | |
| $2.50 | |
| $2.99 | |

| $ | ¢ |
|---|---|
| | 400 ¢ |
| | 406 ¢ |
| | 410 ¢ |
| | 432 ¢ |
| | 457 ¢ |

| $ | ¢ |
|---|---|
| $9.25 | |
| $5.07 | |
| | 615 ¢ |
| | 891 ¢ |
| $3.79 | |

**Use the chart to solve.**

Snack Bar Menu

Chips ............................ $0.90
Pretzels ........................ $1.10
Crackers ........................ $1.00
Fruit Snacks .................. $0.70
Granola Bar ................... $0.80

How much does it cost to buy chips and a granola bar?

How much does it cost to buy fruit snacks and pretzels?

How much more do crackers cost than chips?

How much less does a granola bar cost than chips?

You buy fruit snacks. You give the clerk $1.00. How much change do you get?

★ You buy pretzels. You give the clerk $2.00. How much change do you get?

## Review

**Complete.**

| | | | | |
|---|---|---|---|---|
| $\begin{array}{r} 3 \\ \times\ 9 \\ \hline \end{array}$ | $\begin{array}{r} 10 \\ \times\ 10 \\ \hline \end{array}$ | $\begin{array}{r} 9 \\ \times\ 5 \\ \hline \end{array}$ | $\begin{array}{r} 4 \\ \times\ 3 \\ \hline \end{array}$ | $\begin{array}{r} 2 \\ \times\ 9 \\ \hline \end{array}$ |
| $\begin{array}{r} 5 \\ \times\ 8 \\ \hline \end{array}$ | $\begin{array}{r} 7 \\ \times\ 4 \\ \hline \end{array}$ | $\begin{array}{r} 10 \\ \times\ 7 \\ \hline \end{array}$ | $\begin{array}{r} 4 \\ \times\ 9 \\ \hline \end{array}$ | $\begin{array}{r} 1 \\ \times\ 8 \\ \hline \end{array}$ |

**Complete.**

52 - 47 = ☐

51 - 46 = ☐

50 - 45 = ☐

94 - 88 = ☐

84 - 78 = ☐

74 - 68 = ☐

**Solve.**

You give the clerk $30.
How much change do you get?

$16

Change
$ ____

You give the clerk $50.
How much change do you get?

$39

Change
$ ____

## Lesson Activities

### A

You pay the clerk $9.
How much change do you get?

$8.90

Change
$ ____

$8.90 + ____ → $9.00

You pay the clerk $5.
How much change do you get?

$3.50

Change
$ ____

$3.50 + ____ → $4.00 + ____ → $5.00

### B

## Pretend Store

$7.80

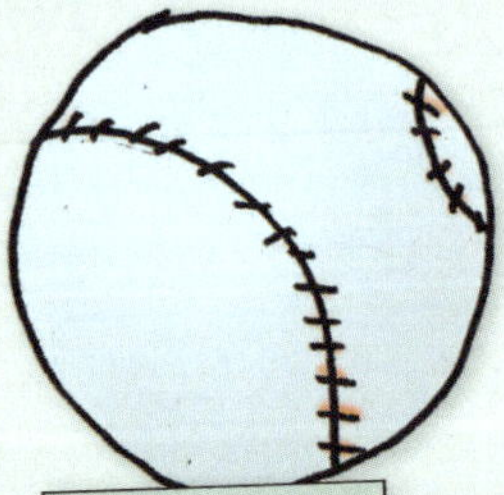

$6.50

$8.30

$8.95

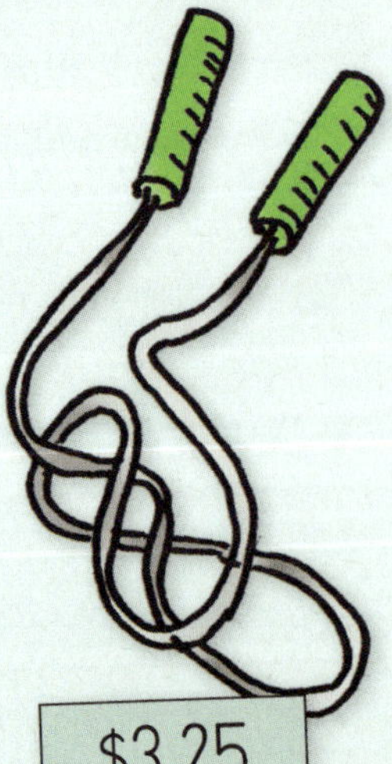

$3.25

$7.59

## Practice

**Complete.**

$2.80 + [$ 0.20] = $3.00

$4.75 + [$ ] = $6.00

$3.40 + [$ ] = $4.00

$6.95 + [$ ] = $8.00

$5.75 + [$ ] = $10.00

$7.50 + [$ ] = $10.00

$6.70 + [$ ] = $10.00

★ $3.79 + [$ ] = $10.00

**Solve.**

You pay the clerk $3.00.
How much change do you get?

Change
$

You pay the clerk $5.00.
How much change do you get?

Change
$

You pay the clerk $10.00.
How much change do you get?

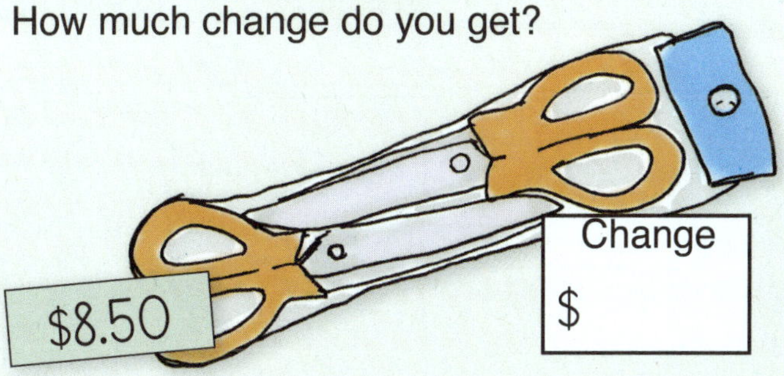


Change
$

★ You pay the clerk $20.00.
How much change do you get?

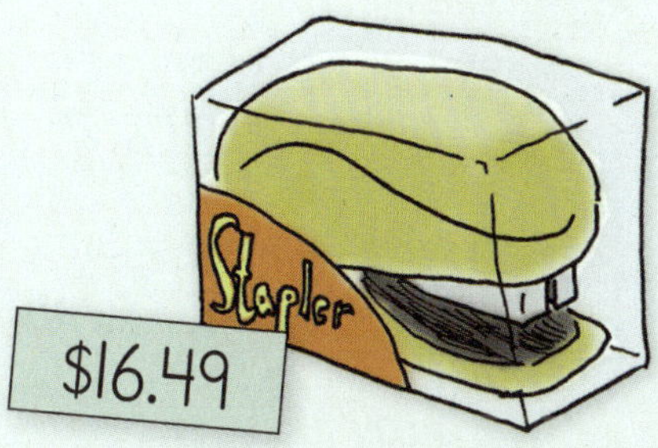


Change
$

# 7.3

## Review

Complete with <, >, or =.

| | | |
|---|---|---|
| $\frac{1}{8}$ ◯ $\frac{1}{4}$ | $\frac{2}{8}$ ◯ $\frac{2}{4}$ | $\frac{3}{8}$ ◯ $\frac{3}{4}$ |
| $\frac{8}{8}$ ◯ $\frac{2}{4}$ | $\frac{7}{8}$ ◯ $\frac{1}{4}$ | $\frac{4}{8}$ ◯ $\frac{2}{4}$ |

Match.

| | | | |
|---|---|---|---|
| 4 × 7 | 32 | 3 × 8 | 24 |
| 3 × 6 | 18 | 4 × 9 | 27 |
| 4 × 8 | 28 | 8 × 5 | 36 |
| 3 × 7 | 24 | 3 × 9 | 40 |
| 4 × 6 | 21 | 9 × 5 | 45 |

Complete.

| | | | |
|---|---|---|---|
| | 4 | 8 | 6 |
| + | 3 | 9 | 0 |
| | | | |

| | | | |
|---|---|---|---|
| | 6 | 4 | 0 |
| - | 1 | 7 | 3 |
| | | | |

Complete.

$1.50 = ☐ ¢

$2.96 = ☐ ¢

$5.74 = ☐ ¢

$ ☐ = 174 ¢

$ ☐ = 800 ¢

## Lesson Activities

A

$7.00 + $1.40 = ☐

$7.00 +$1.00 → ☐ +$0.40 → ☐

$3.90 + $4.30 = ☐

$3.90 +$4.00 → ☐ +$0.30 → ☐

## 7.4

## Practice

**Complete.**

Start

\$4.00 + \$2.00 = ____

\$4.00 + \$2.50 = ____

\$4.50 + \$2.50 = ____

\$2.80 + \$0.20 = ____

\$2.80 + \$0.30 = ____

\$2.80 + \$0.50 = ____

\$3.10 + \$2.00 = ____

\$3.10 + \$2.70 = ____

\$3.10 + \$2.90 = ____

\$5.60 + \$0.40 = ____

\$5.60 + \$0.60 = ____

\$5.60 + \$2.60 = ____

**Use the chart to solve.**

How much does it cost for a pony ride and a ferris wheel ride?

### Carnival Activities

| Activity | Price |
|---|---|
| Ferris Wheel Ride | \$3.50 |
| Ring Toss Game | \$2.80 |
| Carousel Ride | \$4.10 |
| Face Painting | \$6.50 |
| Pony Ride | \$5.00 |

How much does it cost to have your face painted and take a ferris wheel ride?

You go on the carousel ride and pay \$5.00. How much change do you get?

## Review

**Round to the nearest dollar.**

| $7.05 | $7.55 | $7.50 | $17.05 | $17.55 | $17.50 |
|---|---|---|---|---|---|
| | | | | | |

**Complete.**

$\frac{3}{8} + \frac{2}{8} = \frac{\square}{\square}$

$\frac{7}{8} - \frac{5}{8} = \frac{\square}{\square}$

$\frac{4}{6} + \frac{2}{6} = \frac{\square}{\square}$

$\frac{6}{6} - \frac{6}{6} = \frac{\square}{\square}$

**Connect each number to its place on the number line.**

898 | 901 | 903

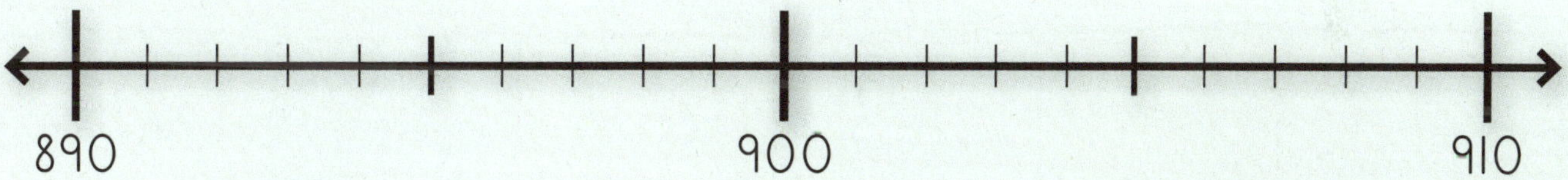


899 | 902 | 904

**Color the problems that match the number in the star.**

| 100 | 150 | 200 |
|---|---|---|
| 10 × 10 | 2 × 60 | 10 × 20 |
| 2 × 50 | 3 × 50 | 2 × 100 |
| 3 × 30 | 5 × 30 | 4 × 40 |

## Lesson Activities

A

$6.00 - $2.00 = ☐

$7.50 - $4.00 = ☐

$5.50 - $2.20 = ☐ — $5.50 -$2.00 → ☐ -$0.20 → ☐

$3.00 - $1.20 = ☐ — $3.00 -$1.00 → ☐ -$0.20 → ☐

★ $4.10 - $2.70 = ☐ — $4.10 -$2.00 → ☐ -$0.70 → ☐

B

## Practice

**Complete.**

Start

| | |
|---|---|
| $3.50 - $1.00 = ____ | $6.10 - $3.00 = ____ |
| $3.50 - $1.40 = ____ | $6.10 - $3.10 = ____ |
| $3.50 - $1.50 = ____ | ★ $6.10 - $3.20 = ____ |
| $7.00 - $2.00 = ____ | $8.00 - $3.50 = ____ |
| $7.00 - $2.50 = ____ | $9.00 - $3.50 = ____ |
| $7.00 - $2.90 = ____ | $10.00 - $3.50 = ____ |

**Use the chart to solve.**

**Winter Festival Menu**

| Item | Price |
|---|---|
| Pretzel | $4.50 |
| Hot Chocolate | $1.75 |
| Soup | $5.25 |
| Cookie | $2 |

How much less does a cookie cost than a pretzel?

You have $3. If you buy hot chocolate, how much money will you have left?

★ You have $10.
You buy soup and a cookie.
How much money will you have left?

## Review

**Write the time.**

:

:

:

:

**Complete.**

| | | |
|---|---|---|
| $5 \times 7 =$ ☐ | $8 \times 4 =$ ☐ | $5 \times 4 =$ ☐ |
| $3 \times 5 =$ ☐ | $0 \times 9 =$ ☐ | $7 \times 3 =$ ☐ |
| $4 \times 6 =$ ☐ | $5 \times 6 =$ ☐ | $2 \times 8 =$ ☐ |
| $2 \times 5 =$ ☐ | $8 \times 3 =$ ☐ | $3 \times 6 =$ ☐ |

**Solve. Write the equations you use.**

Alana read two books.
One book had 128 pages.
The other book had 306 pages.
How many pages did she read in all?

Alana read two books. One book had 128 pages. The other book had 306 pages. How many more pages did the longer book have than the shorter book?

## Lesson Activities

**A**

$1.89

$4.37

|   | 1. | 8 | 9 |
|---|---|---|---|
| + | 4. | 3 | 7 |
|   |   |   |   |

Estimate

+ ______

$2.64

$3.99

|   | 2. | 6 | 4 |
|---|---|---|---|
| + | 3. | 9 | 9 |
|   |   |   |   |

Estimate

+ ______

**B**

## SPIN TO WIN!

| + |   |   |   |
|---|---|---|---|

| + |   |   |   |
|---|---|---|---|

| + |   |   |   |
|---|---|---|---|

| + |   |   |   |
|---|---|---|---|

| + |   |   |   |
|---|---|---|---|

| + |   |   |   |
|---|---|---|---|

| + |   |   |   |
|---|---|---|---|

| + |   |   |   |
|---|---|---|---|

| + |   |   |   |
|---|---|---|---|

| + |   |   |   |
|---|---|---|---|

## Practice

Complete.

| | 3 | .5 | 6 |
|---|---|---|---|
| + | 2 | .2 | 6 |
| | | | |

| | 1 | .7 | 4 |
|---|---|---|---|
| + | 2 | .4 | 3 |
| | | | |

| | 4 | .3 | 8 |
|---|---|---|---|
| + | 0 | .6 | 2 |
| | | | |

★

| | 7 | .9 | 4 |
|---|---|---|---|
| + | 8 | .6 | 7 |
| | | | |

## Review

Complete the equivalent fractions.

$\frac{1}{4} = \frac{\square}{8}$

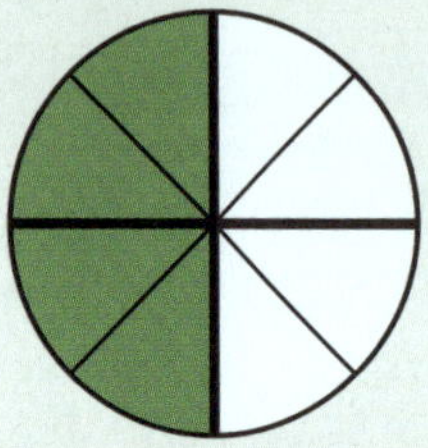

$\frac{2}{4} = \frac{\square}{8}$

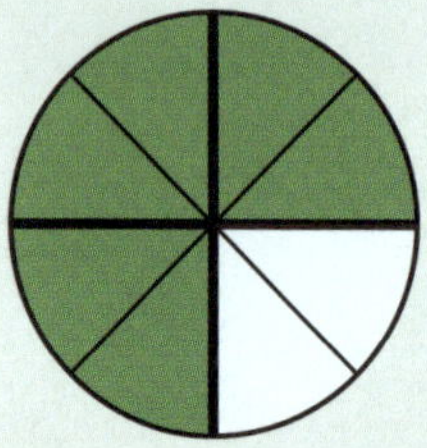

$\frac{3}{4} = \frac{\square}{8}$

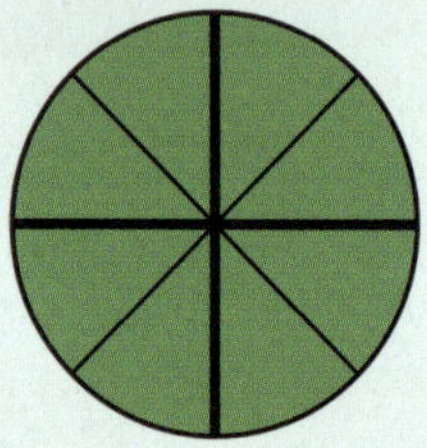

$\frac{4}{4} = \frac{\square}{8}$

Match.

| | | |
|---|---|---|
| 2 × 60 | 110 | 4 × 30 |
| 2 × 70 | 120 | 11 × 10 |
| 2 × 55 | 130 | 3 × 50 |
| 2 × 75 | 140 | 7 × 20 |
| 2 × 65 | 150 | 10 × 13 |

## Lesson Activities

**A**

$3.45

| | 7 | .1 | 9 |
|---|---|---|---|
| - | 3 | .4 | 5 |
| | | | |

Estimate

\-

$6.32

| | 9 | .0 | 0 |
|---|---|---|---|
| - | 6 | .3 | 2 |
| | | | |

Estimate

\-

**B**

$1.68

$1.59

$2.17

$2.09

$2.36

$1.95

| | 9 | .5 | 0 |
|---|---|---|---|
| - | | | |
| | | | |

# 7.7

## Practice — Complete.

$$7.77 - 3.33 = \square$$

$$8.90 - 3.68 = \square$$

$$4.38 - 2.98 = \square$$

$$6.00 - 2.37 = \square$$

## Review — Complete.

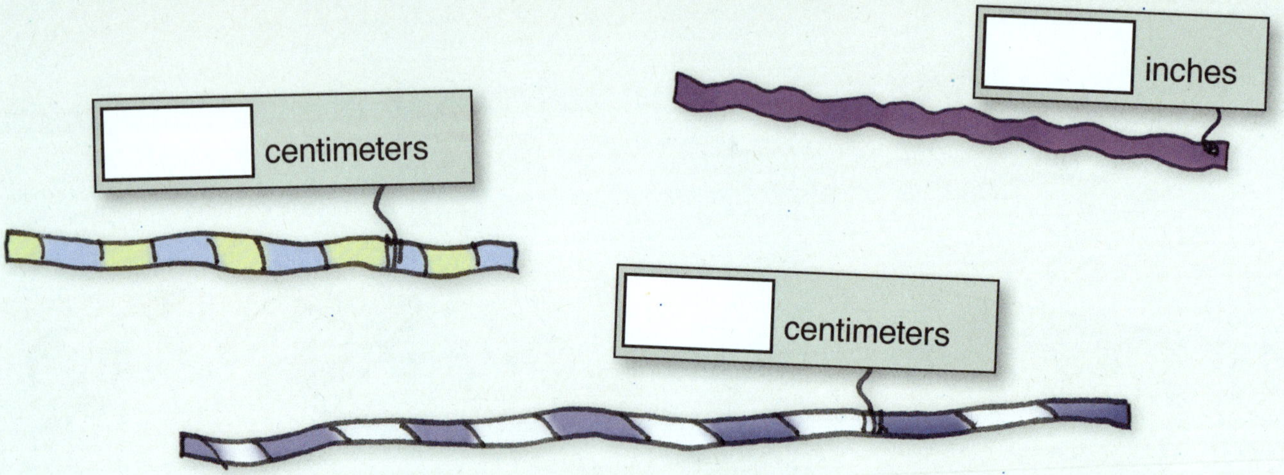


**Jacob made a graph to show how much it snowed each month.**
**Use the graph to complete the chart.**

| Month | Inches of Snow |
|---|---|
| December | |
| January | |
| February | |

## Unit Wrap-Up

**Round to the nearest dollar.**

| | |
|---|---|
| $2.98 | |
| $0.74 | |
| $7.07 | |
| $9.49 | |
| $9.50 | |

**Complete.**

| $ | ¢ |
|---|---|
| $3.50 | |
| | 175 ¢ |
| $4.07 | |
| | 316 ¢ |

**Complete with <, >, or =.**

56 pennies ◯ $0.50

5 dimes ◯ $0.49

7 nickels ◯ $0.40

4 quarters ◯ $1.00

**Match.**

| | | |
|---|---|---|
| $3.00 + $1.80 | $5.70 | $6.90 - $1.40 |
| $2.20 + $3.50 | $4.50 | $5.70 - $1.70 |
| $2.40 + $1.60 | $4.80 | $7.00 - $2.20 |
| $3.90+ $0.60 | $5.50 | $6.50 - $0.80 |
| $3.90 + $1.60 | $4.00 | $8.00 - $3.50 |

## Unit Wrap-Up

Use the chart to answer the questions.
Write the equations you use.

# Thelma's Bakery

| Item | Price |
|---|---|
| Pie | $9.49 |
| Large cake | $8.57 |
| Small cake | $4.99 |
| Cookie | $1.25 |
| Cupcake | $2.86 |

How much does it cost to buy a cookie and a cupcake?

How much less does a small cake cost than a large cake?

You have $9.00. You buy a large cake. How much money do you have left?

A loaf of bread costs $1.43 more than a cupcake. How much does a loaf of bread cost?

You buy a pie. You give the clerk $10. How much change do you get?

★ You have $25. Do you have enough to buy a pie, large cake, and small cake?

## Lesson Activities

### A

$6 \times 1 = \square$

$6 \times 2 = \square$

$6 \times 3 = \square$

$6 \times 4 = \square$

$6 \times 5 = \square$

$6 \times 6 = \square$

$6 \times 7 = \square$

$6 \times 8 = \square$

$6 \times 9 = \square$

$6 \times 10 = \square$

### B

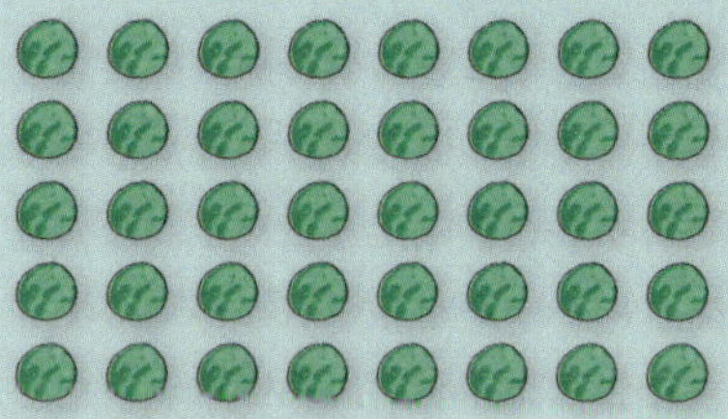

$5 \times 8 = \square$

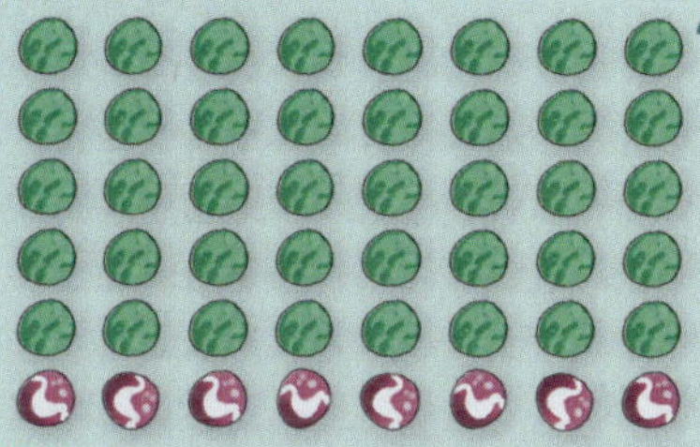

$6 \times 8 = \square$

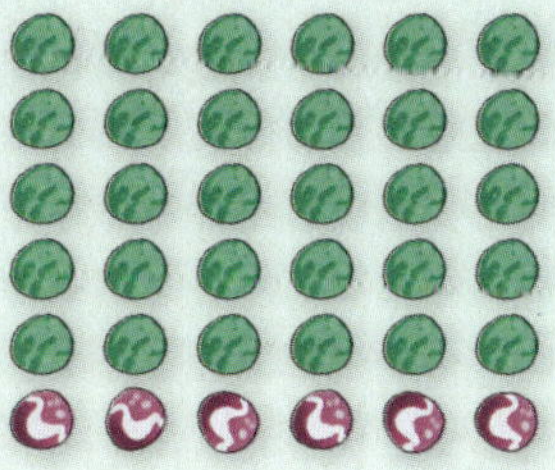

$5 \times 6 = \square$ $6 \times 6 = \square$

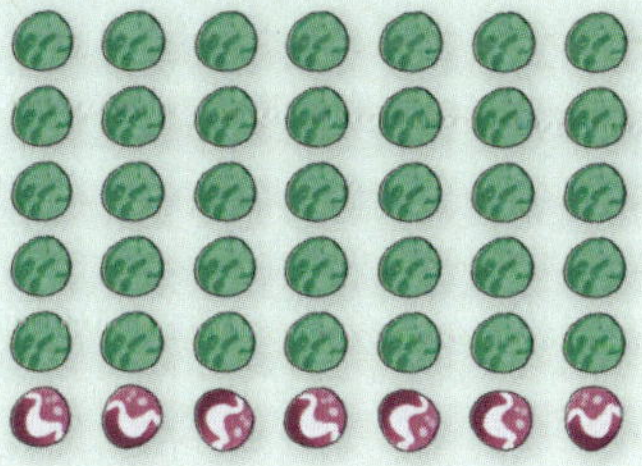

$5 \times 7 = \square$ $6 \times 7 = \square$

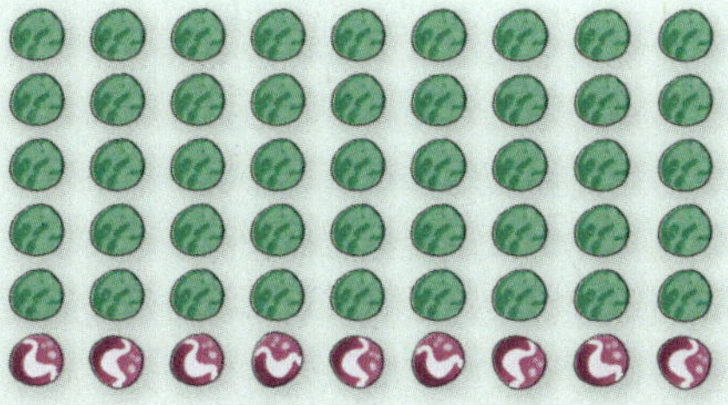

$5 \times 9 = \square$

$6 \times 9 = \square$

C

# Tic-Tac-Toe Crash (×6)

| | | |
|---|---|---|
| 6 | 12 | 18 |
| 24 | 30 | 36 |
| 42 | 48 | 54 |

## Practice

**Complete.**

$6 \times 8 =$ ☐

Start $5 \times 8 =$ ☐

$6 \times 6 =$ ☐

$5 \times 6 =$ ☐

$6 \times 9 =$ ☐

$5 \times 9 =$ ☐

$6 \times 7 =$ ☐

$5 \times 7 =$ ☐

## Review

**Complete.**

35 + 7 = ☐

28 + 42 = ☐

36 + 36 = ☐

72 - 8 = ☐

81 - 45 = ☐

56 - 49 = ☐

**Match.**

$\frac{2}{2}$

$\frac{3}{3}$

$\frac{4}{4}$

$\frac{6}{6}$

$\frac{8}{8}$

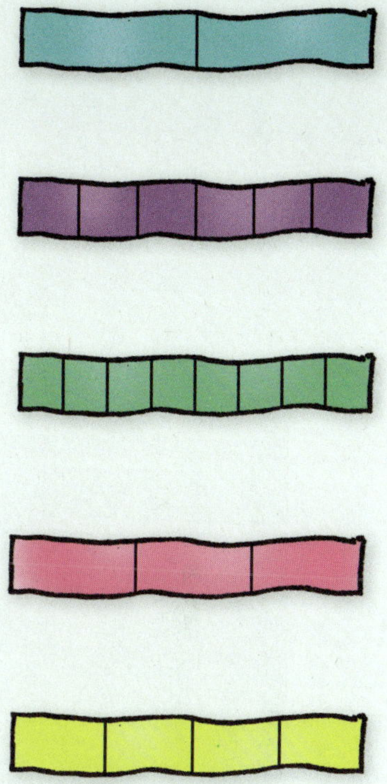

**Complete.**

| | 4 | .9 | 0 |
|---|---|---|---|
| - | 2 | .4 | 8 |
| $ | | | |

| | 6 | .7 | 5 |
|---|---|---|---|
| - | 3 | .4 | 0 |
| $ | | | |

| | 8 | .1 | 0 |
|---|---|---|---|
| - | 3 | .1 | 2 |
| $ | | | |

**Solve. Write the equations you use to solve the problems.**

Jerome has $7.50.
He spends $2.00 on a toy car.
Then, he spends $3.50 on a deck of cards.
How much money does he have left?

One day, Anna does 50 exercises.
She does 23 jumping jacks and 8 push-ups.
The rest of the exercises are sit-ups.
How many sit-ups does she do?

## Lesson Activities

### A

5 × 7 = ☐

6 × 7 = ☐

5 × 8 = ☐

6 × 8 = ☐

5 × 9 = ☐

6 × 9 = ☐

### B

## Multiplication Bingo (×6)

| B | I | N | G | O |
|---|---|---|---|---|
| 42 | 36 | 60 | 6 | 24 |
| 36 | 18 | 12 | 48 | 30 |
| 6 | 60 | 42 | 54 | 48 |
| 48 | 54 | 30 | 60 | 42 |
| 24 | 36 | 54 | 18 | 12 |

| B | I | N | G | O |
|---|---|---|---|---|
| 36 | 24 | 6 | 18 | 30 |
| 6 | 48 | 12 | 60 | 42 |
| 12 | 24 | 36 | 54 | 18 |
| 54 | 30 | 18 | 48 | 60 |
| 6 | 42 | 30 | 12 | 24 |

### C

☐ × ☐ + ☐ = ☐

☐ × ☐ + ☐ = ☐

☐ × ☐ + ☐ = ☐

## Practice

**Complete.**

$$\begin{array}{r} 6 \\ \times\ 3 \\ \hline \square \end{array} \quad \begin{array}{r} 6 \\ \times\ 8 \\ \hline \square \end{array} \quad \begin{array}{r} 6 \\ \times\ 2 \\ \hline \square \end{array} \quad \begin{array}{r} 6 \\ \times\ 9 \\ \hline \square \end{array} \quad \begin{array}{r} 6 \\ \times\ 4 \\ \hline \square \end{array}$$

$$\begin{array}{r} 6 \\ \times\ 7 \\ \hline \square \end{array} \quad \begin{array}{r} 6 \\ \times\ 1 \\ \hline \square \end{array} \quad \begin{array}{r} 6 \\ \times\ 6 \\ \hline \square \end{array} \quad \begin{array}{r} 6 \\ \times\ 5 \\ \hline \square \end{array} \quad \begin{array}{r} 10 \\ \times\ 6 \\ \hline \square \end{array}$$

**Complete the equations to match the pictures.**

$\square \times \square + \square = \square$

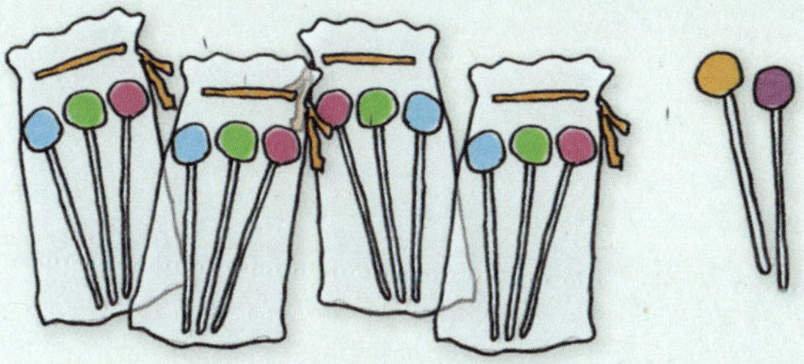

$\square \times \square + \square = \square$

$\square \times \square + \square = \square$

$\square \times \square + \square = \square$

$\square \times \square + \square = \square$

$\square \times \square + \square = \square$

8.2

## Review

**Complete.**

$\frac{7}{8} + \frac{1}{8} = \boxed{\frac{\phantom{0}}{\phantom{0}}}$

★ $\frac{6}{8} + \boxed{\frac{\phantom{0}}{8}} = \frac{8}{8}$

$\frac{5}{8} + \frac{3}{8} = \boxed{\frac{\phantom{0}}{\phantom{0}}}$

★ $\frac{4}{8} + \boxed{\frac{\phantom{0}}{8}} = \frac{8}{8}$

**Solve.**

You pay the clerk $5.00.
How much change do you get?

Change
$

You pay the clerk $10.00.
How much change do you get?

Change
$

**Write the time.**

:

:

:

:

**Complete.**

| | | | |
|---|---|---|---|
| | 5. | 3 | 2 |
| + | 0. | 8 | 9 |
| $ | | | |

| | | | |
|---|---|---|---|
| | 8. | 3 | 2 |
| - | 0. | 8 | 9 |
| $ | | | |

## Lesson Activities

**A**

$9 \times 1 = \square$

$9 \times 2 = \square$

$9 \times 3 = \square$

$9 \times 4 = \square$

$9 \times 5 = \square$

$9 \times 6 = \square$

$9 \times 7 = \square$

$9 \times 8 = \square$

$9 \times 9 = \square$

$9 \times 10 = \square$

**B**

$10 \times 7 = \square$

$9 \times 7 = \square$

$10 \times 9 = \square$

$9 \times 9 = \square$

$10 \times 8 = \square$

$9 \times 8 = \square$

C

# Multiplication Crash (×9)

| 9 | 18 | 27 | 36 | 45 |
|---|---|---|---|---|
| 54 | 63 | 72 | 81 | 90 |

## Practice

**Use the chart to answer the questions.**
**Write a multiplication equation for each question.**

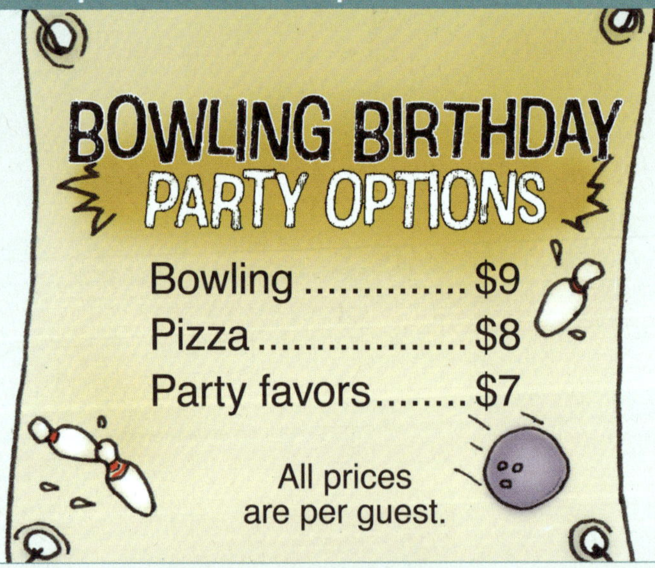


How much does bowling cost for 10 guests?

☐ × ☐ = $☐

How much does bowling cost for 9 guests?

☐ × ☐ = $☐

How much does pizza cost for 10 guests?

☐ × ☐ = $☐

How much do party favors cost for 10 guests?

☐ × ☐ = $☐

How much does pizza cost for 9 guests?

☐ × ☐ = $☐

How much do party favors cost for 9 guests?

☐ × ☐ = $☐

## Review

**Complete.**

$\frac{3}{4} - \frac{1}{4} = \frac{\square}{\square}$

★ $\frac{2}{3} - \frac{\square}{\square} = \frac{1}{3}$

$\frac{4}{4} - \frac{1}{4} = \frac{\square}{\square}$

★ $\frac{\square}{\square} - \frac{5}{8} = \frac{3}{8}$

**Complete.**

| | 4. | 7 | 3 |
|---|---|---|---|
| + | 2. | 9 | 1 |
| $ | | | |

| | 6. | 7 | 8 |
|---|---|---|---|
| - | 2. | 5 | 5 |
| $ | | | |

| | 7. | 1 | 0 |
|---|---|---|---|
| - | 4. | 3 | 9 |
| $ | | | |

**Complete.**

$6 \times 3 + 2 = \square$

$4 \times 4 + 1 = \square$

$9 \times 4 + 3 = \square$

$10 \times 6 + 5 = \square$

$8 \times 4 + 4 = \square$

**Color the even numbers red.**
**Color the odd numbers yellow.**

## Lesson Activities

**A**

$10 \times 8 =$ ☐

$9 \times 8 =$ ☐

$10 \times 7 =$ ☐

$9 \times 7 =$ ☐

$10 \times 9 =$ ☐

$9 \times 9 =$ ☐

**B**

### Climb and Slide

**C**

Allie bought 6 packs of plain hair bows. Each pack had 5 hair bows. She also bought 2 fancy hair bows. How many hair bows did she buy in all?

Tyler's parents bought tickets to a play. They bought 4 adult tickets for \$10 each. They bought 3 child tickets for \$5 each. How much more did they spend on adult tickets than child tickets?

## Practice

**Color the multiples in order from Start to End.**

Multiples of 9 (Start: 9; END: 90)

| | | | | |
|---|---|---|---|---|
| 9 | 3 | 20 | 64 | 75 |
| 18 | 27 | 36 | 42 | 90 |
| 12 | 24 | 45 | 72 | 81 |
| 15 | 48 | 54 | 63 | 56 |
| 8 | 16 | 30 | 60 | 35 |

Multiples of 6 (Start: 6; END: 60)

| | | | | |
|---|---|---|---|---|
| 25 | 20 | 32 | 63 | 60 |
| 16 | 27 | 28 | 56 | 54 |
| 12 | 18 | 24 | 45 | 48 |
| 6 | 20 | 30 | 36 | 42 |
| 4 | 16 | 32 | 40 | 45 |

**Complete.**

$9 \times 5 =$ ☐

$9 \times 10 =$ ☐

$6 \times 6 =$ ☐

$6 \times 9 =$ ☐

$9 \times 9 =$ ☐

$9 \times 8 =$ ☐

$6 \times 10 =$ ☐

$6 \times 8 =$ ☐

$9 \times 7 =$ ☐

$9 \times 6 =$ ☐

$6 \times 7 =$ ☐

$6 \times 5 =$ ☐

**Solve. Write the equations you use.**

Miriam bought 3 packs of large cups and 2 packs of small cups for a party. Each pack of large cups had 8 cups. Each pack of small cups had 16 cups. How many cups did she buy in all?

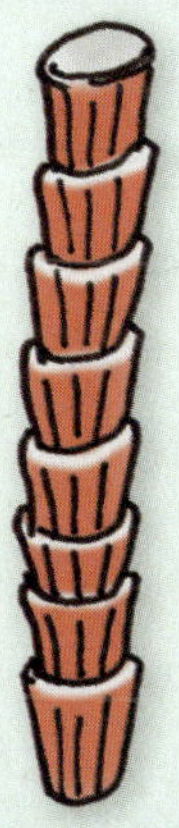

Micah bought 7 packs of trading cards. Each pack had 4 cards. He gave 5 of the cards to a friend. How many cards did he have left?

## Review

**Complete.**

\$3.50 + \$2.20 = ______

\$6.80 + \$1.30 = ______

\$3.50 + \$3.50 = ______

\$4.00 - \$1.00 = ______

\$4.00 - \$1.50 = ______

\$4.00 - \$2.50 = ______

**Complete with <, >, or =.**

$\frac{8}{8}$ ◯ $\frac{6}{8}$

$\frac{1}{2}$ ◯ $\frac{5}{6}$

$\frac{2}{4}$ ◯ $\frac{3}{6}$

$\frac{1}{3}$ ◯ $\frac{1}{8}$

$\frac{0}{4}$ ◯ $\frac{0}{8}$

**Draw a shape to match.**

Quadrilateral

Pentagon

Hexagon

**Use a ruler to draw a line that matches each length.**

4 inches

10 centimeters

## Lesson Activities

A

| | | | |
|---|---|---|---|
| 8 × 1 = | ☐ | 8 × 6 = | ☐ |
| 8 × 2 = | ☐ | 8 × 7 = | ☐ |
| 8 × 3 = | ☐ | 8 × 8 = | ☐ |
| 8 × 4 = | ☐ | 8 × 9 = | ☐ |
| 8 × 5 = | ☐ | 8 × 10 = | ☐ |

B

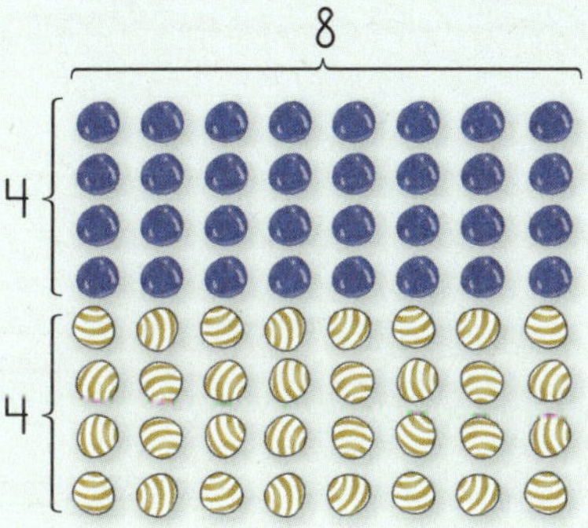


4 × 8 = ☐

8 × 8 = ☐

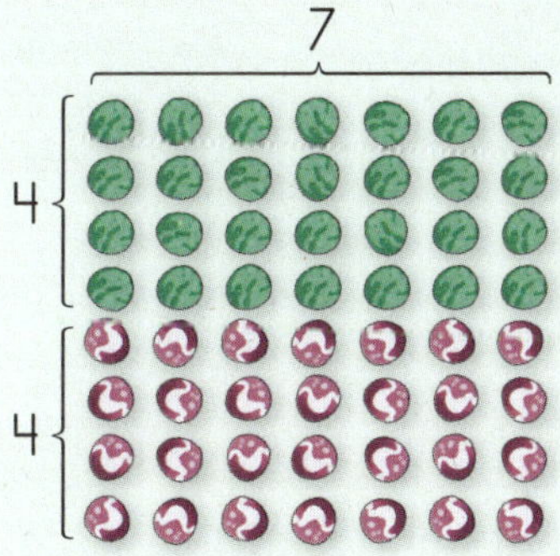


4 × 7 = ☐

8 × 7 = ☐

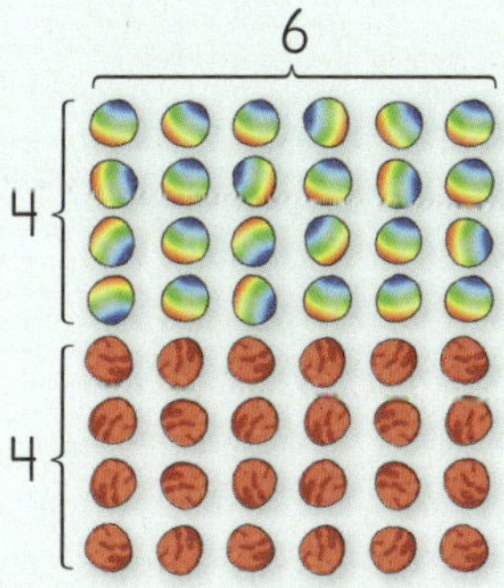


4 × 6 = ☐

8 × 6 = ☐

C

## Multiplication Cover Up (×8)

| | | | | | | | | | | |
|---|---|---|---|---|---|---|---|---|---|---|
| Player 1 | 8 | 16 | 24 | 32 | 40 | 48 | 56 | 64 | 72 | 80 |
| Player 2 | 8 | 16 | 24 | 32 | 40 | 48 | 56 | 64 | 72 | 80 |

8.5

## Practice

**Complete.**

Start

$8 \times 5 =$ ☐

$4 \times 5 =$ ☐

$8 \times 6 =$ ☐

$4 \times 6 =$ ☐

$8 \times 7 =$ ☐

$4 \times 7 =$ ☐

$8 \times 8 =$ ☐

$4 \times 8 =$ ☐

$8 \times 9 =$ ☐

$4 \times 9 =$ ☐

$8 \times 10 =$ ☐

$4 \times 10 =$ ☐

$8 \times 4 =$ ☐

$4 \times 4 =$ ☐

$8 \times 3 =$ ☐

$4 \times 3 =$ ☐

**Solve. Write the equations you use to solve the problems.**

Silas' family bought 6 packs of cupcakes for a party. Each pack had 8 cupcakes. How many cupcakes did they buy?

Alisha's family bought snacks for a party. They bought 3 bags of chips. Each bag cost $4. They bought 5 bottles of soda. Each bottle cost $2. How much did they spend?

## Review

**Draw lines to split each ribbon into the fractional part listed.**

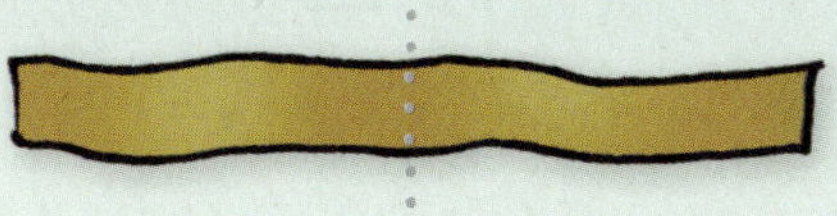

Halves

Fourths

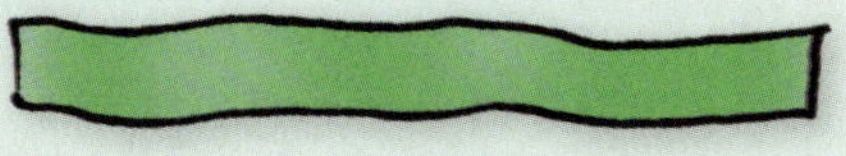

Eighths

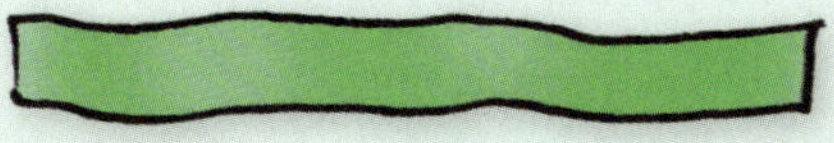

Thirds

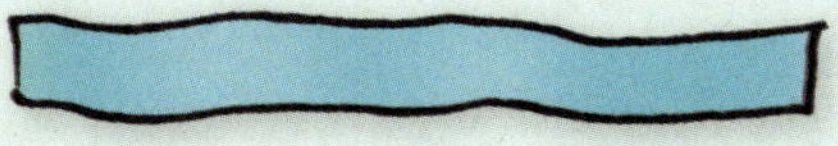

Sixths

**Complete.**

$6.05 = ☐ ¢

$3.25 = ☐ ¢

$4.97 = ☐ ¢

$ ☐ = 150 ¢

$ ☐ = 346 ¢

**Complete.**

1 foot = ☐ inches

1 yard = ☐ feet

1 yard = ☐ inches

1 meter = ☐ centimeters

**Color the problems that match the number in the star.**

| 90 | 100 | 110 |
|---|---|---|
| 3 × 30 | 5 × 20 | 11 × 10 |
| 2 × 45 | 3 × 40 | 2 × 65 |
| 4 × 20 | 2 × 50 | 2 × 55 |

## Lesson Activities

**A**

$4 \times 7 =$ ☐

$8 \times 7 =$ ☐

$4 \times 9 =$ ☐

$8 \times 9 =$ ☐

$4 \times 8 =$ ☐

$8 \times 8 =$ ☐

**B**

### Escape the Maze (×8)

| | | | | |
|---|---|---|---|---|
| PLAYER 1 40 START | 56 | 72 | 48 | PLAYER 2 64 END |
| 72 | 48 | 64 | 40 | 56 |
| 64 | 40 | 56 | 72 | 48 |
| PLAYER 2 56 START | 72 | 48 | 64 | PLAYER 1 40 END |

**C**

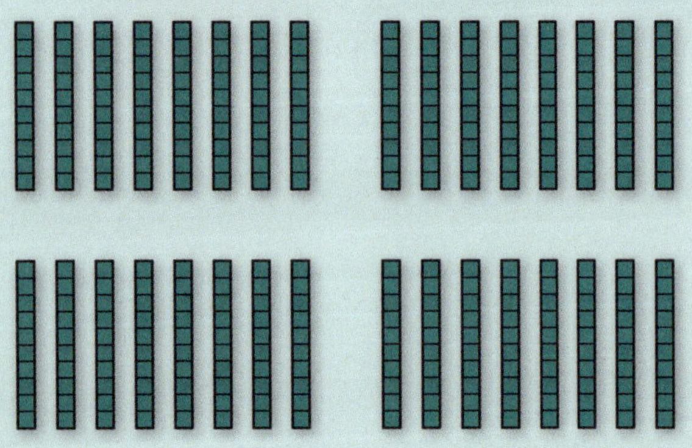

$4 \times 80 =$ ☐

$4 \times 8$ tens = ☐ tens

$5 \times 80 =$ ☐

$5 \times 8$ tens = ☐ tens

$7 \times 60 =$ ☐

$7 \times 6$ tens = ☐ tens

$9 \times 90 =$ ☐

$9 \times 9$ tens = ☐ tens

## Practice

**Complete.**

| 4 × 8 | 5 × 8 | 2 × 8 | 6 × 8 | 8 × 8 |
|---|---|---|---|---|
| | | | | |

| 3 × 8 | 9 × 8 | 10 × 8 | 7 × 8 | 1 × 8 |
|---|---|---|---|---|
| | | | | |

**Color the multiples in order from Start to End.**

Multiples of 8

| | | | | | |
|---|---|---|---|---|---|
| | 16 | 24 | 32 | 40 | 44 |
| Start → | 8 | 20 | 36 | 48 | 54 |
| | 14 | 28 | 40 | 56 | 64 |
| | 18 | 36 | 44 | 63 | 72 |
| | 12 | 21 | 35 | 70 | 80 → END |

Multiples of 7

| | | | | | |
|---|---|---|---|---|---|
| Start → | 7 | 14 | 21 | 28 | 35 |
| | 12 | 16 | 54 | 49 | 42 |
| | 24 | 48 | 64 | 56 | 60 |
| | 45 | 36 | 40 | 63 | 70 → END |
| | 35 | 30 | 32 | 72 | 80 |

**Color the problems that match the number in the star.**

| 540 | 300 | 480 | 560 |
|---|---|---|---|
| 9 × 60 | 5 × 60 | 6 × 90 | 8 × 70 |
| 9 × 50 | 6 × 60 | 6 × 80 | 7 × 80 |
| 9 × 70 | 6 × 50 | 6 × 70 | 9 × 50 |

## Review

**Circle the fractions that equal one whole.**
**X the fractions that do not equal one whole.**

$\frac{4}{4}$ $\frac{3}{4}$ $\frac{6}{6}$ $\frac{2}{3}$ $\frac{8}{8}$ $\frac{1}{2}$

$\frac{5}{8}$ $\frac{2}{2}$ $\frac{1}{4}$ $\frac{1}{8}$ $\frac{3}{6}$ $\frac{3}{3}$

**Ethan made a pictograph about the cookies he baked.**
**Use the pictograph to answer the questions and complete the equations.**

How many chocolate chip cookies did he bake?

☐ × ☐ = ☐

How many oatmeal raisin cookies did he bake?

☐ × ☐ = ☐

How many lemon cookies did he bake?

☐ × ☐ = ☐

**Solve. Write the equation you use to solve the problem.**

Sophia saved $64. Then, she earned $7 shoveling snow and spent $19 on a game. How much money did she have left?

## Lesson Activities

### A

| | |
|---|---|
| $1 \times 7 = \square$ | $6 \times 7 = \square$ |
| $2 \times 7 = \square$ | $7 \times 7 = \square$ |
| $3 \times 7 = \square$ | $8 \times 7 = \square$ |
| $4 \times 7 = \square$ | $9 \times 7 = \square$ |
| $5 \times 7 = \square$ | $10 \times 7 = \square$ |

### B

## Multiplication Crash (×7)

| | | | | |
|---|---|---|---|---|
| 7 | 14 | 21 | 28 | 35 |
| 42 | 49 | 56 | 63 | 70 |

### C

3 weeks = $\square$ days

$3 \times 7 = \square$

5 weeks = $\square$ days

4 weeks = $\square$ days

7 weeks = $\square$ days

8.7

## Practice

**Complete.**

| | | 3 |
|---|---|---|
| × | | 7 |
| | | |

| | | 2 |
|---|---|---|
| × | | 7 |
| | | |

| | | 5 |
|---|---|---|
| × | | 7 |
| | | |

| | | 6 |
|---|---|---|
| × | | 7 |
| | | |

| | | 1 |
|---|---|---|
| × | | 7 |
| | | |

| | 1 | 0 |
|---|---|---|
| × | | 7 |
| | | |

| | | 9 |
|---|---|---|
| × | | 7 |
| | | |

| | | 4 |
|---|---|---|
| × | | 7 |
| | | |

| | | 8 |
|---|---|---|
| × | | 7 |
| | | |

| | | 7 |
|---|---|---|
| × | | 7 |
| | | |

**Complete.**

2 weeks = ☐ days

6 weeks = ☐ days

10 weeks = ☐ days

9 weeks = ☐ days

**Solve. Write a multiplication equation for each problem.**

Mary Anne bought 7 packs of gum.
Each pack had 8 sticks.
How many sticks of gum did she buy?

☐ × ☐ = ☐

Logan bought 8 packs of gum.
Each pack had 7 sticks.
How many sticks of gum did he buy?

☐ × ☐ = ☐

## Review

**Round to the nearest dollar.**

| $4.75 | $3.99 | $4.09 | $0.99 | $3.50 | $3.70 |
|---|---|---|---|---|---|
| | | | | | |

**Match pairs whose sum equals one whole.**

$\frac{3}{4}$ $\frac{1}{6}$ $\frac{3}{8}$ $\frac{3}{6}$ $\frac{1}{8}$ $\frac{2}{3}$

$\frac{5}{8}$ $\frac{1}{4}$ $\frac{5}{6}$ $\frac{7}{8}$ $\frac{1}{3}$ $\frac{3}{6}$

**Complete.**

Start

74 - 67 = ☐

71 - 67 = ☐

70 - 67 = ☐

★ 750 + 170 = ☐

750 + 70 = ☐

750 + 50 = ☐

★ 620 - 230 = ☐

620 - 30 = ☐

600 - 30 = ☐

7 × 60 = ☐

6 × 70 = ☐

6 × 7 = ☐

## Lesson Activities

### A

| × | 6 | 7 | 8 | 9 | 10 |
|---|---|---|---|---|---|
| 5 | 30 | 35 | 40 | 45 | 50 |
| 6 | | | | | 60 |
| 7 | | | | | 70 |
| 8 | | | | | 80 |
| 9 | | | | | 90 |
| 10 | 60 | 70 | 80 | 90 | 100 |

### B

3 weeks, 1 day = ☐ days

$3 \times 7 + 1 =$ ☐

2 weeks, 4 days = ☐ days

5 weeks, 2 days = ☐ days

4 weeks, 5 days = ☐ days

10 weeks, 6 days = ☐ days

C

# Multiply and Add

| | Score |
|---|---|
| ☐ × ☐ + ☐ | |
| ☐ × ☐ + ☐ | |
| ☐ × ☐ + ☐ | |
| ☐ × ☐ + ☐ | |
| ☐ × ☐ + ☐ | |
| Player 1 Total | |

| | Score |
|---|---|
| ☐ × ☐ + ☐ | |
| ☐ × ☐ + ☐ | |
| ☐ × ☐ + ☐ | |
| ☐ × ☐ + ☐ | |
| ☐ × ☐ + ☐ | |
| Player 2 Total | |

## Practice

**Complete.**

| | | |
|---|---|---|
| $6 \times 6 =$ ☐ | $9 \times 9 =$ ☐ | $6 \times 8 =$ ☐ |
| $5 \times 7 =$ ☐ | $8 \times 8 =$ ☐ | $7 \times 9 =$ ☐ |
| $7 \times 7 =$ ☐ | $7 \times 6 =$ ☐ | $7 \times 4 =$ ☐ |
| $9 \times 8 =$ ☐ | $8 \times 7 =$ ☐ | $9 \times 6 =$ ☐ |

**Complete.**

| | |
|---|---|
| 2 weeks, 1 day = ☐ days | 3 weeks, 5 days = ☐ days |
| 10 weeks, 3 days = ☐ days | 7 weeks, 1 day = ☐ days |

8.8

## Review

**Complete.**

- The pineapple costs 30¢ more than the bananas.
- The avocado costs \$1.10 more than the bananas.
- The avocado costs \$1.50 more than the celery.

**Complete the sequences.**

| Count by 12s | 12 | | | | | | | 96 |
|---|---|---|---|---|---|---|---|---|
| Count by 15s | 15 | | | | | | | 120 |
| Count by 20s | | | 100 | | | | | |

**Circle the fractions equivalent to $\frac{1}{2}$. X the fractions that are not equivalent to $\frac{1}{2}$.**

$\frac{2}{4}$ $\frac{3}{4}$ $\frac{4}{6}$ $\frac{5}{8}$ $\frac{2}{3}$ $\frac{3}{8}$

$\frac{1}{3}$ $\frac{2}{6}$ $\frac{3}{6}$ $\frac{7}{8}$ $\frac{4}{8}$ $\frac{6}{6}$

## Unit Wrap-Up

**Color the multiples in order from Start to End.**

Multiples of 6

| | | | | |
|---|---|---|---|---|
| 8 | 10 | 14 | 56 | 60 (END) |
| (Start) 6 | 12 | 15 | 48 | 54 |
| 21 | 18 | 25 | 42 | 45 |
| 20 | 24 | 30 | 36 | 40 |
| 25 | 27 | 32 | 52 | 39 |

Multiples of 7

| | | | | |
|---|---|---|---|---|
| 14 | 21 | 28 | 35 | 48 |
| (Start) 7 | 25 | 32 | 42 | 49 |
| 12 | 15 | 40 | 54 | 56 |
| 16 | 18 | 30 | 60 | 63 |
| 24 | 20 | 81 | 72 | 70 (END) |

Multiples of 8

| | | | | |
|---|---|---|---|---|
| (Start) 8 | 16 | 24 | 32 | 40 |
| 14 | 12 | 36 | 56 | 48 |
| 27 | 44 | 54 | 64 | 72 |
| 15 | 25 | 45 | 70 | 80 (END) |
| 20 | 21 | 50 | 49 | 100 |

Multiples of 9

| | | | | |
|---|---|---|---|---|
| 24 | 30 | 32 | 35 | 80 |
| 18 | 27 | 36 | 40 | 90 (END) |
| (Start) 9 | 12 | 45 | 48 | 81 |
| 15 | 20 | 54 | 63 | 72 |
| 21 | 25 | 56 | 70 | 64 |

**Complete.**

$6 \times 3 + 4 =$ ☐

$5 \times 8 + 3 =$ ☐

$10 \times 7 + 5 =$ ☐

$9 \times 4 + 2 =$ ☐

**Match.**

| | |
|---|---|
| $8 \times 50$ | 280 |
| $7 \times 40$ | 400 |
| $9 \times 80$ | 490 |
| $7 \times 70$ | 720 |

## 8.9 Unit Wrap-Up

**Complete.**

$$\begin{array}{r} 6 \\ \times\ 6 \\ \hline \end{array} \qquad \begin{array}{r} 8 \\ \times\ 9 \\ \hline \end{array} \qquad \begin{array}{r} 9 \\ \times\ 6 \\ \hline \end{array} \qquad \begin{array}{r} 8 \\ \times\ 8 \\ \hline \end{array} \qquad \begin{array}{r} 9 \\ \times\ 7 \\ \hline \end{array}$$

$$\begin{array}{r} 8 \\ \times\ 6 \\ \hline \end{array} \qquad \begin{array}{r} 7 \\ \times\ 7 \\ \hline \end{array} \qquad \begin{array}{r} 7 \\ \times\ 8 \\ \hline \end{array} \qquad \begin{array}{r} 6 \\ \times\ 7 \\ \hline \end{array} \qquad \begin{array}{r} 9 \\ \times\ 9 \\ \hline \end{array}$$

**Solve. Write the equations you use.**

Spiders have 8 legs.
How many legs do 7 spiders have?

Katelyn earns $6 for washing the car.
If she washes the car 9 times, how much will she earn?

Liam's family is buying doughnuts for a party.
There are 8 doughnuts in each box.
They buy 3 boxes of plain doughnuts and 5 boxes of chocolate doughnuts.
How many doughnuts do they buy?

Kate's family is going on vacation in 5 weeks and 3 days.
How many days away is their trip?